Also by Richard Grant

American Nomads:
Travels with Lost Conquistadors, Mountain Men,
Cowboys, Indians, Hoboes, Truckers, and Bullriders

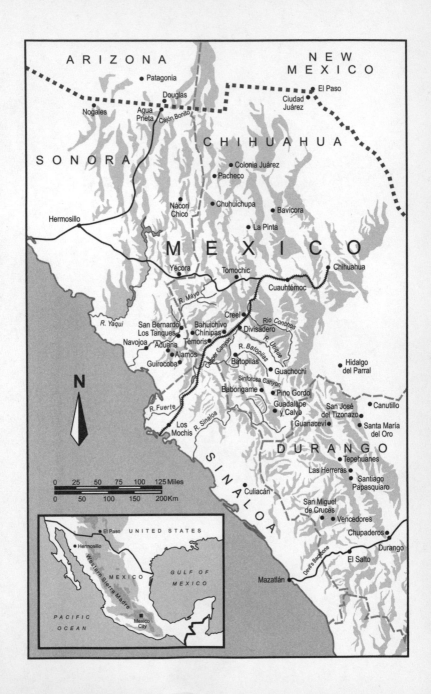

ARIZONA

NEW MEXICO

● Patagonia

Douglas

Nogales ●   Agua
             Prieta   Cajón Bonito

● El Paso

Ciudad
Juárez ●

SONORA

CHIHUAHUA

● Colonia Juárez
● Pacheco

Nácori
Chico ●   ● Chuhuichupa   ● Bavícora

Hermosillo ●

● La Pinta

M E X I C O

Yécora ●   ● Tomochic

Chihuahua ●

Cuauhtémoc ●

R. Mayo

R. Yaqui

Creel ●
San Bernardo   Bahuichivo   Rio Conchas
Los Tanques ●   ● Chínipas   Divisádero ●
Navojoa ●   Aduana   Témoris ●   R. Urique
           ● Álamos   R. Batopilas
Guirocoba ●   Batopilas ●
                              ● Guachochí

Copper Canyon

Sinforosa Canyon

Baborigame ●   ● Pino Gordo

R. Fuerte

Los
Mochis ●   R. Sinaloa

● Hidalgo
del Parral

Guadalupe
y Calvo ●   San José
             del Tizonazo ●   ● Canutillo
        Guanacevi ●   ● Santa María
                                  del Oro

S I N A L O A

D U R A N G O

● Tepehuanes

Las Herreras ●   ● Santiago
                   Papasquiaro

San Miguel
de Cruces ●
        ● Vencedores

● Chupaderos

Durango

● Culiacán

El Salto ●

Mazatlán ●

Devil's Backbone

N

0   25   50   75   100   125 Miles

0   50   100   150   200 Km

● El Paso   UNITED STATES

● Hermosillo

Western Sierra Madre

MEXICO

GULF OF
MEXICO

PACIFIC
OCEAN

■ Mexico
  City

God's Middle Finger

Into the Lawless Heart of the Sierra Madre

RICHARD GRANT

Free Press

New York   London   Toronto   Sydney

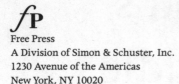

Free Press
A Division of Simon & Schuster, Inc.
1230 Avenue of the Americas
New York, NY 10020

First Free Press paperback edition March 2008

FREE PRESS and colophon are trademarks of
Simon & Schuster, Inc.

For information about special discounts for bulk purchases,
please contact Simon & Schuster Special Sales at 1-800-456-6798
or business@simonandschuster.com

Map © 2008 by Russ Billington (www.vector-redraw.co.uk)

Manufactured in the United States of America

10   9   8   7   6   5   4   3   2   1

Library of Congress Cataloging-in-Publication Data
Grant, Richard.
    God's middle finger : into the lawless heart of the Sierra Madre /
Richard Grant.
        p. cm.
    1. Sierra Madre Occidental (Mexico)—Description and travel. 2. Grant,
Richard.—Travel—Mexico—Sierra Madre Occidental. I. Title.
    F1340.G73 2008
    917.2'10484—dc22
ISBN-13: 978-1-4165-3440-2
ISBN-10:   1-4165-3440-7

For Kezia

Contents

During the revolution Martín Luis Guzmán rode the train through Navojoa and looked over at the sierra and felt what we all do when we see its green folds rising up off the desert. We all wonder what is up there and in some part of us, that rich part where our mind plays beyond our commands, we all dread and lust for what is up there.

—Charles Bowden, *The Secret Forest*

The real Sierra Madre...the wondrous cruelty of those mountains.

—J. P. S. Brown, *The Mulatos River Journal*

Our art movement is not needed in this country.

—André Breton, French surrealist visiting Mexico

God's
Middle
Finger

Prologue

SO THIS IS WHAT it feels like to be hunted. My spine is pressed up against the bark of a pine tree. My heart hammers against my rib cage with astonishing force. Here they come again. Here comes the big dented old Chevy pickup with its engine roaring and its high-beam lights swinging through the darkness and the trees. The men in the truck are drunk and they have rifles and now there are other men on foot looking for me with flashlights.

Why? I have done nothing to them. I pose no threat. Nor do the men imagine that I pose a threat. They are hunting me because I'm a stranger in their territory and the nearest law is three hours away over a potholed and bandit-infested road and because they are the type of men who pride themselves on their willingness to kill.

"We are the real killers here," the tall one growled at me in gruff mountain Spanish, back when I was desperately trying to make friends with them. "Further north they grow more drugs but here we are hundred percent killers." He had a silver scorpion fixed to his white straw cowboy hat and the first moment I saw him I knew I was in bad trouble.

The lights are swinging closer now and I press back into the corrugated bark of the tree. I turn my face to the side, afraid that it might reflect the light. My breath comes short and fast and it makes no sound. The lights swing away and I take off running again. Deeper into the forest and the darkness, with the wide eyes and edgy floating gait of a frightened deer.

I come to a creek with a high undercut bank and wedge myself into a shallow cave under its lip. The earth is damp and cold. It feels like a good place to hide. Then I realize that I can't see them coming from here and I can't hear anything except the water rushing through the creek. I have neutralized my two key senses. They could be twenty feet away. What if the men with flashlights are following my tracks? The ground I ran across was bare and dusty with a scant covering of pine needles and the men in these mountains grow up hunting game and tracking stray livestock.

I unwedge myself from the cave and step from one pale silver rock to the next across the creek. My eyes are well adjusted to the starlight from all the watching and waiting and I fear the rise of the moon. Like all hunted creatures, I want darkness and deeper cover.

On the other side of the creek I start climbing a steep slope covered with dry crunching leaf litter and find a thicket of oak saplings with a large boulder in front of it. I work my way into the thicket, concerned about rattlesnakes and scorpions, and hunch down behind the boulder. My breathing slows and lengthens. My heart no longer feels like it's going to smash its way through my rib cage and bounce off through the forest.

These mountains have already taught me more than I ever wanted to know about fear. It comes in many forms and normally has an element of numbness and panic but not this time. I feel focused and alert, clearheaded and agile, with a deep black dread in my core. I stand up and peek over the boulder. The lights are still strafing the darkness. The fuckers are still out there. How can they be so drunk and yet so persistent? Ah yes, the cocaine. Instead of snorting it like gentlemen, they poured out white mounds of it on the palms of their hands, threw it down their throats, and chased it back with more beer.

"You say you're alone and unarmed," said the short fat one. "Aren't you afraid someone will kill you?"

"Why would anyone want to kill me?"

The tall one smiled and said, "To please the trigger finger."

The short fat one smiled and said, "Someone could kill you and throw your body down a ravine and no one would ever know."

I should have grabbed that warm fleece-lined corduroy shirt when I bolted away from them into the forest. I can keep running and hiding all night but we're high up in the mountains, at eight thousand feet or so, and I'm already shivering in jeans and a T-shirt and by dawn the temperature will be close to freezing. If I had matches or a lighter, I would walk a long way from here and light a fire. If I had a shirt with sleeves, I would stuff it with dead oak leaves and pine needles for insulation. If I had half a goddamn brain, I wouldn't be here in the first place.

And now another problem: what sounds like a large wild animal is walking through the dry leaf litter toward me. Its footfall is too stealthy, graceful, and purposeful to be a cow or a donkey or a goat. A coyote perhaps? It sounds bigger. A mountain lion? The men said these mountains were full of them. They also said there were *onzas*— a kind of mutant mountain lion or lion-jaguar cross that has never been photographed and has never furnished a verifiable pelt to a scientist. I don't believe in the existence of *onzas* and yet now I see one in my mind's eye. The brindled elongated torso. The tufted elbows. The low skulking gait.

Whatever it is, this creature needs to know that I'm here and willing to fight. The human voice would be the most effective warning. Wild animals are extremely wary of people here, because the custom of the mountains is to shoot all wild animals on sight. But I daren't make a human sound. I'm afraid human ears might pick it up. So I make a low snarling growl and the animal stops. I growl again and the footsteps veer away.

Deprived of language, hunted through the woods like an animal— what in the whoremothering bastard name of Jesus am I doing here? That's the way they talk around here: grubworm sons of their disgraced mothers, filthy offspring of the grand raped whore. What in the goat-fornication was I thinking?

Those people up there will look at you like a great big pork chop. They'll want to render your fat and eat your meat . . .

You can't say I wasn't warned. From the early planning stages of this long twisted journey, I have been bombarded and deluged with warnings. They came in such quantity that I stopped listening to them. I started trusting to luck and I was luckier than I deserve to make it as far as this thicket.

If you go up there alone, you become prey . . .

As I shiver through the long cold hours on the wrong side of midnight, growling to keep the wild animals away, waiting for the men to give up and go home so I can get back to my truck and leave these mountains forever, one quiet husky voice keeps echoing in my head.

1

Boiled Vultures

THE FIRST TIME I saw him, he was standing in his front yard in Patagonia, Arizona, with a pack of dogs roiling at his feet and a high-stepping emu penned off to the side. Fifth-generation Arizona cowboy and cattleman, former U.S. Marine, occasional gold prospector, and a well-respected novelist, J. P. S. Brown spent the best part of forty years on horseback in the Sierra Madre Occidental—the Mother Mountains of the Mexican West—a rugged, forbidding, lawless region for which I felt an unfortunate fascination.

The dogs came forward and sniffed politely at my legs and he shut them away in the screened front porch of his house. He was a big, broad-shouldered, stout-bellied man in his early seventies, an aging alpha male with a bad knee, a white mustache and small smoky green eyes that were shot through with intelligence and authority. "Joe Brown," he said, extending a leathery right hand.

We exchanged opinions on the likelihood of rain and then I asked him about the emu. It was standing by the fence now studying us. It bore a strong resemblance to Samuel Beckett. "You can pet him if you want to," Joe said. "He likes affection but you have to watch him."

I went over and started stroking the emu's neck. The skin on its neck was blue under a patchy covering of feathers. The neck began to undulate as I stroked it, the eyelids lowered and fluttered with pleasure and then it made a sudden, vicious, lunging peck at my ear. I whipped back my head and let slip an involuntary oath.

"Yup, he's a feisty one all right," said Joe Brown, smiling proudly.

"Where did you get him?" I asked.

"There was a fad for emu ranching around here a few years back. When the ranchers went bankrupt, a lot of them just let their stock go loose in the desert. Most of them got killed by coyotes or starved to death. This one showed up starving for water at my horse trough and fell in with my horses. He thought he was a horse for a while but he's getting over it now. He's a good old emu."

He pronounced it *eh-moo,* as if it were a Spanish word.

"Does he have a name?"

"We call him Eh-moo."

I judged that the preliminary courtesies had now run their proper course and started wheeling the conversation around to the Sierra Madre. Joe Brown surveyed me from under his hat brim and listened carefully to what I had to say.

"How's your Spanish?" he asked.

"Pretty basic but I'm working on it."

"How are you horseback?"

"Not good. I've been on a horse four times in my life and none of them were happy experiences."

"Well," he said curtly. Joe Brown learned to ride at the age of three and once wrote most of a novel from a horse's point of view. "You're not going to find anyone who speaks English up there. And they're not going to wait for you to catch up afoot."

He limped over to his pickup truck, planted his cowboy boots, and started unloading fifty-pound bags of horse feed as if they were feather pillows. The truck was an old white Ford. A sticker in its rear window declared, "BEEF: It's What's For Dinner." There were low gray clouds scudding overhead and the smell of rain falling somewhere else on the desert.

Joe Brown finished unloading. He gave me another long searching look. "Let's say you were fluent in Spanish and a horseman," he said. "I still don't see how you can do this without getting killed."

"I was hoping you might have some advice for me about that. I was thinking about posing as an academic of some kind, a historian maybe, and trying to steer clear of the really dangerous places."

"Look," he said and now his eyes bored into mine in deadly earnest. "I don't know you but you're a friend of someone who's been a very good friend to me. If you go up in those mountains, what you're going to find is murder. Lots of murder. The last place you want to find is the heart of the Sierra Madre, because that's where you'll get shot on sight, no questions asked, and the guy who shoots you will probably still have a smile on his face from saying hello."

"That's the type of place I want to avoid."

"Well, stay out of the Sierra Madre then."

"I don't think I can. And I don't think it's as dangerous as it used to be."

The sky was a dark pearl color now and the first fat raindrops came spattering down. "I guess you'd better come inside," he said.

FROM JOE BROWN'S front yard the foothills of the Sierra Madre are ninety miles away. He used to fly down there in a Cessna, back in his cattle-buying and gold-prospecting days, and he is still enowned in the town of Navojoa, Sonora, for buzzing the roof of the local whorehouse while flying drunk. On the second pass, with his favorite whore beside him in the passenger seat, he managed to knock off the TV aerial so the madam could no longer watch her soap operas.

Farther east in the border town of Douglas, Arizona, the foothills of the Sierra Madre are only twenty miles away and from the southwestern bootheel of New Mexico they are closer still. The mountains climb out of the desert on bony, outlying fingers and knuckled ridges, rising up into high cliffs, peaks, and battlements, with further ranges stacked up behind them in paler shades of blue. Crossed by only one railway and two paved roads, lacking a single city or large town, the Sierra Madre Occidental extends away behind those northern ramparts for 800 miles.

Or it extends for 930 miles. There are quarrels among cartographers, wild discrepancies on the maps. Where does the Sierra Madre end and a new chain of mountains begin? When the king of Spain asked Cortéz to describe the geography of Mexico, the country he had just conquered, Cortéz is said to have crumpled up a piece of paper and thrown it down on the table.

The worst mountains, the most crumpled and impenetrable, were the Sierra Madre Occidental and the Spanish authorities, like the Aztec emperors before them, were never able to bring them under government control. Some isolated mines, missions, haciendas, and military colonies were established but the population remained predominantly Indian and largely unsubdued.

Apaches terrorized the northern 250 miles. The warlike Yaquis were in the northwest and a nightmare horde of Comanches ravaged the eastern flanks every September, riding down from Texas and Oklahoma on horses festooned with human scalps, blowing on eaglebone whistles, raping, killing, torturing, snatching up children, and riding away with the livestock.

The Spaniards and mixed-blood *mestizo* Mexicans who made their ranches and villages in the Sierra Madre developed a rough, violent, fiercely independent culture that had more in common with the American frontier than the civilized parts of central Mexico. Feuds and vendettas flourished. So did banditry, alcoholism, a fanatical machismo, and a deep distrust of law, government, or any kind of outside authority.

In the 180 years since independence from Spain, the Mexican nation-state has made a few inroads into the Sierra Madre but it still relies on the army to defend the small pockets of control it has managed to establish. Local power is in the hands of feuding mafias and regional strongmen who usually operate outside the law. Bandit gangs are still at large and some of them are still riding horses and mules like their cinematic counterparts in *The Treasure of the Sierra Madre* ("Badges? I don't have to show you any stinking badges!").

The Sierra Madre Occidental still contains unconquered and largely unassimilated Indian tribes. Three hundred miles south of the U.S. border, in the early years of the twenty-first century, it is still possible to find Tarahumaras wearing loincloths and living in seasonal caves. At the southern end of the Sierra Madre are some twenty thousand Huichol Indians, most of whom are still guided by their shamans and the hallucinogenic visions they experience on peyote cactus.

The range is mostly volcanic, a southern continuation of the Rocky Mountain chain, rising up to nearly eleven thousand feet at its highest point and torn apart by plunging ravines, gorges, and the immense, steep-sided canyons known in Spanish as *barrancas*. Four of them are deeper than the Grand Canyon of Arizona, three others are nearly as deep, and there are six more only slightly less daunting. You can stand on the rimrock in high pine forest with snow on the ground and look down on the backs of parrots and macaws flying over semitropical jungle at river level—a sight guaranteed to wow the passing traveler and sink the hearts of any army or police force.

The Sierra Madre Occidental was the last refuge for the Apaches, some of whom were still living free and raiding Mexican homesteads into the 1930s, and in the last thirty years it has become one of the world's biggest production areas for marijuana, opium, heroin, and billionaire drug lords. It was my bright idea to travel the length of the Sierra Madre and write a book about it.

JOE BROWN HUNG up his hat, smoothed back his thinning hair, and limped with stately dignity across the kitchen linoleum to the coffeepot. He poured out two cups and we sat down in opposing armchairs in the front room. The house was clean, modestly furnished, and decorated almost exclusively with images of cows, horses, cowboys, and Indians.

"It's always been dangerous, it's always been an anarchy, but now nearly all the decent people have been killed or run out and all the bad guys have automatic weapons, at least in the part of the Sierra that I know," he said. "It's become the kind of anarchy that gives anarchy a bad name."

A few months previously, Joe Brown had won the Lawrence Clark Powell award for his lifetime contributions to the literature of the American Southwest and northern Mexico, mainly in light of his first novel, *Jim Kane,* which was filmed as *Pocket Money* with Paul Newman and Lee Marvin, and *The Forests of the Night,* the best novel ever written about the Sierra Madre with the arguable exception of B. Traven's *The Treasure of the Sierra Madre.* The more Joe Brown talked, in that gentle, husky, authoritative voice, the more I wished he was an ignorant drunk sounding off in a bordertown saloon.

"In San Bernardo, which is just a very small town in the foothills, there were twenty-six young men that I knew killed in one year. The bus, the old rattletrap local bus, was getting held up about once a month. This was in the mid-1980s. They would rape the women by the side of the road and strip the men of all their belongings and clothes, including a couple of Americans who were up there bird hunting. Now it's even worse. People are getting killed up there now for no reason at all, because some drug guy with an automatic weapon is drunk or bored and he wants to see how his new gun shoots."

At that moment, for some unaccountable reason, my pen leaped out of my fingers and clattered on the floor between us. He paused while I reached down and picked it up, then took another swig of coffee and continued.

"They can't have social gatherings because there's always trouble. But what happens is that people go mad from the isolation. There was always a couple of them on the loose when I was up there, just wandering around, eating grass, and killing people because they got the idea in their heads that they were good at it, that it was their destiny to be a great killer of men. There's this idea in the Sierra that you're not a man until you've killed a man, like it was with the Apaches, and now you add alcohol and cocaine and AK-47s into the equation . . ."

I thought he was exaggerating, making bold, forthright, unsustainable declarations like that sticker on his truck. Much as I love beef, it isn't always for dinner. I also thought his information was out of date. Joe Brown stopped going to the Sierra Madre in the 1980s and my scattered reports indicated that things had calmed down since then. I knew of American botanists who had traveled safely in the northern Sierra, although one group was robbed at gunpoint and a woman in the party was raped. I had been to the Sierra Madre myself but only in the two small areas where it was safe for tourists to visit.

In the early 1990s I spent most of a summer in Álamos, Sonora, an old colonial town in the foothills with a winter population of expatriate Americans. That was where my fascination began. The mountains loomed above the town and stories would come down of the latest killings and vendettas between the drug mafias and also of lost gold mines, buried treasure, mythical beasts, bandit gangs, the gigantic canyons that lay deeper into the mountains. There's no law up there, people kept saying. They made it sound like a remnant Wild West and, like Martín Luis Guzmán riding that train during the revolution, I gazed up there with a mixture of dread and yearning.

Then I took the train into the Copper Canyon country, the other part of the Sierra where tourists travel freely. I gawped at the *barrancas* and found my way into some remote Tarahumara huts, skirting marijuana fields along the way, meeting a cantankerous old gold prospector on a mule, suffering a mild but persistent vertigo because so much of the landscape was vertical, and generally wandering around in a state of wide-eyed confusion and wonderment.

Sitting there in Joe Brown's front room, I tried to explain to him how raw and alive I had felt in the mountains and how consistently baffled and intrigued I was by the things I saw there. In Álamos there were big, healthy marijuana plants growing in the tree wells at the state judicial police headquarters—the very agency charged with fighting drug cultivation in the area. I knew some *judiciales* were corrupt, but were they actually growing the stuff, too?

"No, no," one of the locals said. "They sit out there on the front steps and roll their joints and throw the seeds into the tree wells and Mother Nature does the rest."

"But they don't pull out the plants. They're right there for everyone to see."

"They will pull them out but what's the hurry? Look, the buds are nearly ready."

In the raucous, accordion-driven, cocaine-fueled *cantinas* of Álamos and Batopilas, a small town at the bottom of one of the deepest *barrancas,* I drank with a succession of extravagantly costumed drug traffickers—ostrich skin boots, gold chains, silk cowboy shirts, white straw cowboy hats—and discovered that nearly all of them were devotees of Jesús Malverde, a nineteenth-century bandit who has been claimed as the patron saint of Mexican *narcotraficantes,* although stringently denied by the Catholic Church.

The *narcos* wore scapulars of the mustachioed bandit around their necks and took their loads of marijuana, heroin, and Colombian cocaine to Malverde shrines to get them blessed for safe passage north into the United States. Hit men went to the shrines to get their bullets blessed, so they would fly straight and true and lethal.

At Satevo, a village not far from Batopilas, I went to an old white cathedral built by the Jesuits. At the nave was an effigy of Christ lying horizontal in a glass box and both his eyes were covered by blue Smurf stickers. I asked around. Why does Christ have these cartoon stickers over his eyes? My question was met with shrugs or stony silence. No one else seemed to find it odd or noteworthy. Finally an old woman set me straight. "We covered his eyes because Our Lord has seen enough suffering."

Joe Brown liked these stories. They made him laugh and brought back memories. "Sometimes I really miss it down there," he said. He poured more coffee. I told him about my encounters with Tarahumaras, seeing their caves, being served a bowl of goat stew with the uncleaned guts floating in it, watching them run a hundred mile footrace in sandals cut from old truck tires. The Tarahumaras are generally agreed to be the greatest long-distance runners on the planet, and in one of those bizarre, surreal paradoxes that Mexico is always throwing at you, they are also one of the drunkest tribes on earth, getting utterly smashed on fermented corn beer once or twice a week, often for two or three days straight.

"I remember coming up on these Tarahumaras once and they were roasting a rat over a fire by the side of the trail," said Joe Brown. "They had it on a stick and its tail was hanging down and the tail caught fire and it started scorching the meat and they didn't care in the very least bit. The fare is a little bleak, to say the least, but that's going to be the least of your problems."

Now we were getting somewhere. He was talking about my travel plans as though they were actually going to happen. "I read somewhere that rat tastes better than squirrel," I said. "And a lot better than boiled whole vulture, which is supposedly eaten in the Sierra Madre during lean times and also considered a cure for venereal disease."

"Well, I've never been served vulture but it's a terrible rudeness to refuse the food that someone offers you," he said. "That's the kind of thing that gets you started on the wrong foot and can end up getting you killed."

He rose with stifled pains and opened a kitchen cupboard. He pulled out a large plastic Coke bottle with a handwoven rope handle and poured out one shot of a clear and slightly oily liquid.

"This is what they call *lechuguilla,* the bootleg tequila of the Sierra Madre," he said. Joe Brown had given up drinking twelve years ago, having worked up a habit that reached four bottles of whiskey a day, but he still enjoyed watching other people drink.

The *lechuguilla* had a green, spiny taste with a strong burn and the first swallow seemed to lift up the back of my brain and send it skidding across the top of my skull. "Suffering gods, what proof is that?"

He poured a little into a glass ashtray and set fire to it with a cigarette lighter. "It's pure alcohol," he said. "If you're ever offered *lechuguilla* straight from the still, take only a little sip or else your throat might get permanently damaged."

I asked him where he got the stuff and he said that Oscar Russo, the nephew of his ex-partner, had gone back up into the Sierra and started up the family cattle ranch again, along with the *lechuguilla* still.

"If Oscar is up there again, it probably means the drug turf wars have calmed down, at least temporarily," he said. "He might be able to get you in and that's the only way you're going to be able to do it. The rest of the Sierra is not like Álamos or that Copper Canyon country. You can't just turn up there. You need someone from there to take you in there under their protection."

"Do you think Oscar Russo would be willing to do it?"

"That's for him to decide. Bringing a stranger into the country might put his life in danger, especially a *gringo*. But I'll get in touch with him and see what he says. If you get up there, say you're researching cattle and ranching and the history of the area, and whatever you do, don't mention drugs. If *they* mention drugs, don't show any interest. And if you can't make friends with the people there in twenty minutes, get out immediately."

"Any other advice?"

"Learn Spanish and learn to ride a horse."

2

Dead Soldiers

WE ALL HAVE OUR own acceptable level of risk. Is it cycling without a helmet? Is it having unprotected sex or walking through a bad neighborhood after midnight? Is it strapping on your crampons at three in the morning and climbing up a glaciated mountain where one false step might send you plunging over a precipice? Is it joining the army and trusting that your training and equipment will keep you from getting killed? Is it flying into the latest war zone with a camera, laptop, and satellite phone, telling yourself yes this will be a bad one and a lot more war correspondents are getting killed these days but you have good instincts and a good fixer lined up and you won't take any unnecessary chances?

When it comes to assessing danger we all have our own justifications, phobias, and delusions. I have a mountaineering friend who will happily sleep in a hammock hammered into the sheer face of a two-thousand-foot cliff but is gripped with fear when paddling a canoe down a placid river. A few years ago I met America's preeminent expert on venomous snakes, Harry Greene of Cornell University, who picks up rattlesnakes and fer-de-lance with casual aplomb but is so afraid of spiders that he jams a towel under his bedroom door to keep them from coming in at night. Statistically one of the most dangerous things we do is to drive. The United States averages fifty thousand traffic fatalities a year—sixteen times the death toll from the September 11 attacks, year after year after year—but to be afraid of driving is considered a pathology.

If someone had come up to me in my early twenties, when men are supposed to be at their most reckless, and offered me a fortune to go into a place like the Sierra Madre, I would have thought about it for about three seconds before saying no. Except for alcohol and drugs, I was a fairly cautious young man, afraid of heights, roller coasters, high-speed driving, the police, guns, snakes, big spiders, and venereal disease. I avoided fights and adventure sports and I tended to doubt the sanity of those who put themselves deliberately in harm's way, much as some people now doubt my own sanity. So what happened?

In my mid-twenties I left London and started traveling around America, doing a lot of hitchhiking and later picking up a lot of hitchhikers. Americans kept telling me I was crazy, that I didn't understand their countrymen, that psychopaths would feast on my liver and use my scrotum for a tobacco pouch, but nothing bad happened. I grew bolder and more curious and started venturing into poor black neighborhoods and poor white trailer parks, biker bars, cowboy bars, American Indian bars full of alcoholics, and I was robbed once and beaten up twice but not badly. I kept going back to the places that people warned me against because there were wilder times and better storytellers there, and because I wanted to know what it was like to live in a culture so different from my own and see the world from such a different point of view.

I turned myself into a freelance magazine journalist and spent many years covering crime and the American underbelly. I wrote about the gangs in South Central L.A., where I had a gun pointed at me for the first time and another very bad scare involving a Jheri-curled barber on PCP, a straight razor, and an accusation that I had come to South Central because I wanted to get raped by a black man. I wrote about the Chicano gangs in East L.A. and the Mexican American prison mafia and I rode the freight trains to write about hobo gangs. I went down to Chiapas for the Zapatista uprising and my second look down the barrel of a gun. Riots in Haiti, riots in Ecuador, feral shantytowns around Ciudad Juárez on the Mexican border, down to Culiacán to write about the Mexican drug cartels. Between stories I took long solo walks across the desert, three or four days with a backpack and no cell phone, and people warned me against that too.

What happened was this. I learned that most places are not as dangerous as people say. I learned to trust my instincts in dangerous situations, because I kept emerging unscathed. Slowly and almost imperceptibly, my acceptable level of risk kept rising. I began to feel comfortable in situations that would have frightened me a few years earlier. I began to enjoy that edgy, adrenaline-hyped feeling that comes with pushing your luck in a place you don't belong, getting by on your wits and charm and trying to make sense of it all at the same time.

At the same time I grew increasingly dissatisfied and irritable with what we are prone to call normal life. Except for wine, music, and books, I disliked shopping. Television grated on my nerves, the commercials in particular, so I got rid of the television. I found it harder and harder to rouse any interest in sports, celebrities, electronic gadgets, the chatter of the culture, the latest this or that. Nor did I have any desire to own a house, or get rich, or start a family. I wanted to keep traveling and see the world, live an eventful, unpredictable life with as much personal freedom as possible, and have a few adventures along the way. When people ask me now what compelled me to go to such a dark and dangerous place as the Sierra Madre, I tell them that I get bored easily, that I wanted an adventure, that I was curious, that I didn't think it would be that dangerous, that it was intellectual curiosity about the nature of anarchy and surrealism, that the forbidden mystique of the Sierra got the better of me, that it had nothing to do with my marriage falling apart.

A bright spinning band of gold, rising against the blue sky and falling into blue water. That was my wedding ring when I threw it off the back of a Long Island ferry and left my wife for the last time. She understood why I needed to do things like go to the Sierra Madre. That wasn't the problem. I left because of her drinking and the awful fights about her drinking and the way she would promise to come back from the bar for supper and then roll in at two or three or five in the morning without having called to say anything at all. I loved her but I couldn't take it anymore.

From Long Island I went to Mississippi and licked my wounds in a trailer attached to a friend's recording studio. He was recording the last of the old bluesmen in Mississippi and one of them had a song that was all too familiar.

Stop your crazy ways
Woman you know you drink too much
You stay out all night woman
You know I stay awake the whole night through
Woman you know you ain't treat me right
Woman you know you're breaking my heart
Lord you stay out all night long
And drinking all that liquor and wine

—Robert Belfour, *Crazy Ways* (Fat Possum Records)

Then I came back to Tucson, filed divorce papers, and went down to Mexico, thankful that I had a big, long, difficult, all-consuming project to hurl myself into. The first stage was to improve my Spanish. I went down to the cultured central Mexican city of Guanajuato and enrolled in a Spanish-language immersion course. I was interested to see that the teachers at the school and the journalists and intellectuals I met in the plaza cafés knew almost nothing about the Sierra Madre. They had heard about the train ride you could take through the Copper Canyon country and the existence of Tarahumara Indians and the rest of it they dismissed like New Yorkers talking about backcountry Appalachia or northern Italians talking about the interior of Sicily. It was a remote, barbarous hinterland peopled by sinister clanfolk. There was no reason for a civilized person to go there and nothing of value to learn from such a place.

After a month at language school, I went back to Arizona and started taking riding lessons with Joe Brown. We would walk the horses up and down the mountain trails near his house and Joe would tell stories over his shoulder and charge me twenty dollars an hour except when I was short of money. I knew he had been a gold prospector, a Marine, a cattle trader, rodeo cowboy, and ranch hand. Now I learned that he had also been the heavyweight boxing champion of his university (Notre Dame) and had sparred for a couple of weeks in the early 1950s with Rocky Marciano. Later he boxed professionally in northern Mexico and would sometimes throw fights for money. "I'd pretend that I'd been knocked down or knocked out and the audience would go wild. They just loved to see a big *gringo* get beaten down by one of their own."

He also worked on an alpine search-and-rescue unit in the Sierra Nevada of California, wrangled horses for Hollywood westerns, smuggled whiskey and guns into Mexico, and became drinking buddies with Lee Marvin. They met during the making of *Pocket Money,* which was filmed in Tucson and Álamos in 1971. I asked Joe how he liked the film, and he said it made him want to puke and hurt somebody.

"Paul Newman was playing Jim Kane, the central character, which was me just as honestly and accurately as I could set myself down on paper. He followed me around for two weeks, studying the way I walked, the way I spoke, asking me all these questions about myself. I guess I got to feeling a little flattered by the attention and my hat size might have gone up a couple of notches. Then I saw the movie and that sonofabitch played me as this dumb, stupid, cowboy jackass, just as dumb as he could possibly be and still move the plot along and not walk into a fence post."

Sometimes as we rode he would tell me the Spanish names for various birds, plants, landforms, pieces of horse tack and equine behavior, but he wasn't offering much in the way of riding instruction. On trotting technique, for example, he had only this to say: "Don't let your ass hit the saddle in an undignified manner." When I asked him how this might be done, he said the only way to learn was to spend enough time on the back of a horse. No one ever taught Joe Brown how to ride. They just threw him up on the saddle every day or two, starting at the age of three.

One bright blue November afternoon I was aboard an aging roan called Mike. Red-tailed hawks and golden eagles soared overhead and the air was so dry and clear that you could see mountain ranges eighty miles away. Joe's faded black cowboy hat was bobbing up and down ahead of me and over his shoulder came the story of his first trip to Mexico in 1936.

"I must have been six years old. I remember it was the first time I had full responsibility for my horse. It was me and my father and a couple of cowboys. We rode down into Sonora and up to a cow camp in the mountains and all these Yaqui Indians came streaming down the trail past our camp. The women had their possessions stacked on their heads and they were wearing all the dresses and skirts they owned at once. They were fleeing from Mexican soldiers sent after them by General Calles and my father swore there were a few Apaches in there with the Yaquis. If that's true, and my father grew up around Apaches, they were probably the last of the renegades that stayed up in the Sierra Madre after Geronimo surrendered."

All we have is Joe's word on his father's supposition but if the story is true it answers one of the enduring questions about the history of the Sierra Madre. How late did free or "wild" Apaches survive in the mountains and what became of them?

Old Mike was wheezing hard by now and sodden with sweat and the saddle was starting to slip. We stopped to let him breathe. I dismounted to tighten the cinch and Mike went down with a huff and a groan onto his knees. "What does that mean?" I asked. "Have I cinched him too tight?"

"No, he's just tired," said Joe. "We better head back down."

"How old is Mike?" I asked.

"He's twenty-four but that's got nothing to do with it," Joe said curtly. "He just needs to be ridden more and worked harder. That's all."

We got the horses turned around on the narrow, brush-lined trail and began our descent. Then Joe told a story about coming down from the Sierra Madre in the early 1970s with the handwritten manuscript of *The Forests of the Night* in a leather satchel. He knew he had something special and to celebrate its completion he went on a four-day drinking binge in Douglas, Arizona, with two cowboy friends. Somewhere along the way he realized the leather satchel was gone.

"We looked up and down and all over that town. The cowboys kept asking me, 'What are you going to do, Joe?' and I was full of piss and vinegar and I kept saying, 'I'll write another goddamn book.' Eventually we found the manuscript emptied out into a garbage can behind the B&P bar and of course that called for another toot."

Like most of Joe's fiction, *The Forests of the Night* borrows heavily from Joe's personal experience. He told me that the central character, Adán Martinillo, who goes on a long, reluctant quest through the Sierra Madre after a jaguar that has been killing livestock, is a straight rendition of his old friend Adán Martinez, "the greatest outdoorsman and tracker I ever saw."

The man was sitting high on the top of a cliff in the Sierra Madre Occidental of Mexico in the dark shade of an *aliso* tree. He had been waiting for afternoon shade to cover the face of the cliff so he could climb down and pluck an *enjambre,* a wild beehive, from the face. . . . He felt akin to all who made their living in the Sierra. *Tienen derecho,* they have a right to do what they do, he felt.

The man was tall and wiry. He was strong. He tied tire treads on the soles of his feet with leather thongs that cost him more than he could afford. These *huaraches* were all the protection he had ever used and needed for getting from one place to another. His name was Adán Martinillo and few people in the world knew him. He did not care or worry about being known by anyone. He was a calm man who waited, watched, and hoped for dark, high, heavy clouds to come, day or night, early or late, with rain. He was a man who was a friend of lightning, friend of the torrent and the flood, and an enemy of death. He was friend to beasts and growing corn. He was enemy to hunger, cruelty, devastation, wasted fat, oil, and wood, to raucous women and wooing.

—J. P. S. Brown, *The Forests of the Night*

Adán was now living in the coastal city of Hermosillo and running a dry goods business but for a reasonable fee Joe thought he might take me into the Sierra and guide me around. "I'll give him a call. And I'll write you a letter of introduction to Oscar Russo."

Then, as we rode down to the foot of the mountains and the horse trailer came into view, Joe happened to mention that he himself was thinking about going back into the Sierra Madre, to research the sequel for *The Forests of the Night,* and would I be interested in joining him?

"Joe," I said. "Does a wooden horse have a hickory dick? What can I do to make this happen?"

He had applied to the Guggenheim Foundation for a grant to finance the trip and support himself, his fourth wife, Patsy, and the dogs and horses and the emu while he wrote the book. He had lined up glowing letters of recommendation from various well-known authors, scholars, and previous Guggenheim winners and I thought he had an excellent chance of getting it. Just in case, I offered to cover his travel expenses if he would take me along.

I left Patagonia that day in a state of high excitement and low humming fear. Joe Brown and the model for Adán Martinillo . . . who could imagine better guides to the northern Sierra Madre? Now it was a question of whether my Spanish, my horsemanship, and my nerve were up to it and that I didn't know.

A week later I came back for another riding lesson. We caught the horses in the corral, led them into the trailer and drove out to a trailhead in the Patagonia mountains. We had been riding for about twenty minutes when Joe said there had been a setback. Drug mafiosos (Mexicans have borrowed the word from Italians) had killed six soldiers not far from Oscar Russo's ranch.

To try to enforce its own drug laws and look good to the United States, and because its federal police force has been so thoroughly corrupted by the drug mafias, the Mexican government sends army units into the Sierra Madre every harvest season. Sometimes the army officers take bribes to ignore the growing and movement of drugs and sometimes they don't. Sometimes they find fields of marijuana or opium and burn them. Sometimes they harvest the drugs and take them out of the Sierra in military helicopters, airplanes, and other trucks and vehicles, because a mafioso has paid them to do so, or because the army commander is a man of ambition and initiative. Sometimes a mafioso will snitch to the army about a rival's crop and the soldiers will destroy it and it will be proudly photographed, videotaped, and reported to the media and the United States government as further evidence of Mexico's proud commitment to the war on drugs.

The relationship between the army and the drug mafias is dark, bloody, ever-shifting, and nightmarishly treacherous, but with six soldiers gunned down there was little doubt about what would happen next. The army would be out for vengeance and not particular about who felt it. There would be bloodletting and brutalities. Marijuana and opium crops would be destroyed. The drug growers and traffickers would be angry and temporarily out of a living and they would start robbing and kidnapping people instead. It was an old familiar cycle by now, and the Russos and the other people Joe Brown knew in that part of the Sierra had come downhill until it played itself out.

"How long?" I asked him.

"Could be a few months," he said. "If you're going to be traveling in Mexico, you'd better not get too attached to your plans."

3

Bad Man in a Dress

FOR A LONG TIME it seemed that I was never going to get up into the mountains. One way and another, access kept getting denied. In Tucson I wasted a lot of time and hope on a group of academics, environmentalists, and wealthy donors who had bought a big ranch in a remote part of the northern Sierra Madre and turned it into a preserve for wild jaguars. I tried going back to Álamos and finding the Mexican friends I had made there. I knew that some of those friends had relatives higher in the mountains and I thought it might be possible to climb someone's family tree through the Sierra Madre. But alas, another eight soldiers had just been killed above Álamos, including a captain and a lieutenant, allegedly for refusing to take a bribe, although my friends found that part very hard to believe indeed. They advised me to come back in a few months when things might have cooled off.

Then I woke up one morning with an idea, raced over to my desk, and wrote a letter to the Tecate brewing company, saying that I was a devoted drinker of their splendidly refreshing beer (true), that my observations so far had shown me that Tecate was the basic fuel of life in northwest Mexico (also true) and that I would dedicate this book to Tecate if they would let me accompany one of their delivery drivers into the Sierra Madre. It would have been a great way to see the mountains and great publicity for Tecate but sadly my request was denied by their public relations department.

The months rolled by and the violence and mayhem in the Sierra only got worse. Oscar Russo abandoned his ranch and came downhill for good. Joe Brown failed to get his Guggenheim grant and then went into the hospital for a knee operation. In the state of Sinaloa, where all the big mafia clans had originated and the Sierra was supposed to be at its most dangerous, the newspapers were reporting that homicide was now the leading cause of death for adult males, having overtaken drunk driving accidents and cirrhosis of the liver.

Then a friend in Tucson gave me the number of a local documentary filmmaker and musician called Ruben Ruiz, whose family had a ranch in the northernmost part of the Sierra Madre. We met for coffee and Ruben was excited about my project and eager to help—"It's like a fucking Wild West up there, *hombre,* right there on America's back doorstep and no one knows about it."

Ruben was an openhearted, good-humored man in his late forties, a Mexican American who had spent most of his life in Tucson. He had a boyish enthusiasm for life and music that belied his years and a vocabulary peppered with curses in both Spanish and English. He offered to take me on a mule trip to the wildest, most remote part of his ranch, a high mesa called El Contrabando where smugglers, bad men and renegades have hidden out from the law and traded contraband for hundreds of years.

"You'll love it up there, man," he said. "There's bears all over the place *y mas leones que la chingada* [and more mountain lions than fornication]. Last time I was up there we found lion kills all over the place. We found a bunch of shallow graves too. I don't know what the story is with them. But hey, that's what we're going to do, *hombre,* sleep with the lions and a bunch of dead fuckers. Hah! We'll bring a big-ass bottle of tequila and have a fucking blast."

We made our plans and we grew attached to them. Two days before we were scheduled to leave, a cold front came in from the west and deluged southern Arizona and northern Mexico with heavy rains. It would be fine, we told ourselves. It wasn't that much rain.

We left on the appointed morning in bright sunshine. We crossed the border at Douglas, passed through two Mexican army checkpoints looking for guns and drugs, and then entered the foothills of the mountains on a muddy dirt road. My grand adventure was under way at last. I rolled down the window and feasted my eyes on the landscape. I felt a rush of excitement, a sensation of being fully alive and immersed in the present moment. This was why I traveled so compulsively and why I fared so poorly under conditions of domestic routine and the feeling was always more intense when I traveled in places with an edge of danger. I wondered if hunters, poets, soldiers, or mystics reached a similar state of mind and then Ruben slammed on the brakes and said, "Holy shit, *cabrón*."*

The creek that flows through the Cajón Bonito, a small tree-lined canyon that descends prettily from the high mountains, is normally a placid stream a few inches deep. Now it was in full roaring flood from the rains, ripping down trees from its banks and sending them careening downstream through whitewater rapids. The water was five or six feet deep, as near as we could determine, and the road to the ranch lay on the other side of it.

We waited there for two days and spent much of that time soaking in a hot spring said to have been favored by Geronimo. On the morning of the third day, with the water knee-deep and still flowing swiftly, we put Ruben's truck into four-wheel drive, rolled out into the current, made it across to the far bank and promptly sank up to our axles in wet slimy mud. *"Puta madre de la pinche chingada,"* groaned Ruben. Whore mother of stinking fornication, or thereabouts.

It took us three hours to dig out the wheels and get rocks and branches wedged under them and another half hour of mud-splattering failed attempts before we managed to slither out of there. It would have taken a lot longer without the hard work and expert instruction of a local cowboy nicknamed Cuate (Twin), who also

*Cabrón: Literally means a big male goat but the word is used in Mexico to denote the type of man who will start a lot of fights and win them, swindle you in business, screw your wife, and get the last laugh. It is often used affectionately between male friends, in the same way that an Englishman might greet a friend with "you old bastard."

showed us some beautiful carvings he had made from found objects in the mountains. Ruben bought a sandhill crane carved from a cow horn that glowed when the sun shone through it. I admired a deer antler pipe, turning it over in my hands.

"Who buys these pipes?" I asked.

"The people around here. Cowboys, ranch people."

"What do they smoke in them?"

"These days it's mostly little white rocks," he said, meaning crack cocaine.

We were all covered in mud. We shook hands and wished each other well and the best of health to our respective families. Cuate, who was forty, told us with a grin that he had fathered five children by five different women and now had a sixteen-year-old girlfriend. We thanked him profusely for his help and he got back on his horse and insisted it had been nothing. We got back into Ruben's truck and started bucking and lurching our way up what I thought at the time, in my dewy innocence, might be described as a bad road in the Sierra Madre.

An hour later, ten miles deeper into the mountains, we were driving alongside the high ridge that divides the states of Sonora and Chihuahua and the drainage of the continent. Any rain or snow that fell on the east side of the ridge would find its way into the Atlantic; anything on the west side would flow into the Pacific. A few gaunt cattle grazed the rocky slopes and occasionally a deer bounded away from us. Vultures wheeled overhead. Every twenty minutes or so, I would get out to open another crudely strung ranch gate of barbed wire and sticks and the wind would bite through two shirts and a thick jacket.

Ruben started pointing out local landmarks. That dark shadowed cleft disappearing into the rocks to the west was the Cañon de Los Embudos. On March 26, 1886, shortly before surrendering for the second and penultimate time, Geronimo posed there on his horse with three warriors and an infant for a Tombstone photographer with the pimpadelic name of Camillus Fly. It's one of the few photographs ever taken of North American Indians while at war with the

United States Army and a copy of it hangs by the front door of my house in Tucson.

To the south were the dramatic rock spires of the Sierra Las Espuelas, splayed out like the rowels on a set of spurs, which is what they were named after. The Espuelas were one of the last refuges for the unsurrendered Apaches, who survived there by hunting, gathering, and stealing cattle and horses from the ranches below the mountains. Occasionally they also stole Mexican children and raised them as Apaches to bolster their flagging numbers. One of their camps was found in the Espuelas in 1931 and its remains were still supposed to be visible. I wanted to go there but Ruben said it wasn't a good idea.

"There's a ranch in the way that's owned by a young guy from Sinaloa who offered my dad a million dollars in cash for our ranch. His *pistoleros* [gunmen] all wear black leather jackets and carry big fucking machine guns. They say they're up here raising rodeo cattle, which no one believes."

To the west was another big ranch owned by a suspected *narcotraficante* and there were others farther south. Ruben knew of five different marijuana-growing camps within ten miles of his ranch. They were all staffed by men with guns and one of them produced a ton and a half every summer. The road we were driving along was a major smuggling route for the marijuana coming out of the area—all of which is grown for U.S. consumption—and the machine guns coming in.

There was a debate among North American geologists and other academics about whether this stretch of mountains—the Sierra San Luis and Sierra Las Espuelas—was the beginning of the Sierra Madre cordillera or an outlying range. Ruben thought it was pointless nitpicking and I agreed with him. The local Mexicans called these mountains the Sierra Madre. Historically they had always been considered part of the Sierra Madre, by Anglos, Mexicans, and Apaches alike. And the present-day culture was pure Sierra Madre: cowboys, drug smugglers, machine guns, crack pipes made out of deer antlers.

It was hard to believe the U.S. border was only twenty miles away. Up here there was no electricity, telephone lines, or cell phone service. There was functionally no law. Even if we'd been carrying a satellite phone, it would take the police three hours to reach us and it was entirely likely that they would be corrupt and predatory.

I had always rankled against the police, the law, and governments in general. Now I was in a place where the law was absent and government was a vague and distant entity and I felt both liberated and distinctly uneasy. Ruben and I were unarmed, mainly because it's illegal to bring a firearm into Mexico. If the army had found a pistol at one of those roadblocks we would be facing a ten-year prison sentence. There are no jury trials in Mexico and you are presumed guilty unless you can prove yourself innocent before a judge or engineer a well-placed bribe.

I also thought that having a gun would increase the likelihood of one or both of us getting shot in a tense situation and that the people most likely to shoot us would have machine guns. Intellectually I still thought we had made the right decision but instinctively it felt stupid and wrong to be in such a violent, heavily armed, lawless place without any means of defending ourselves.

WE CAME TO the entrance of the ranch in a rocky broken country of scrub oak, juniper, and cactus. Then we inched down an irrefutably bad road into a canyon with high rocky pillars on the other side. This was the upper Cajón Bonito and there by the creek stood a low brick-and-stucco ranch house with a tin roof. There was also a sagging bunkhouse, a dilapidated barn, a well with a broken pump, and a corral containing a few horses and mules. Leading a pale Appaloosa horse toward us across the bare gray earth was a scrawny, lanky, leathery old rooster of a cowboy named Guillermo Plutarco Santa Cruz Romero.

He wore a battered white straw hat and a thin poly-cotton western shirt in the cold wind. His legs were long and bandy and there were spurs on his boots. My language school in Guanajuato had left me completely unprepared for his accent, which was slurred and grunted and composed almost entirely of gutturals. The letters s, t, d, n, b, and v were all gone from the alphabet. *Buenos días,* for example, sounded like *weh-oh ee-ah*. This was the accent of the northern Sierra Madre, as I came to discover, and I still wonder if it stems from generations of toothlessness.

We had brought sacks of flour, beans, rice, oranges, and other goods and Guillermo clucked and fussed around in the low-ceilinged kitchen of the bunkhouse, making sure everything got put away in its right and proper place. There was an old woodstove for cooking and heat, a linoleum-covered table, an oil lantern for light, plastic buckets of well water by the sink. On the far wall was an old calendar photograph of a smiling woman with a basket of fruit on her arm, holding coconut halves over her breasts. By the front door was a current calendar with a photograph of a black stallion. Guillermo tore off today's page—it was a Friday—and jabbed his finger at the page underneath, which was marked with both Saturday and Sunday.

Ruben translated: "I brought him this calendar last time and he doesn't like it. He likes one day per page. What he does is pull off a page every day, keep the pages in a drawer and that way he knows how many days he's worked."

Guillermo had been alone up here for nearly six weeks and that was the way he liked it. "Sometimes he stays up here four or five months," said Ruben. "Guillermo's a good guy and the best cowboy we've ever had but he doesn't care much for company. We tried to get another guy up here to help him and he threatened to quit."

"It must be difficult to find good help up here."

"Oh man, you have no fucking idea."

THE NAME OF the ranch was Pan Duro, Hard Bread, and it occupied some ten thousand acres or fifteen square miles of land. That night, sipping good Hornitos tequila by the fireplace in the ranch house, we went over Pan Duro's recent history. Neither Ruben nor Guillermo, who had grown up here when it was a rough and murderous logging camp, knew how the place got its name but they assumed it had something to do with the difficulty of making a living in such steep, rocky, drought-prone, mountain-lion-infested country.

The ranch had been in receivership at the bank for many years when Ruben's father, a hardcase Sonoran cattleman who had hunted up here as a boy, bought it in the early 1990s. He stocked it with cattle and hired a cowboy with a big black beard to look after them. The man's name was Jesús Otero, known as Mule Tamer or The Bearded One.

"The first winter he was up here, Mule Tamer lost a mule," said Ruben. "He rode out into the *monte* [the wilds], found the mule and roped it to his horse. Then he got caught in a blizzard on the way down. The trail was really steep and nasty and his horse slipped on the snow and all three of them went over a cliff—Mule Tamer, his horse, and the mule."

The Bearded One shattered his jaw in the fall but he managed to struggle back to the ranch in a blizzard at night with the two injured animals. Then he found he was unable to eat food or drink liquids. There was no telephone or other means of communicating with the outside world and he couldn't ride out because the snow was too deep. Ruben's father went up to the ranch ten days later and found him half-starved, severely dehydrated, unable to talk, and barely alive. "Dad drove him to the hospital in Agua Prieta and that was the last we saw of him. He never set foot in the Sierra again."

His replacement was a young Tarahumara Indian from the deep *barranca* country to the south. He refused a horse and covered phenomenal distances on foot. Neither Ruben's father nor anyone else could pronounce his Tarahumara name so they called him Indio. He lasted only a few weeks. "He couldn't handle all the lions and bears and my dad yelling orders at him," said Ruben. "He basically got stressed out and left."

Then came the notorious Raúl Sala, who wasn't the worst of the Pan Duro cowboys but certainly left the most vivid impression. "I'll never forget the first time I saw that fucker," said Ruben. "I came up here with my cousin Billy and the place looked totally deserted. It's kind of spooky here anyway—women don't like it, very few of them, my wife hates the fucking place—and all abandoned like that it was just eerie. Then this guy walks out of the trees wearing a fucking dress. He points a Winchester rifle at us and he says, *'¿Quienes son?'* Who are you?"

"I say, 'I'm Ruben Ruiz, son of Alfonso Ruiz. This is my ranch. Who are you?' It turns out that he's the new cowboy my dad hired."

The dress was flowery and brightly colored and he was also wearing clumsily applied mascara, lipstick, and daubings of rouge on his stubbled cheeks. Over supper that night he told them all about the famous mafiosos he had worked for, the loads of marijuana and cocaine he had packed in trucks and small planes, the gun battles he had fought with rival drug runners and the *federales*. "You took one look into that fucker's eyes and you knew he was dangerous and crazy as shit," said Ruben.

"He was a killer," said Guillermo, nodding with great solemnity. "A very bad man."

There was nothing feminine in the way Raúl Sala walked, talked, rode a horse, or handled a gun. Some of the time he wore Wranglers and a snap-button western shirt like any other Sierra Madre cowboy. Then a change of some kind would come over him and he would walk out of the bunkhouse in the morning wearing his dress and makeup and carrying his Winchester, then saddle his horse, mount it, and ride away in full regalia, looking "strange on the range," as Ruben put it.

Guillermo said that Raúl Sala had grown up in Agua Prieta and had been a good kid who was always talking about becoming a cowboy when he grew up. Then he went to Hermosillo, the big fast city near the coast, and that's where he went bad. He came back with his mafia stories and women's clothes and a well-established reputation as a killer.

"He lasted here one summer," said Ruben. "He grew a big crop of marijuana upstream from the ranch house, harvested it, packed it up in a truck, stole a bunch of saddles and bridles and left without telling anyone. Word got around that the ranch was unguarded and it was raided by these guys from Monte Verde, which is this *ejido** full of outlaws and badasses a day's ride south of here. They stole some cattle and horses and my dad's favorite mule."

Raúl Sala's replacement was a man called Roberto Caperon who had spent time in prison for cattle rustling and rape. "He was the worst," said Ruben. "He moved his whole extended family up here and it was a mess, man. There were barefoot, snot-nosed kids everywhere and dogs, chickens, cats. They had a bunch of pigeons up here too for some fucking reason. The boys all had *pistolas* and they would blast away at any bird or animal that came near the ranch and there was always a commotion, a dog chasing a chicken, a woman screaming at a kid, a kid drowning puppies, something. They captured a bear cub and they had it on a chain and they would basically torture it and try to get it to fight the dogs."

"Why would your father hire a known rapist and cattle rustler?" I asked.

"Maybe he was just desperate to find somebody," said Ruben. "But I've always heard that he had an arrangement with Caperon to have sex with his teenage daughter. I don't know if it's true or not but shit, my dad was compulsive that way."

Ruben had also heard many times that Caperon kidnapped Raúl Sala, brought him up to Pan Duro, shot him, and buried him somewhere on the ranch, in order to please Ruben's father, who was furious about the loss of his mule. That had always been the story on the Sierra Madre bush telegraph. But just recently two agricultural inspectors had told Ruben that Raúl Sala was alive and well, still wearing women's clothes and moving a lot of drugs through Cananea, Sonora. The people there had nicknamed him Marimar, after a popular female soap opera character who was born poor and has to use her looks to land a rich husband and save her family.

"No, no, no," said Guillermo. "He was already called Marimar and I know the man who killed him. It was not Caperon but Caperon's

---

Ejido: a communally owned area of agricultural land, granted to Mexican peasants after the revolution.

partner, a man called Cuate but a different Cuate to the one you met. He told me how it happened. They were in a truck with Caperon, Caperon's son, and a little girl. They found the cross-dresser working in a marijuana camp. Cuate shot him in the head but he wouldn't die quick enough and Cuate didn't want to waste a bullet. So he grabbed a pitchfork and stuck that through Sala's head and that's how he died. The little girl saw it all. The little girl knows this is the truth."

With that, Guillermo stoked up the fire, poured himself a large nightcap, gulped it down, and went off to bed. Ruben and I stayed up talking about the elusive, confounding nature of truth and facts in Mexico. A writer friend of mine called Chuck Bowden suggests that all events in Mexico go through three stages. First there is the event. Then there are the rumors and theories about what happened. Then comes the final stage. It never happened.

Another friend of mine summed up his impressions of Mexico like this. If a man was sitting on a chair and the chair turned into a giant bird and flapped away, the man would simply dust himself off and look around for another chair. Obviously these are crude generalizations, designed to get a point across, but there can be no doubt that Mexicans live in a very different version of reality from the one subscribed to in the United States and Britain, the two countries I know best.

"In Mexico reality has always this quality of the absurd," writes the Mexican novelist Paco Ignacio Taibo II. "And on those rare occasions when it doesn't, we have to assume the worst, the deceitful curtain of words, the false language of the system."

Throughout Mexico's history the government has always lied, the courts have always been arbitrary and corrupt, the press has always been unreliable at best, the police have behaved like criminals, and power—whether official or otherwise—has always operated in secret behind a mask of lies. The official version of events is automatically suspect and probably a cover-up. We Anglos also complain about our dishonest governments, corrupt politicians, biased courts, and partisan newspapers but our institutions have always been more open and far less corrupt and dishonest than their Mexican counterparts. Consequently most of us still believe that the facts of what happened—a crime, for example—can be established by official investigations, procedures, and media scrutiny, whereas almost no one in Mexico believes this, and with good reason.

But it's not just Mexican institutions that habitually blur and conceal the truth. The condition runs much deeper than that and probably has its roots in the Indian ways of coping with the Spanish conquest.

"Dissimulation . . . is almost habitual with us," writes the Mexican Nobel Prize winner Octavio Paz in *The Labyrinth of Solitude,* his classic study of the Mexican character. "We tell lies for the mere pleasure of it, like all imaginative peoples, but we also tell lies to hide ourselves and to protect ourselves from intruders. Lying plays a decisive role in our daily lives, our politics, our love-affairs and our friendships, and since we attempt to deceive ourselves as well as others, our lies are brilliant and fertile, not like the gross inventions of other people."

I once spent a week following around a television crime reporter in Ciudad Juárez, the Mexican border city across the river from El Paso, Texas. We arrived at a crime scene late one night and saw a dead woman slumped back on a couch. Her brains were splattered over a velvet painting of a tiger on the wall behind her. We interviewed the neighbors, filmed the dead woman, and broadcast the footage the next morning, there being no restrictions on blood and gore in Mexican television.

The next day we went back for a follow-up story. The velvet painting was gone, presumably taken away by the police, but the neighbors were insisting that it had never existed. The velvet tiger painting was a false rumor, they told us. A real tiger had been living in the house and the woman's boyfriend had fed her to it.

To me it was a fascinating glimpse into the malleable, magical fabric of Mexican reality but when I told the story to Ruben that night he yawned wearily and got up to go to bed. "Fucking *Mexicanos,* man," he said. "I get so sick of their bullshit."

4

Sleeping with Lions

THE NEXT MORNING RUBEN and I went for a walk. Guillermo, who had the usual cowboy disdain for traveling on foot, stayed behind to make tortillas from the flour we had brought him. We had slept well and escaped without hangovers and we set out in fine spirits. We walked upstream into the deepening, narrowing canyon and found a bear skull polished smooth by the weather and saw orioles and blue jays and about twenty other species of birds. In the damp ground by the side of the stream we saw the footprints of bears, mountain lions, coyotes, foxes, deer, javelina (or collared peccary),* raccoons, and bobcats. Ruben wanted to get rid of the cattle on the ranch, which kept starving to death in the droughts and losing their calves to the mountain lions, and turn the whole place into a protected nature reserve.

"Get in a few deer and turkey hunters to pay the bills, fix up the house, get a deeper well, get the solar electricity running, and start doing a little ecotourism, mule rides into the *monte* and shit like that." It sounded good to me although it was a long drive on a bad road to get there, and there was no law or emergency medical services, a lot of rattlesnakes and scorpions around the house in the summer, and some of the neighbors carried machine guns and crack pipes. Per-

---

* Javelina: a snouty animal that looks like a wild pig but is actually of the deer family. Also known as a collared peccary.

haps it was more of a niche market than a mainstream ecotourism experience.

We got back to the ranch house and after studying animal tracks for most of the morning, an amateurish hobby of mine, I completely missed the four sets of fresh mule tracks. It was Guillermo who pointed them out to us and explained what had happened while we were gone.

Two riders had come down the trail from Monte Verde. They were young men with rifles on their saddles and pistols in their belts and they were leading two mules packed with bales of marijuana. They were looking for Roberto Caperon. They had heard that he paid good money for marijuana.

Guillermo told them that Caperon had been fired (for butchering Ruiz cattle and selling the meat on the sly; he was now in prison for drugs and guns). They asked if he bought *yerba*. Guillermo told them no. They asked if he could give them any tortillas for their journey. Again he said no and told them to be on their way because the boss would be back any time and if he found them on his ranch he would make short work of them.

"Jesus, can you imagine?" said Ruben. "I'm probably the most peaceful guy in the whole fucking Sierra."

"Monte Verde," growled Guillermo. "They are sons of their double-whore mothers." It wasn't their drug trafficking that bothered him. Everyone knew it was the only way to make any money in the Sierra and it carried no shame or disapproval. *Tienen derecho,* as the saying went. They have a right to do what they do. But Monte Verde was different. It was personal.

When Guillermo's daughter Ofelia was a teenager, a group of drug growers from Monte Verde rode up to the ranch where Guillermo was living and asked her to come with them to their marijuana camp. She refused. The men insisted. She refused again so one of the men shot her in the stomach and another shot her through the wrist and they rode away.

"They are lucky she didn't die," said Guillermo. "I would have killed all of them or got killed trying."

"How many men would you have tried to kill?"

"All the fucking whoreson *cabrones* from Monte Verde. You have to kill all of them, or they will come back and kill you. That is how it is in the Sierra."

The mule tracks went up the trail to El Contrabando, a high tableland named for all the stolen cattle, horses, human captives, and other goods traded up there by Apaches and other thieves and outlaws. During Prohibition, Mexican smugglers known as *tequileros* would pack their mule trains with cases of tequila and send them across and down and over the border. Now the contraband was marijuana. Guillermo thought the riders would probably cross the mesa and then descend by a steep trail on its northwest flank, ride toward Agua Prieta, cache their load in the desert, and then ride into town to find a buyer. We decided to give them a day's head start before riding up to El Contrabando ourselves.

AT DAWN THERE was frost on the ground and a low hanging mist. Guillermo was already splicing together a broken set of reins with an old piece of electrical wire. He was wearing the warm, lined flannel shirt I had given him and making odd little hooting noises to himself. I asked him how he had slept.

"Not well," he said. "There were a lot of spirits in the night, banging on the walls and windows and calling out Ofelia's name. It's all the people who were killed here."

He finished with the reins and then went over and fixed a broken packsaddle with a piece of baling wire and some frayed nylon rope. When that was done, he went off to catch his horse and three mules. Joe Brown had taught me how to catch a horse but I didn't offer to help because I had broken my thumb.

The night before, I'd been whacking dead branches over a rock to break them into smaller pieces for the fireplace and I got a little carried away. I picked up a thickish branch about eight feet long, lifted it up behind my head and swung it down on the rock with all my might. The branch didn't break and the force of the blow somehow traveled back up through the wood and broke my thumb. It was now black and swollen and taped up with two twigs that I had used as splints.

Guillermo brought back the *bestias,* the animals, and tied them to a fence rail. He started loading up the pack mule, yanking the weathered blue nylon ropes around the packsaddle and letting fly an extravagant stream of oaths. I was tuning in to his accent now, growing accustomed to all the dropped consonants and the endless variations on the same few curses. "Son of a . . . *Ay cabrón* . . . Hold still, you son of the grand whore." Somewhere I had read that a proper macho Mexican is impervious to insults, which is why you have to insult his mother. Apparently the mules in Mexico were equally impervious.

He got the beasts saddled and packed and then we were ready. It was my first experience with a mule but I had read innumerable stories about the animals in my growing collection of Sierra Madre literature. Mules were tougher and more sure-footed than horses in the steep, rugged terrain. On that point all authors and witnesses were agreed. And yet the books were full of descriptions of mules losing their footing and falling off cliffs. As I swung aboard the saddle I remembered something Joe Brown had told me: "The horse is a noble animal who performs his service with grace. A mule will wait his whole life for the opportunity to kill a man."

We rode in the tracks of the men from Monte Verde, who were nearly a day ahead of us and probably down off El Contrabando by now. Ruben was ahead of me, also on a mule. Guillermo scouted ahead on his Appaloosa and then waited for us to catch up. My mule required a lot of kicking in its ribs to get out of first gear but then it had a nice steady trot, a sure step on the loose rocky trail and a magnificent swiveling pair of ears. And here I was at last, riding an outlaw trail into the high wilds of the Sierra Madre.

The air was crisp and pine-scented and as we climbed big views opened up of mountains and canyons. Ruben was grinning and relaxed, feet dangling out of the stirrups. "So far, so good," he said. "Can you believe how fucking gnarly and wild this country is? You wait till we get to El Contrabando, man. It's just fucking primal up there."

By midday we had gained its flanks and were climbing slowly through a sparse forest of pine and juniper. Guillermo was riding close now. He pointed out the tracks of deer and wild turkey on the trail. Then a set of fresh mountain lion prints. Then a fresh lion turd scraped over and half-buried. The big cats are amazingly similar to the small cats in so many ways.

Ruben's mule got jumpy. He put his feet back in the stirrups and called it *cabrón*. My mule was jumpy, too. It had scars on its hide from a mountain lion attack when it was young and Ruben had warned me that it was spooky around lions. I shortened the reins and tightened my grip and the next thing I knew Ruben's mule had bolted out from under him. Ruben came off backward but his left foot was caught in the stirrup and he was getting dragged along the ground at a horrifying speed. My mule tried to bolt in the same direction and I yanked back on the reins and a fierce pain flashed in my thumb and Ruben's foot must have come out of the stirrup because his body was slumped on the ground seventy yards away like a piece of meat.

Maybe he's just knocked out, I thought. I dismounted and led my mule toward him, feeling numb with shock, not knowing what to do. Then Ruben clutched his leg and started writhing and roaring in pain—long, deep, catastrophic roars, one after another. Guillermo leaped off his horse like a man forty years younger and told me to ride back down and get the pickup truck and meet him at some place on the ranch I had never heard of and then drive Ruben to the hospital in Agua Prieta. All this came slurring out of his mouth at full speed and I understood it all perfectly except where to meet him and how to get there.

Ruben stopped roaring. He lay back and was still. Then he puffed and groaned and got up on his elbows with a blank look on his face. "Ruben," said Guillermo. "Where are you hurt?" Ruben rolled onto his side, got on all fours, paused for a few moments, and then staggered up to his feet. He stood there wavering. It seemed like an absolute miracle. "Ruben, you had me so scared," said Guillermo.

"Fuck," said Ruben. "I think I'm all right."

There were bloody cuts on his face and lumps and scrapes and contusions all over his head and legs and back. His left ankle, left foot, and left thigh all felt wrenched and torn but he could stand and limp about. "It happened so fast," he said. "I saw his ass, I saw him kick. Then I'm spread out like a wishbone and his hooves are flying in my face and the whole world of the *monte* is rushing into my head in stereo. I knew if I didn't get my foot out of that stirrup I was toast. Fuck! I feel like killing that fucking mule. Where is that motherfucker?"

"Your father would have killed that mule," said Guillermo. He went off into the trees, following the tracks, and came back a few minutes later with the mule. We went over to the spot where the mule had bolted and found fresh mountain lion urine. The mule had bolted out of fear but it was the only animal to do so and Guillermo said it was *muy desgraciado,* an absolute disgrace.

"I'm not riding that fucker," Ruben said to Guillermo. "Give me the pack mule or your horse."

"Ruben," I said. "Are you sure? I can go back and get the truck."

"Fuck it," he said. "We're nearly there."

Guillermo put Ruben on the horse and packed our supplies on the spooky mule, whose name was Macho Grullo, Gray Male, whose mother's profession was not in the slightest doubt, and we rode up to El Contrabando. It was shaped like an immense horseshoe, scalloped away at the sides by stupendous canyons, an island left high and dry in the sky. We rode out across it and almost immediately came upon a lion-killed fawn and then a lion-killed calf. The ground was flat and rocky and there were ancient juniper trees with bark like alligator skin, twisted and gnarled by three or four hundred years of wind.

Toward the middle of the mesa was a shallow bowl-like depression with an old wooden corral and a stock pond. As we approached it, a large black bear ran away from us and then a buck deer with eight-point antlers. We found another lion-killed calf. There were big fresh piles of bear shit all over the place. "We camp here," said Guillermo. "There is water and grass for the animals and they can go loose in the corral. If we tie them or hobble them, it is too easy for the lions. The lions may come for us, too."

I thought that was highly unlikely. An adult male mountain lion weighed about 160 pounds and was perfectly capable of taking down an adult human but it seldom happened. And these mountain lions were shot on sight and had surely associated the smell and presence of human beings with the smell of guns and death. A hungry bear was more likely to come into our camp, but not if we hung our food in a nearby tree. I was more worried about the two armed men from Monte Verde. What if they were still up here? What if other dope smugglers were riding up the trail behind us? Once again I wished we had a gun. And since I was wishing, why not something sturdy and reliable like an AK-47?

Guillermo unsaddled the animals and put them in the corral. Ruben limped over to a log and sat down heavily. He got his boot off and I taped up his swollen left foot and ankle. The ankle looked broken to me but it turned out to be his foot that was fractured. One of the lumps on his head was the size of half a golf ball. "Do you know how lucky you were, Ruben?" said Guillermo. "A runaway horse opens the tomb. I have seen men die like that."

"'So far, so good,'" said Ruben. "I can't believe I said that shit. I've always said I wanted to be buried on El Contrabando. I was nearly buried a little sooner than I had planned."

Guillermo got a fire going, flapping the flames into life with his hat. I pitched two tents. Then Guillermo began cutting brush with a machete and arranging it like a low fence around the back of the tents. I was puzzled. Was it to keep lions and bears away? Would the disturbance in the landscape give them pause? Surely the smell of us and our fire would be a far greater deterrence.

"It's against the snakes," he said, and I was even more puzzled. It was the middle of winter and far too cold for snakes to be out. And if there had been snakes, wouldn't they prefer the cover of the brush to slithering across open ground? "There is a very bad snake here that bites you with its tail," said Guillermo and I realized we were in the realm of superstition and mythology, building a remedy that wouldn't work against a creature that didn't exist. And the snake wasn't the only mythical creature Guillermo was worried about.

There was a bad-luck bird with a blue light shining out of its fore-head. And there were *onzas*.

Guillermo had never seen one but everyone in the Sierra Madre knew about *onzas*. Some said the *onza* was the runt of a litter of lions and that was why its appearance and behavior was different from that of a regular lion. Others said it was a cross between a lion and a jaguar.

"They can fly for fifty meters in one leap and they have special intestines and must eat all the time," said Guillermo. "Their favorite thing to eat is dogs. A friend of mine had a dog that was chased by an *onza*. The dog ran into the house and into my friend's bedroom and the *onza* came in after the dog and leaped up on the bed. He would have killed my friend and eaten him but the *onza* had just killed a porcupine and there were quills sticking out of its face. The quills prevented it from getting a good bite on my friend."

I got out that big bottle of tequila and passed it around. We baked potatoes wrapped in tinfoil in the fire and then laid down our steaks directly on the coals. We were so hungry that we ate in silence. Then Guillermo built up the fire again, scratched in the dirt with a twig, and told a story about a family he used to know that was inordinately fond of its dog. One day the dog was biting at the legs of a horse rid-den by a man who lived nearby. The man shot the dog. The family was furious and took revenge by shooting one of the man's brothers. That was how the feud began and by the time it was over both fami-lies had been wiped out. "Except the wives," he said. Then he told a story about two families that had wiped themselves out in a feud over a bull.

It was hard to know how much truth was in Guillermo's stories. He belonged to an oral culture that drank heavily and swapped, em-bellished, half forgot, and re-formed its legends and stories around campfires and kitchen tables and sitting on barstools in the *cantinas* of Agua Prieta. But it did seem significant that all his tales were about violence and menace and that he appeared to have an endless supply of them.

"Ricardo," he said. "Another little swallow of that tequila." I passed him the bottle and he took a big swig and started in on the story of Chuy Villalobos and his brother. Chuy's old blue pickup broke down on the road from Pan Duro to Agua Prieta. They couldn't fix it so they started walking. Chuy's brother was attacked and eaten by an *onza*. They knew it was an *onza* because it had eaten nearly all his clothing and left only a few scraps of flesh. Chuy got away from the voracious *onza* but a storm boiled up and farther down the road he was pelted to death by giant hailstones. Guillermo's world, with its blend of the real, the imaginary, and the mythological, was nothing if not hostile and dangerous.

He had lived a hard, violent, poverty-stricken life in a hard, violent, poverty-stricken place. He had been widowed three times by disease and never married again. Three of his five children were dead. His surviving daughter, Ofelia, was living in Agua Prieta with four children by four different men, none of whom had stepped up with anything in the way of money or love. He had lost count of how many friends and acquaintances had been killed in horse, mule, and pickup accidents, or by knives and bullets.

He pulled up his shirt and showed us the scar of a knife wound in his stomach. He pulled up one leg of his jeans and showed us the scar from a rattlesnake bite. Scorpions? "Ah yes. I like being stung by scorpions. I put them on my bare feet and get them to sting me because I like the feeling. It's strange, no? I don't know of anyone else who does this."

I had heard of cowboys with bad knees putting bees on them. They said the bee sting numbed out the knee pain and allowed them to ride. But I've never heard of anyone, before or since, who deliberately sought out scorpion stings. The stars came up and the moon rose. On and on he went with his stories, scratching in the dirt with his stick, hawking and spitting, throwing up his right hand to dismiss an objection, cocking his elbow like a chicken wing and hooting with laughter at the funny parts in his stories.

He had a friend in Colonia Oaxaca called Evaristo who was exceedingly proud of his big steel-capped boots. One day a truck rolled into the *colonia* that Evaristo didn't recognize. He wanted to know what the driver was doing there so he motioned for him to stop and put one of his steel-toed boots in front of the wheels. The driver kept going and the steel-toe cap buckled down and sliced off Evaristo's toes.

Guillermo was laughing so hard that he could barely croak out the punch line to the story, which was delivered at the scene by his friend Aristeo: "Next time try putting your head in front of the wheels." Now Guillermo exploded in mirth, slapping his thigh, hooting and cackling and pointing again at the tequila bottle. That was how we spent most of the night. Guillermo told one story of violent death and gruesome dismemberment after another, Ruben clarified the translation, and I made painful notes with my broken-thumbed writing hand.

When the bottle was empty we crawled into our tents. Guillermo had never slept in one before, being accustomed to a blanket under the stars, and was delighted by the "little house," as he called it. I tried sharing the other tent with Ruben but he was groaning in his sleep and farting to beat the band. I found a piece of flat ground near the fire and lay down there in my sleeping bag, too drunk and exhausted to worry about lions, bears, or anything at all.

AT DAWN I made coffee and the smell of it brought Guillermo out of his tent. I'm not proud to admit it but I'm something of a coffee snob and I always bring my own into Mexico. Thirty years ago, when the economy in the Sierra Madre was self-sufficient, people grew and roasted their own coffee but now everyone drank instant Nescafé and I found it a depressing start to the day. I handed Guillermo a tin cup of dark-roasted, organic, shade-grown jibber-jabber. He looked at it, sniffed it, took a slurp, and exclaimed, *"Ay, que rico!"* (Oh, how rich!) with a kind of hunching orgasmic pleasure. I keep thinking that someone should restage that scene and use it for a coffee commercial.

Ruben was stiff and sore and hungover but determined to show me around El Contrabando. After breakfasting on leftover steak and tortillas, which he hung in a tree overnight to keep the bears out of camp, he limped around on his broken foot and found one of the shallow graves, covered over with lava rocks and with a small wooden cross made of twigs. He asked Guillermo about it, and he shrugged that particularly eloquent Mexican shrug—the one that says, "Who knows?" with absolute finality.

Guillermo made his bandy-legged way over to the corral and saddled the Appaloosa and two mules, leaving El Desgraciado in the corral. We mounted up and rode around the rim of the mesa. To the north you could see over a hundred miles of desert reaching well into Arizona and New Mexico. Diving off the edge to the northwest was the vertiginous switchback trail that led down to the desert below and on to the border. Sure enough, there were four sets of mule tracks heading down it. I felt an odd sense of kinship with our fellow travelers now and I imagined them getting a good price for their crop and blowing the money in the bars and whorehouses of Agua Prieta.

"You can see why outlaws and people on the run have always used this place," said Ruben. "You can see anyone coming after you, hours before they get here. And if you need to escape, you can disappear into all of that."

He pointed south to a rocky tangle of peaks, crags, caves, and canyons called the Sierra de las Cuevas. Behind it were bigger mountains, higher mesas, and deeper canyons, more narco-ranches and marijuana camps and doubtless hundreds more stories of violent death, extending as far as the eye could see and for at least eight hundred miles beyond.

5

Intrepid Norwegian

WHAT I SHOULD HAVE done was stick with Guillermo, a fourth-generation Sierra Madre cowboy who had worked at twenty-eight different ranches in and around the northern mountains. He knew all the trails and who was who and except for those slithering grub-worm fornicators from Monte Verde and a certain *narcotraficante* rancher of appalling maternal ancestry who had pulled a gun on him last week and accused him of rustling cattle, Guillermo appeared to have few enemies. For a very reasonable fee, he could have threaded my passage through the drug camps and narco-ranches, delivered me into the safekeeping of reliable cowboys and cattlemen farther south, and asked them to do the same. Pass the *gringo,* handle with care. He is a friend of Guillermo Plutarco Santa Cruz Romero.

The problem was that Ruben had a broken foot and needed to get to the hospital, I had a broken thumb (and raw silver-dollar-sized saddle sores), Guillermo had forty-five days in his kitchen drawer and was going into Agua Prieta to get drunk for two weeks, and I didn't think of the plan until it was too late. By then I'd reentered the mountains eighty miles south, in the Gavilán River country of north-west Chihuahua, and abandoned my dream of pure linear ground travel from one end of the Sierra Madre to the other.

I knew of only three people in history who had completed that journey and one of them was a murky figure at best. In the Sierra they called him Johnny Mula, meaning Johnny Mule. He showed up in the Cajón Bonito in the early 1990s with six mules and hardly any Spanish. He was a retired cowboy and mule wrangler from California, an ornery old cuss who had decided to ride the length of the Sierra Madre, right down the goddamn spine of the thing, because he couldn't stand to be around modern people and he had always wanted to see the old stomping grounds of Geronimo, Pancho Villa, and Humphrey Bogart as Fred C. Dobbs in *The Treasure of the Sierra Madre.*

Crack Pipe Cuate (as opposed to Pitchfork Cuate) put him up for the night and Cuate's cousin wrote him a note of safe passage in Spanish. The note recommended Johnny Mula as *buena gente,* good people, and a friend of Francisco Javier "Cuate" and said to please sell him beans and gasoline for his little camp stove.

The way Cuate tells it, Johnny Mula made it all the way and then rode his mules to Mexico City. I heard other stories about him in the Tarahumara country to the south. Some said Johnny Mula had passed through and that was all they knew. Others said he was killed in a drug camp in the Golden Triangle, an area where the borders of Chihuahua, Sinaloa, and Durango come together, most of the opium is grown and the murder rate is astronomical.

When I reached the Golden Triangle later in my travels, I asked a state police officer if he knew anything about an old *gringo* traveling through the Sierra with a string of mules. "Ah yes," said the cop. "Yohnny Mula."

Fate had smiled on the old *gringo.* He had found a lost gold mine, made his fortune, and was living on a farm in the mountains with a Mexican woman. Where in the mountains? The cop shrugged his shoulders and said, *"¿Quién sabe?"* Who knows? And that is the best I can do if you ask me which is the true story of Johnny Mula.

The travels of the other two men are well documented. In 1997 a journalist from Chicago called Paul Salopek unloaded a three-hundred-dollar mule near the Cajón Bonito and told the local cowboys he was intending to ride it all the way. No sooner had he mounted the mule than it bucked him off and broke his nose. He wiped away the blood and got back on the mule and the Cajón Bonito cowboys still talk about his fortitude. Nine months later, after nine hundred miles in the saddle and the requisite near-death experiences with armed men in drug camps, Salopek emerged from the southern end of the mountains, rode south for another four hundred miles, and wrote a story about it for *National Geographic*.

The story was mainly about Salopek's predecessor and inspiration, a genial Norwegian explorer and ethnographer called Carl Lumholtz. He was the first man to ride the length of the Sierra Madre and it took him eight years, between 1890 and 1898. Afterward he sat down and wrote a charming two-volume book about his travels and discoveries, full of oddities that he felt compelled to record in rigorous scientific detail.

> Eight people with hair-lip, seven hunchbacks, six men and four women with six toes to their feet, and one or two cases of squint-eyes came under my notice.

Now there was a song for the Sierra Madre. On the first day of Christmas, my true love sent to me: eight people with harelip, seven hunching hunchbacks, six men with twelve toes, four twelve-toed women, and a squint-eye in a pear tree.

Carl Sophus Lumholtz. The name has a slightly supercilious air that is not entirely misleading. His sense of humor was clumsy and stilted and perhaps a bit Norwegian. His descriptions of getting drunk on corn-beer with Tarahumara and taking peyote are hilariously earnest. Even by Victorian standards, he was repressed and awkward around the whole subject of sex and romance and he never married. Nor did he leave us with any descriptions of the lithe and well-formed limbs of the native boys, which are the trademark footprint of the gay explorer.

Lumholtz had a few quirks but it's hard not to be charmed by him. He was a kind, intelligent, patient, immensely tolerant man, as well mannered in a Belgravia drawing room as around a campfire with a group of cannibals. In many ways he was the consummate Victorian gentleman adventurer, a straitlaced and eminently civilized man who was never happier than when tramping through some uncharted wilderness, studying the native tribes, bagging specimens with his fowling piece, sitting in a heavy canvas tent at the end of the day, and writing notes about absolutely everything that had come under notice of his keen eyes and ever-curious brain—the birds, animals, and plants, the geology and archaeology, tribal hairstyles, the rules of their gambling games, the ins and outs of sorcery:

> Sorcerers may put snakes into the legs, and such animals as centipedes, toads, larvae, scorpions, or even small bears into the body of some unfortunate person, and these disturbers have to be drawn out at once or else they will eat the sick man's heart.

In other ways he was an atypical Victorian explorer. He wasn't working for an empire. He had no interest in civilizing the tribes he encountered or making money from them. Nor was he driven by a gigantic ego. His only motives were to expand the world's store of knowledge about itself and to satisfy his own curiosities and wanderlust.

"What a misfortune it would be to die without having seen the whole world," he wrote as a young man, shortly after dropping out of seminary school in Norway, and this became the operating principle of his life. In 1880, at the age of twenty-nine, he sailed to Australia to collect zoological specimens for the University of Christiania in Oslo and begin his self-appointed studies as a field ethnographer. He ended up spending four years in the Australian bush, one of them with a group of aboriginal cannibals in the rain forest of northern Queensland. Mostly they preyed on other cannibal tribes, killing and eating men, women, and children alike. White people didn't taste as good, they said, but the Chinese were delicious.

Lumholtz plied them with tobacco, for which they would do anything, and kept them in constant fear of his revolver. At first he was disgusted by their taste for human flesh and finally irritated because they talked about it so much. He was more disturbed by the horrendous beatings that the men kept inflicting on the women, on the slightest of pretexts, and thought it "simply ridiculous" to see a grown man with a nine-year-old wife. Lumholtz never overcame his prejudices toward the cannibals but he thought of them as "friends and comrades" and found them endlessly intriguing.

He returned to Norway with the first-ever specimen of a tree kangaroo, as well as three new species of opossum, and wrote a readable and modestly successful book called *Among Cannibals*. Then he turned his attention to the American Southwest and the mysterious, uninhabited cliff dwellings that had been discovered there. No one knew what had happened to the people who built them—the Anasazi, or Old Ones as the Navajo called them. We still don't. Did they die out or migrate because of drought? Was it warfare or disease? Was it social collapse brought on by marauding Anasazi cannibal gangs, as the archaeologist Christy Turner argues with considerable evidence in his 1999 book, *Man Corn*?

Lumholtz's theory was that the Anasazi or their descendants might still be living in cliff dwellings in the unexplored wilds of the Sierra Madre. So he sailed to New York and organized an expedition to find out.

They set off from Bisbee, Arizona, in the late summer of 1890, with backing from the American Museum of Natural History in New York and letters from Porfirio Díaz, the president and dictator of Mexico. Lumholtz had eight scientists under his command, twenty-one mule whackers, guides, and helpers, and more than a hundred horses, mules, and donkeys to carry their provisions and equipment. They were traveling in style with the latest in folding wooden camp furniture, state-of-the-art scientific equipment, an arsenal of firearms in every conceivable caliber, and boxes of dynamite for any explosions that might need setting. Lumholtz's own personal library of books was packed in heavy wooden traveling crates, along with his large cumbersome camera, photographic plates, and luxury foodstuffs like fruit preserves and several cases of honey. Lumholtz had acquired a taste for honey and hot water among the cannibals in Queensland. He found the beverage most refreshing and beneficial to the constitution and drank it in tremendous quantities.

They rode down the western flanks of the Sierra to Nácori, visiting every hut and village on the way. Like most of the great explorers, Lumholtz always stopped and asked for directions and he was surprised how little the people knew about the "great and mysterious mountain range" that dominated their eastern skyline. Even at Nácori in the foothills, where the main trail leading into the mountains originated, reliable information was hard to find. There was a very good reason for this ignorance and it also explained why scientists knew so little about the mountains. Until very recently the northern 250 miles of the Sierra had been controlled by the Apaches.

> From their mountain strongholds these marauders made raiding expeditions into the adjacent states, east and west, sweeping down on the farms, plundering the villages, driving off horses and herds of cattle, killing men and carrying off women and children into slavery. Mines became unworkable; farms had to be deserted; the church, built by the Spaniards, mouldered into decay.

Now, with Geronimo's final surrender in 1886, the long reign of terror had come to an end. There were still a few bands of Apaches in the wilder reaches of the Sierra Madre and others were running off from the reservations in Arizona to join them, but it was now possible, for the first time in centuries, for a large, well-armed party to travel into the Sierra Madre in relative safety.

From Nácori they climbed the outlying ranges and then the main cordillera. Lumholtz sent men ahead to cut zig zag switchbacks in the forty-degree slopes to save strain on the pack animals, and discovered a perennial truth about the Sierra Madre: "To look at these mountains is a soul-inspiring sensation; but to travel over them is exhaustive to muscle and patience." Even in a pickup truck, as I was to discover, it can take you ten hours to cover thirty miles and all the bouncing and jolting will leave you punch-drunk and hurting all over.

Dense fog and hard rains brought them to a halt for three days. Then their main guide fell ill and had to be carried back to Nácori where he died. The weather cleared, they moved on, the trails became ever steeper and more precipitous. In places they had to lead the mules one by one along thin exposed ledges. "Whenever a mule runs accidentally against some projection, or its foot slips, the poor beast invariably loses its balance, and over it goes. . . ."

At one point Lumholtz heard a noise above him on the switchbacks and looked up to see a donkey with its pack come hurtling past him, "turning over and over with astounding speed," sailing over a pillar of rock below him, landing heavily at the base of it, and rolling over twice more before coming to a halt. To Lumholtz's amazement the animal then stood up in the midst of its scattered cargo, which turned out to be a case of dynamite. Two of his Mexican drovers scrambled down the slope after it, repacked the dynamite, and led the donkey up to the trail "as coolly as if nothing had happened."

So it went. One ridgetop was so steep that it required two men pushing from behind and one man in front pulling on a rope to get each of the hundred pack animals over it. Progress was desperately slow, grueling to the body and the nerves, but onward and upward they pressed.

Climbing, climbing, climbing, one massive cordon after another, at the start through dense oak thickets, and over hills flattened and eroded with countless deep, precipitous gashes seaming the rock in every direction.

Climbing, climbing, climbing, with no idea that it would be eight years until he reached the end of his journey.

In those first few weeks they found some ancient ruins but no inhabited cliff dwellings. They rode through somber and immense pine forests with trees more than a hundred feet high. They shot three of the biggest and most beautiful woodpeckers in the world—the scarlet-crested imperial woodpecker, two feet tall and found only in the Sierra Madre. Apaches were never far from their minds. They came across fresh moccasin tracks and small bunches of yucca leaves tied together and the stacked-up stones known as Apache monuments. Trotting alongside Lumholtz's horse was a dog that he had named Apache. On January 5, 1891, they stopped at an old Apache campsite near the Gavilán and decided to rest there for a few days and recover their strength on the abundant deer and the "overwhelming" number of trout in the river.

Lumholtz was off scouting for cliff dwellings when he encountered his first human inhabitant of the Sierra Madre, a white Mormon farmer, "a frank and intelligent man, very pleasant to talk to," from the nearby Mormon colony of Pacheco.

In 1885, in response to growing pressure from the U.S. government to abandon polygamy, the Mormon Church dispatched several hundred colonists to northern Mexico to extend the Mormon empire and continue to practice polygamy undisturbed. President Díaz was happy to sell them big tracts of land and unruffled by their marital practices. "It makes no difference to Mexico whether you drive your horse tandem or four abreast."

The Mormons established eight colonies in northern Mexico, three of which were in the Sierra Madre of Chihuahua. Lumholtz visited Pacheco and Chuhuichupa (pronounced Chewy-chew-pa) farther south and got on well with the people there. As a man of science he found some of their beliefs hard to sustain—that three biblical races of people had emigrated to the Americas, that Jesus came to North America after the Resurrection—but they were friendly, helpful, honest, and reliable people, and he didn't see fit to mention to his readers that the men usually had more than one wife.

I WAS TAKEN into the Gavilán country by the great-grandson of one of the original Mormon colonists. Ruben Ruiz recommended him to me as a knowledgeable and trustworthy guide to the area. His name was John Hatch and like most Mormons in Chihuahua these days he had only one wife. There were still a few polygamist families left and a cultish nest of them in the town of Le Baron but the Church itself had long since succumbed to outside pressure and renounced the practice. John wasn't the sort of man to go around passing judgment—*tienen derecho,* he felt, they have a right to do what they do—but he couldn't help wondering about the motives of those who kept on marrying new and younger wives: "You have to ask yourself if they're really driven by religious desires."

John was fluent in Spanish and he spoke English with a faintly Scottish accent, reminiscent of Sean Connery, although there were no Scots in his family tree. Like so many of the orginal Mormon converts, his great-grandparents came from the English Midlands. A sturdy, capable, energetic man in his midfifties, John had a wind-burned face and he wore steel-rimmed glasses and a cap with a picture of a leaping trout on the front panel. He made most of his living growing apples and peaches on the Chihuahua plains and in his spare time, for one hundred dollars a day plus expenses, he guided curious outsiders into the Sierra Madre. Most of his clients were Mormons with family connections to the old mountain colonies but he also took occasional fly fishermen, ecologists, and scientific researchers. Last year he took his first Norwegian and was dismayed to find that the man knew more about the Sierra Madre than he did.

Lumholtz and his men came in from the west. We climbed the more forgiving eastern slopes in John's faithful old 1978 Chevy pickup, with his standard Sierra Madre survival kit in the bed: spare gasoline, two spare tires, a battery-powered tire inflater, food, five gallons of water, and a shovel, all packed in around the four fat tires of a small all-terrain vehicle, which would be useful if the truck broke down. Guns? John said there was no need. He grew up hunting and fishing all over these mountains and his father had been the only doctor for an enormous area of the backcountry. "Most people up there know who I am. And if not, I just have to say I'm the son of Doctor Hatch. If they're over the age of thirty-five, there's a good chance that my dad delivered them as babies."

Logging trucks rumbled down the road past us, heavily laden with second-growth timber. The old-growth pine forest had nearly all been logged out of the Sierra Madre now and the imperial woodpecker had gone extinct because of it. We crested the first steep ridge and then reached a long wide mountain valley where we drove through one devastated *ejido* after another. I had seen it in Haiti and Africa and here it was again. Wealthy nations destroyed the environment in big indirect ways like global warming while practicing conservation at home. Poor hungry people laid waste to their immediate surroundings.

Granted a finite amount of land by the government in the 1920s, the people of these *ejidos* had dramatically increased their populations but the land had not increased its capacity to keep people alive. It was arid and marginal with thin soil and a short growing season. The people had done what they could. They cut down and sold the virgin timber. They killed and ate the deer, bear, and wild turkey and most of the rabbits, squirrels, and rats. They worked the soil in their cornfields as hard as they could and their beloved cattle grazed down the rest of it to dust and stones.

Aid and development experts would probably recommend fewer cattle, better fencing, a greater variety of crops, building rock walls across streambeds to catch rainwater, perhaps the manufacture of homespun crafts for sale and export. I saw these well-meaning schemes farther south. Sometimes they helped alleviate things so long as the donor money kept flowing in and outsiders were on hand to make sure the money wasn't stolen. But here, in these bleak mountain *ejidos*, the people had devised two much more rational and effective solutions that required no outside capital.

The first was to grow marijuana in remote camps, sell the crops to the local *narco*, and use the money to buy what they needed, which now included protection from the authorities and guns to defend their camps against rivals. The other solution, less risky and far more popular, was to emigrate illegally to the United States. "The people from this area all go to Phoenix, Arizona," said John. "I suppose they're just following the ones who have gone there already."

We passed a number of abandoned villages. Their wooden shacks were sagging and splintering and slowly returning to the earth. Another village appeared to have only one inhabitant: an old man plowing with a mule and wearing the most broken-down straw cowboy hat I've ever seen. The depopulation had been accelerated by a persistent drought and also by a change in consciousness. Until the early 1980s, the people of the Sierra had been subsistence farmers and ranchers, growing or making everything they needed. Then the *narcos* from Sinaloa arrived in their big new trucks. They started buying up the private ranches in the area, paying in cash, and they had a stock response for the ranchers who refused to sell: "Very well then. I will buy the ranch from your widow."

The *narcos* hired peasant farmers to tend their marijuana fields and paid them in cash. They encouraged other farmers to grow it and sell it to them. An economy of surplus entered the Sierra Madre for the first time. People started buying guns, trucks, boomboxes, solar panels, satellite dishes, and televisions. No one was content being a subsistence farmer anymore. They had become modern people. They wanted money to buy things and there was only one crop that made a profit. "That's what they call it," John said. "'The crop that pays.'"

We turned off the road at a handmade wooden sign with the word PACHECO daubed on it with red paint. When Lumholtz was here in 1891, the Mormon colony was in its infancy. Sixteen families with eighty children were living in wooden houses with a school and a sawmill. By 1910 they had multiplied their numbers to more than a thousand and the houses were brick with gardens, barns, orchards, and wide tree-lined avenues.

Now the avenues were overgrown with weeds. The trees had been cut down for firewood and the ward meeting house was a heap of rubble. Six Mexican families were living among the ruins and all the Mormons were long gone. On the advice of their Church, they had fled the Mexican revolution in 1912 and resettled in Arizona. A few families came back to Pacheco after the revolution but they were discouraged by the isolation and the short growing season and gradually the colony dwindled away.

John showed me his great-grandfather's grave in the overgrown cemetery. Henry Lunt, born July 20, 1824, Wrenbury, Cheshire. Died Colonia Pacheco January 22, 1902. "He was quite a guy," said John. "He crossed the Atlantic five times, crossed the Great Plains three times, and went from Utah to Mexico and back twice. He had four wives and twenty-six children and I believe he had 179 grandchildren."

He also left behind the 30,000-hectare or 115-square-mile Lunt Ranch east of Pacheco. It was now owned by a man from Sinaloa. Driving past it, John pointed out a big new barn and exclaimed with a grin, "Imagine how much weed he can stash in there!" John was a law-abiding, clean-living Mormon who abstained from coffee, alcohol, and tobacco but he had no objection to the growing and trafficking of marijuana in the Sierra and he was on cordial terms with many of the local mafiosos and said they made good neighbors. Some of his Mormon friends were having trouble with an *ejido* encroaching on their ranch lands until the local mafioso sent four gunmen with AK-47s, who fired a burst of rounds over the *ejido* and told them to forget it. There was no law as we would understand it in the Sierra but there were always systems of authority.

We drove on through higher, more remote mountains and second-growth pine forests. Whenever we came across another person, whether on foot, in a truck, or riding a horse or mule, John would stop and they would talk until they found the name of someone they knew in common. It was the custom of the country. You stated where you were going and exchanged your clan credentials. You mentioned any army units that you had seen or heard about in the area. You discussed the condition of the road and the prospects for rain. Then you nodded at each other and went on your way.

We came over the continental divide and soon afterward an immense view opened up of high forested mountain ranges, mesas, and deep canyons. This was the last redoubt of the free Apaches, who almost certainly watched Lumholtz struggle over those mountains. And soon afterward, at the bottom of a stupendous gorge, we saw the shining ribbon of the Gavilán River.

• • •

THE WOMAN WE had come here to see was standing outside her ranch house with a polite, slightly quizzical smile on her face. She had been grinding corn for tamales when we splashed across the Gavilán and into her front yard. There were horses grazing and chickens scratching in the dirt and mangy ranch dogs getting up out of the shade to investigate. Two men in boots and Wranglers and straw hats leaned against an old pickup truck and stared at us. Sheets of raw beef hung from the eaves of the house, drying in the sun.

The woman's name was Nelda Villa and she knew more about the last free Apaches of the Sierra Madre than anyone else alive.

6

For Their Health

THE MEN STOOD UP and the dogs slunk back, wary of a kick from strangers. John announced me as a writer from England who was interested in the history of the Sierra and the Apaches and seeing the country. Nelda's husband, Efren, a tall, lean rancher who looked like original Spanish stock, stepped forward and gave me a formal smile and a leathery handshake. Their son, Walter, tall and languid with a thin mustache and big soulful eyes, welcomed me in passable English. Then Walter's wife appeared from the house, two small boys rode past on horseback, and limping around a stable came a toothless old retainer with a face as deeply and intricately wrinkled as a topographical map of the area.

He looked me up and down and said, "Whirr-ah-hyrrhh-ah-hyrrhh," or something like it. I could find no words or fragments of words there. It sounded like a man trying to dislodge an insect from his throat. I nodded and smiled, stuck out my hand, and said it was a great pleasure to meet him.

"Will you be staying with us?" asked Nelda in perfect English. She was a small slim woman wearing dark slacks, a burgundy sweater, and canvas slippers on tiny feet. Her hair was dyed black and kept short and sensible and she exuded an air of calm grace and kindness.

"Well I . . . it's up to John. It's his truck and I know he wants to get back for a church meeting tomorrow."

"Not a problem," said John. "I can take the four-wheeler and you can bring the truck back in a few days or whenever you're finished here."

From John's house in Colonia Juárez, a Mormon town on the plains of Chihuahua, it had taken us more than five hours of bad road to get here. My neck and shoulders ached and my brain felt battered and stupid from shaking around and banging against the inside of my skull. John said he could make it back in three and a half hours and if it was all right by everybody he'd like to get going now. He unloaded the ATV and handed me his truck keys.

"Things are fairly quiet around here at the moment," he said. "But if anyone wants to know what you're doing, tell them you're a friend of mine and Nelda's and you should be fine."

John zoomed away and I followed Nelda into the kitchen. It reminded me of the kitchen in Ruben's bunkhouse: small windows, concrete floor, wood-burning stove, oil lanterns, linoleum-covered table, giveaway calendars on the wall for decoration. Nelda laid out some corn husks that had been soaking in water and smeared a paste of ground boiled corn onto them. She spooned on a dollop of shredded beef stewed with red chilies, dropped a green olive in the middle, and then folded up the corn husks into little parcels and tied them up with twine. "Oh, don't mind me cooking." She smiled. "We've got family staying this weekend."

"Are you sure there's room for me? I've got camping gear and I'd be happy to sleep outside."

"Oh no," she said, slightly offended. "We've got plenty of room and it's going to be cold tonight."

I dug around in my backpack and pulled out a copy of *The Apache Indians* by Helge Ingstad, another intrepid Norwegian explorer-ethnographer who became fixated on lost tribes in the Sierra Madre. In 1937 he recruited two Apaches from the Mescalero reservation in New Mexico, including one of Geronimo's old warriors, to show him around the Sierra Madre and find the Apaches who were still up there. They came across fresh signs of them and heard them once but never managed to establish contact. Apaches had always been renowned for their uncanny ability to hide, to move undetected and disappear into a landscape, and any Apaches left up in the Sierra by 1937 would have been incredibly wary and secretive. And most of them would have been women.

The book had just been republished in hardback with a new English translation and Nelda's face lit up when I gave it to her. "Oh, thank you," she said. "I'm getting pushed out of my house by all my books and papers but I've been looking forward to this one."

"I was worried you might have it already."

"Oh no. All I have is photocopies of the pages about this area. I haven't even read the whole book."

She made me a cup of tea from an herb she had picked called *yerba anís,* or Mexican tarragon, and got back to making tamales.

"What is it with Norwegians and the Sierra Madre?" I asked. "Wasn't there a Norwegian who settled up here somewhere?"

"Bill Bye," she said. "He lived up near Altamirano with a pack of hunting dogs who got his meat for him. In July 1932 his dogs treed a little Apache girl in the Tasahuinora, which was really a wild remote area back then and still is. There was no sign of her family so Bill Bye took her in and named her Julia Tasahuinora."

Nelda first heard the story from the village elders in the Bavispe Valley. Then she went up to Altamirano and found an old woman who confirmed all the basics and filled in the gaps.

"I kept looking at this woman, Manuela Chafino, and thinking she was Apache herself but every time I tried to bring it up she would change the subject," Nelda said. "It went on like that for days! I just kept coaxing and coaxing and backing off and coaxing a little more and eventually she came out with it. Her grandfather was an Apache who had been taken captive. Bill Bye brought Julia Tasahuinora to him and asked him to explain in Apache that he wanted to adopt her as his daughter."

This was Nelda's great talent as a historian. The old people in the remote Sierra villages would talk to her because Nelda was from the Sierra herself and they all knew her family, at least by reputation. That got her in the door and once inside she had a way of bringing out their family secrets. It wasn't trickery or cajoling but kind, gentle, good-humored persistence and how much she knew already.

In addition to her interviews, Nelda had also read just about every published scrap of information about the Sierra Madre Apaches in books and academic papers and had hunted through civic records offices and local newspaper archives. She had no formal training as a historian. Nor did she have the protective, proprietary attitude toward her knowledge that one finds so often among professional academics. Nelda wasn't trying to build a career out of it. She was happy to meet someone else interested in the subject and share what she knew. All she asked in return was that you got it right. There was a shy self-deprecating quality about Nelda that she covered up with smiles and soft laughter but she had a steel-trap memory when it came to names, places, dates, and family trees and she corrected me firmly when I made mistakes or misinterpreted information.

When the tamales were ready, the men and the small boys sat down at the table. Nelda and her daughter-in-law served the food, planted a big plastic bottle of Coke on the table, and then withdrew to another room. It was a custom that I never got used to. The women and girls waited until the men and boys had finished eating before sitting at the table.

There ensued a slightly awkward tamale-chomping masculine silence, created by my presence rather than the absence of females. I tried to break it by asking about the wildlife in the area.

"There are plenty of deer, javelina, and wild turkey," said Efren. "We are far enough from the *ejidos*. There is still good hunting here."

"There are bears and jaguarundi,"* said Walter.

The old retainer said something. I asked him to repeat it.

"He says there are mountain lions," said Efren.

The retainer said something else. "He says lion is good to eat," said Walter.

"What is it like?" I asked.

---

* Jaguarundi: a small, rare, long-tailed cat.

The old retainer made his right hand into a claw, swiped it in my direction, growled fiercely, and burst into wheezy, uproarious laughter.

"The meat makes you feel like a lion?"

He nodded and hooted.

"What is the worst meat in the *monte*?" I asked.

This took everyone aback. Meat by its very nature was a good thing. They went down a list. Lion, bear, deer, javelina, turkey, fox, rabbit, squirrel, chipmunk, rat, snake, the big lizards known as chuckwallas: they were all *buena comida,* good eating. Then the old retainer raised his finger with great solemnity.

"Skunk," he said.

Efren nodded and chewed.

"It is true," confirmed Walter. "The meat of a skunk is not good."

THE WOMEN CLEARED our plates and we got up from the table. The other male wandered off and I sat down again and asked Nelda about her own family history. "Well," she said. "There's a tradition of people coming down to the Sierra to get away from the law, or 'for their health' as we say here. That's why the Apaches liked it here. It was so hard for the soldiers to find them. Over the years we've had quite a few American bank robbers and outlaws who've come down here for their health. I'll show you where some of them settled tomorrow. My great-grandfather was a Mormon and he came down here for his health too. He didn't want to go to prison."

"How many wives did he have?"

"Four!" She laughed.

"It sounds like a lot of work."

"They used to say the worst thing was dealing with all the mothers-in-law."

I kept looking at her. She had dark eyes, light brown skin, and there was a slightly Asiatic cast to her cheekbones, a feature one often sees in Apaches and other American Indians.

"What about the other side of your family?" I asked. "You don't have any Apache blood, do you?"

"Oh no," she laughed. "My mother was half Japanese. My father met her in Albuquerque, New Mexico, and then they moved down here and bought some land from Efren's family."

Efren's family had lived here on the Gavilán since 1902, when his grandfather Rafael Villa bought the entire western portion of the Pacheco purchase, some fifty thousand acres, from the Mormons, who were pulling in all their outlying settlements because of trouble with the Apaches.

The worst incident had been at the Thompson farm in Cave Valley. Hans Thompson, a Danish polygamist, was away in Colonia Juarez with his other wife. Two Apache men appeared without warning at the corner of a barn. They shot and killed seventeen-year-old Hiram Thompson, then shot and wounded his fourteen-year-old brother Elmer, who played dead and later described what happened next.

His mother came rushing out of the house. "Take anything you want," she said. "Please don't shed any blood."

"We like to shed blood," said one of the Apaches in English. He shot her in the stomach. Then a group of Apache women surrounded her and beat her to death with rocks. The men ransacked the house, smashed everything up, slashed the feather beds. They donned the sacred Mormon temple garments, stole the horses and two large cheeses, and rode away.

At the turn of the twentieth century there were roughly a hundred Apaches left up in the Sierra. They lived in small isolated bands and family groupings and their bloodlines were complicated by the white and Mexican captives they had taken, and also by a few white and Mexican renegades who had joined them voluntarily. They ranged through an area of mountains seventy-five miles wide and two hundred miles long and sometimes descended to steal horses and cattle from ranches in Sonora, Chihuahua, Arizona, and New Mexico. In Arizona they occasionally stole women from the Apache reservations. In the remote bootheel of New Mexico the livestock raids continued into the 1920s.

Armed robbery is always a dangerous business, especially when the people getting robbed are armed too. Nor was raiding essential to Apache survival. The Sierra was still prodigally abundant in wild game in those years. They could have lived peacefully by hunting and gathering but they weren't peaceful hunter-gatherers. They were nomadic raiders and guerrilla fighters, accustomed to preying on their neighbors and winning their honors in war. And the Apaches left in the Sierra were Chiricahuas—the most warlike, recalcitrant, and formidable of all the Apache subgroups. Geronimo was a Chiricahua. So were the great war chiefs Cochise, Victorio, and Mangas Coloradas.

"Rafael Villa told his sons he had bought a big spread of land in the Sierra Madre but there was a problem with it," said Nelda. "There were still wild Apaches in the area. They packed up a wagon and bought a big tent and came here over the mountains by the same route that you and John did. They put the tent up right over there by the river and made a corral for their animals. At night they could see Apaches through the walls of the tent, moving around, looking things over, but Rafael told his sons not to shoot and not to bother them in any way at all."

They never saw Apaches in the daytime, just their tracks, but they managed to form a remarkable unspoken truce. For 250 years the Apaches and the Mexicans had been bitter enemies, with both sides committing horrific atrocities. In other parts of the Sierra the killing, mutilating, and captive snatching was still going on, with the Mexicans doing more of it than the Apaches, but here on the Gavilán the two small family groups managed to leave each other alone. "They never even took a horse or butchered a cow for meat," said Nelda. "The only raid was in 1929 when Apache Juan's band came over from Sonora and stole a bunch of horses and cattle and burned a cow camp."

The raiders drove the stock down the Gavilán so they wouldn't leave any tracks and then turned them uphill to a mesa called Corral de los Indios, which Nelda promised to show me tomorrow. "One of Geronimo's old strongholds is up there," she said. "That's where they would have camped."

She went back into her room and came out with a copy of an old photograph taken by Captain Henry Lawton, a U.S. army officer who traveled more than thirteen hundred miles chasing Geronimo up and down the Sierra Madre in the sweltering, storm-drenched summer of 1886. Lawton never caught a glimpse of Geronimo but he did find the stronghold. The photograph was blurry and indistinct but you could make out a high shelf of rock with a spring and a commanding view of the surrounding crags and canyons.

That night Nelda showed me an old log cabin where Efren's parents had lived. The retainer had warmed it up with a blazing fire. There were hundreds of quivering daddy longlegs on the floor and a pair of child's cowboy boots mounted on the wall in a circle of barbed wire. In the top of each boot was a pink plastic flower.

Lying in bed, resolutely ignoring the daddy longlegs, I kept thinking about that photograph and its caption: APACHE HIDEOUT IN THE HEART OF THE SIERRA MADRES. Naturally I wanted to go there but I was worried about its remoteness, its concealment, and that spring in particular. Geronimo's old stronghold looked like the perfect location for a marijuana camp.

EFREN VILLA HEAVED two big plastic bags full of garbage into the bed of his truck, along with an axe and a shovel. He hung his rifle in the rack across the rear window and fired up the engine. Nelda sat in the middle wearing a black sweater and a silver eagle-feather pendant with an inlaid turquoise. It was given to her by the chairwoman of the Chiricahua/Warm Springs Apache tribe in Fort Sill, Oklahoma, to honor her research and thank her for hosting a delegation of Chiricahuas who came down here in 1988 to find their long-lost cousins.

"I tried to explain that there hadn't been any sightings or incidents since the 1930s but they weren't having any of it," said Nelda. Her tone was kind, forgiving, slightly perplexed, and gently amused. "'You don't know our people,' they kept telling me. 'They can be there but you can't see them.' They said there were thirteen families who never came in and we would find them where the wild horses ran free."

Nelda explained that rugged and remote as the mountains looked, all the land was owned and fenced by private ranchers or *ejidos*. There were no wild horses and it was impossible for anyone to live in the Sierra undiscovered. The Apaches weren't having any of that either. Their oral tradition, passed down by the tribal elders, was very firm and insistent about the thirteen families and the wild horses.

We forded the Gavilán and climbed up the narrow, winding, rocky road that led over the mountains to the west. We passed some freshly discarded Tecate cans but saw no other vehicles. After about forty-five minutes we stopped at a high lookout point on the edge of a precipice that plunged down about fifteen hundred feet. "How do you like the view?" asked Efren, lifting out the garbage bags.

"It's spectacular," I said.

"Yes, we are fortunate to live in such a beautiful place," he said and emptied out the bags over the edge.

"This is the border line between Sonora and Chihuahua," said Nelda. "If you took one step off that cliff you'd be in Sonora, although it might be a while before you touched the ground."

There was a terrifying mule trail that switchbacked down the side of the cliff, clinging to ledges and outcroppings, all the way down into the deep enclosed valley at the bottom. "We call that place The Hole or the Devil's Hole," she said. "Its Spanish name is Taraises. Two American outlaws named Johnny Norcross and Johnny Wright lived there for a while and then got themselves killed doing other robberies. Cabe Adams, he was another one. Cabe lived down there for a long while."

"Are any outlaws or their descendants still living there?"

"Not Anglos," she said. "But there are still a bunch of thieves and cattle rustlers and killers down in The Hole. They do a lot of growing down there too. The Marquez are probably the wildest bunch. And over there is a little sawmill town called El Oro, which you don't want to go to. It's a den of thieves and killers basically and most of them belong to the Jacquez *[Ha-quez]* family. They were French originally— Jacques—but I doubt any of them can still speak French. They're Sierra people now. They've been in a long feud with the Ortegas."

On the other side of the Devil's Hole was the Sierra El Tabaco, one of the few areas in the entire Sierra Madre that logging crews had never managed to penetrate. Farther south and west was the Sierra La India, named after Apache Juan's niece. She was captured there as a teenage girl in 1913 by a tough Sonoran rancher called Francisco Fimbres.

She was the lookout, stationed high on the peak. She had a rawhide rope with bells on it that ran down to their camp. She saw Fimbres and his men coming, trailing their stolen cattle, and tugged on the rope. Apache Juan and the others got away. His niece rushed down to the camp, jumped on a mule, but it bucked her off. She was trying to crawl into some bushes to hide when Fimbres spotted her and dragged her out.

He gave her the name of Lupe and put her to work as a servant in his family. A year later she asked to go back to her people and Fimbres agreed to it. She found them easily, after only a day of looking, and they were not happy to see her. They told her to go back to the Mexicans, that she was no longer Apache. Her brother threatened to kill her. So Lupe returned to the Fimbres family and resumed her duties, looking after the children and becoming attached to them.

She was always afraid of the wild Apaches in the mountains. She knew when they were watching. She said she could smell when they were near. The Fimbres family doubted these abilities at first but she was able to lead them to the tracks and scuffmarks on the ground where the Apaches had been hiding and watching them. She said her uncle was *hombre muy malo,* a very bad man, and she was afraid he wanted the Fimbres children.

On October 15, 1927, Francisco Fimbres was riding with his wife, Maria, and the two youngest children to a new gold mine settlement in the Sierra called Pinos Altos. His rifle was in a scabbard on his saddle. He neglected to take it with him when he switched horses with Maria. Concealed in the bushes by the side of the trail was a small group of women from Apache Juan's band. They waited for Francisco to ride past and then rushed out at Maria, pulled her off her horse, stabbed her, slashed her throat, and threw her body into a ravine. Then they snatched three-year-old Gerardo and disappeared.

Francisco was unarmed and holding his two-year-old daughter. There was nothing he could do. His response to the loss of his wife and the capture of his son, and the awful self-knowledge that he had failed to protect them, was to become obsessed with revenge.

Nelda pointed out another great forested massif in the distance. This was the Sierra de la Nutria, the Otter Range. After nine expeditions and nearly three years of searching, Francisco Fimbres and his men finally caught up with Apache Juan there in April 1930. They killed him and two women and cut off their heads as trophies. One of the women was Lupe's mother. The other was her sister. Lupe called herself a Mexican now but she keened and wailed like an Apache woman when Fimbres brought back the heads.

The other women in the band got away and took seven-year-old Gerardo Fimbres with them. Then they tied him to a tree, stoned him to death, and left the body for his father to find. Meanwhile, televisions were rolling off American production lines, Mickey Mouse had just got his own comic strip, and U.S. Customs officials were seizing copies of James Joyce's *Ulysses* as obscene material. Hollywood had been making cowboys-and-Indians movies for nearly thirty years.

NELDA AND EFREN had another ranch called the Perdido, where the Oklahoma Apaches stayed in 1988. It was set in a small valley enclosed by looming mountains on all sides. There was an old log cabin full of cobwebs and rodent droppings, an overgrown well, a rickety shed, and that was about it. Efren had given up putting cattle on it because they were always stolen by rustlers from The Hole.

"The Oklahoma Apaches were scared as deer the whole time they were in the Sierra," said Nelda. "Afraid of Mexicans, afraid of the Apaches they thought were out there, afraid of wild animals, afraid of their own shadows. Then we brought them out here to do their ceremonies. Most of them had never camped before and the ladies wanted to know where the bathroom was. 'Wherever you want,' I said. 'There must be a bathroom,' they said. 'Sure,' I said.

'Men over there, women over there.' They couldn't get over it. No bathrooms!"

They put up their tents and tepees and held their sacred dances. They prayed and sang and with great trepidation invited the "wild ones," as they called them, to join them. As children in Oklahoma they were brought up in mortal terror of the Sierra Madre Apaches. When they were behaving badly and nothing else worked, their grandparents would threaten to call in the wild ones from Mexico.

There was more relief than disappointment when the wild ones failed to appear and of course it didn't mean that they weren't still out there somewhere and perhaps listening. In the end the visit was deemed a great success. The Chiricahuas had danced and prayed under their sacred peaks in the Sierra Madre for the first time in a century. They were glad to get back to the order, safety, and comfort north of the border but it had been a powerful emotional experience for them and a symbolic reclamation of holy ground.

"They said they wanted to do it again and I told them they were welcome anytime," Nelda reflected. "But I guess that was it."

NOT FAR FROM the Perdido was another spectacular overlook. The lower gorge of the Gavilán yawned open beneath us and jutting out of the far side, looking something like a giant frying pan on a pedestal, was the Corral de los Indios. It was a sheer-sided mesa with a round flat top, connected to the land behind it by a thin panhandle. God must have custom-designed it with Apache horse thieves in mind. All you had to do was pile some brush across the panhandle and the animals had nowhere to go.

Nelda pointed to the soaring forested peak behind the gorge. "That's Cerro Azul, Blue Mountain," she said. "Very sacred peak for the Apache. If you follow a line from the Corral up to the shoulder of the mountain, that's where Geronimo's stronghold is."

"I was thinking about going there and camping for a night."

She asked Efren about it in Spanish. He shrugged and offered to lend me a horse.

"Actually I'd prefer to walk."

"To walk?" he said. The idea of walking for pleasure or recreation does not exist in rural northern Mexico. Walking is what you do when you don't have a truck, horse, mule, or donkey.

"It is a custom of my country," I said. "Maybe it sounds crazy but many of us enjoy walking. How many hours do you think it would take?"

"Three, four, five hours maybe."

"Is anyone growing anything at the spring?"

"No, no," he said. "They used to but the spring is going dry. There isn't enough water to grow anything now."

Early the next morning I filled up my canteens and put my backpack in John's truck. Nelda came out of the house and gave me a bag full of burritos. Efren told me not to leave the truck on the road under any circumstances. "They will strip it, the tires, the seat, the engine, everything."

It was my first time driving in the Sierra and also the first time I broke Joe Brown's cardinal rule and traveled alone in the Sierra. I stashed the truck in a place Efren had recommended, covered it with oak branches, pulled on my backpack, and wondered if I was pushing my luck. Maybe slightly. But I had assessed the situation carefully and it seemed safe enough.

I came to the brink of the gorge and started down the trail, which was composed mainly of those loose baseball-sized rocks that God placed on steep mountain trails so that human beings might sprain their ankles. I slipped and fell twice in the first half hour but here I was at last, striking out alone on foot for an Apache hideout in the heart of the Sierra Madre.

In a high precipitous place where swallows chittered and wheeled in the air below me, I found the ruined cliff dwelling that Nelda had told me about and a few tiny corncobs, two and three inches long. The Apaches didn't reach the American Southwest and northern Mexico until the sixteenth century, after the first Spanish conquistadors. The cliff dwelling was at least five hundred years older than that, built by an agricultural people who had gone extinct under mysterious circumstances, much like the Anasazi. There seemed little doubt that fear governed their architecture. Why else would anyone live an hour's hard climb from the nearest water?

The adobe walls had collapsed or been pulled apart by vandals. The roof beams protruded from the rubble at asymetrical angles, trash and beer cans were strewn around and the name FERGUSON had been painstakingly scraped into one of the fire-blackened cliff walls.

Onward I slipped and stumbled, taking many unwanted diversions on the intersecting cow and deer trails. Eventually I found my way down to the sandy banks of the Gavilán, where a beautiful forest of oaks and white-barked sycamores harbored a wild profusion of bird life. I searched the banks for signs of humans and found only one set of horse or mule tracks that looked at least a week old. I sprawled out in the sand, ate a burrito, and carved off two slices from a slab of Umbrian prosciutto, which had come to Tucson in the suitcase of an Italian filmmaker. Was I the first man to eat Umbrian prosciutto on the Gavilán? Was this what adventure travel had come down to in the twenty-first century?

Crossing the river the water was up to my knees and very cold. I squelched up and down the far bank looking for a trail going uphill and found a rough cattle track that dead-ended at the base of a cliff. From there I scrambled on all fours up a brutally steep slope covered with slippery pine needles. Then I found another dead-end cattle trail. Two hours later, having vomited up my Umbrian prosciutto through over-exertion, I reached the Corral de los Indios, walked out into the middle of it, took off the backpack, and collapsed with my arms and legs in the X formation. It seemed unfathomable that Apaches were able to cover eighty miles of this terrain in a day, on foot, and that Tarahumaras ran hundred-mile races over it.

By the time I dragged myself up to the shoulder of the mountain, all my water was gone, my clothes were sodden with sweat, and I was desperately thirsty. I came to an old logging road and nearly head-butted an owl. It was roosting in a little pine sapling at the exact height of my head, both of us oblivious to each other's presence. I was three feet away when it woke up and shot past my ear. For Apaches and Mexicans, the owl is a bad luck bird but I didn't believe in any of that nonsense.

I recognized Geronimo's stronghold by the weathered coils of black plastic irrigation tubing and old tin cans—the unmistakable signs of a Sierra Madre drug camp. It hadn't been used in a couple of years, by the looks of things, and my heart sank when I saw the reason why. Efren had described the spring as a trickle and said I could fill my canteens there but it was barely a dribble. There went my plan to spend the night at the stronghold and see what dreams I might have. I had no choice but to make the long thirsty walk back down to the river.

THAT NIGHT, SITTING by a fire on the riverbank, refreshed by an icy swim and the last of the burritos, I pulled out my own copy of Ingstad. In many ways his was a quixotic expedition. His Chiricahua companions were more interested in looking for a treasure they had hidden in a certain cave but couldn't seem to find. At one point they tried to mutiny and Ingstad was forced to draw his gun on them. Soon afterward the Apaches went off by themselves and it may well be that they were warning the wild ones that a strange white man was looking for them.

Any Apaches still living in the Sierra in 1937 would have been severely demoralized. Earlier in the decade, Francisco Fimbres and other Mexican ranchers had staged a series of self-described "extermination campaigns." They hunted for Apache camps and almost invariably found no men living in them. The men had either absconded or more likely been killed while raiding. The ranchers killed as many women as they could and snatched up the children.

The most interesting part of Ingstad's book is when he tracks down the captive children and interviews them. One was a broad-faced girl with a shy charm living in the suburbs of Los Angeles. She was twelve years old and her name was now Carmela Harris. Ingstad asked her what she remembered.

They called me Bui (Owl Eyes). There were only women in the camp—four young women and three children besides me. Nana decided everything and she was very strict. We lived in caves and small huts made out of grass. We were always afraid someone would come, so we moved often from mountain to mountain. . . . We ate mescal (baked agave cactus) and dried meat, sometimes grass. We didn't have much—some skins, a knife, nails, a cup, that's about it . . . Nana had just sewn me a nice new dress for me out of leather, but then I was captured.

This was in the mountains above Nácori Chico in Sonora. She was three or four years old. Mexican cowboys came on horseback, killed her grandmother, and took her away. There was an American woman called Dixie Harris living in Nácori Chico with her rancher husband and they adopted the little Apache girl and took her to Los Angeles. Carmela spoke good English now and was doing well in high school. Ingstad asked her if she had liked her life in the mountains.

I was often afraid. Nana was so strict, and I wasn't allowed to do anything. Once a little child cried very loudly and she held its mouth so that it died. . . . Every evening we got down on our knees and reached our hands to the heavens. All was quiet, no one said anything. But I don't know what God we prayed to.

Carmela Harris graduated from high school in Tujunga, California, and went on to become a nurse. She never married and lived out the rest of her life with Dixie. In 1972 they left California and emigrated to a stone farmhouse in the Italian hill town of Perugia, in the province of Umbria where my prosciutto originated. Carmela took with her the little buckskin dress that her grandmother had sewn for her in the Sierra Madre. She was happy in Umbria and loved to explore the cities and towns. She died suddenly in her midforties, cause unknown, and is buried in Perugia.

There are theories that the last free Apaches in the Sierra went south and blended in with the Mountain Pimas or the Tarahumaras, or north to blend in with Mexicans in Arizona. There are certainly stories and folklore to support these theories but Nelda doesn't believe them. By 1940, she thinks, all the Sierra Madre holdouts had been killed or captured, or died out from starvation, disease, or misadventure.

It was a cold, windy night full of stars on the Gavilán. I lay down by the fire in my sleeping bag, watching the flames flatten and flare and listening to wind hissing in the trees. I had just fallen asleep when I heard a rustling in the undergrowth. I snapped on my flashlight and illuminated a big skunk in the act of raising its tail and spraying. Luckily the wind caught most of it but my sleeping bag still carried a skunky smell for the next few months.

LOOKING BACK ON that trip to the Gavilán, it is all overshadowed by an incident that happened on the way out and the conclusion I drew from it. John's truck kept overheating on the uphill grades. I was standing there by the side of the road with the hood up. A beaten-up truck pulled over and four rough-looking, unshaven, steely-eyed men got out.

"Broken down, eh," said their leader. "You're out here alone?"

"The engine is overheating. I have to wait for it to cool down. This is the truck of my friend Juan Hatch, the son of Doctor Hatch."

"What are you doing here? Where are you coming from?"

"I am a friend of Juan Hatch and Nelda Villa. I was staying with Nelda at the Gavilán."

"The Gavilán?" He raised his eyebrows and looked at the other three, as if to share the improbability and ridiculousness of this answer. They grunted distractedly. They were gazing covetously at the tools and spare tires in the bed of John's truck.

"The Rancho Gavilán. Nelda is the wife of Efren Villa."

"Ah," he said. Then to the others: "He says he knows Efren Villa."

"Yes," I said. "Efren and Nelda and their son, Walter."

"Efren Villa is a good man."

"A very good man."

He nodded a few times and said it was well. They got back into their truck, pulled away, and lifted their chins good-bye. That was all it took. Joe Brown was wrong. It wasn't dangerous to travel alone in the Sierra Madre. All you needed was the right name and you were perfectly safe.

7

Lofty's Gold

IT WAS CRACK PIPE Cuate who first told me about Nachito the folk healer and the wonders he could work with roots and herbs and the eggs of a married hen. John Hatch had never heard of him but since we were in the area, exploring the mountains south of the Gavilán River, he agreed to help me track him down. Mainly I was curious to see how Nachito operated but I also had some troubles and ailments that were weighing me down. Despite my skepticism about the eggs and the marital status of the hens that laid them, I couldn't help wondering if he had some other treatment that might cure me or at least alleviate the symptoms a little. It took several hours of driving and stopping and asking for directions but eventually we found Nachito's compound at the end of a rough dirt track a few kilometers beyond the tiny village of Nuevo Ser.

Nachito was suspicious. There were two white men outside his gates and this had happened only once before. "You are Germans," he said accusingly. He was a big man with a sagging belly and a withered leg and he looked like a malevolent old toad.

"No, *señor*, I am British and my friend here is a Mormon from Colonia Juarez."

"And is your friend a Mormon mafioso? Huh? Answer me that. I know about these Mormons."

It was true that a few Chihuahua Mormons, including a friend of

John's, had got caught up in the marijuana-growing and -trafficking business a few years ago; John's friend had been forced to reverse the usual direction and go north for his health. "Oh no," said John politely. "I grow a different crop. Apples and peaches."

"What are you doing here, a Mormon and a what now?"

"Un britanico," I said. "I have a cowboy friend in Sonora who said I should come here. You healed his shoulder. I have a bad shoulder also and I was traveling in the area—"

"Why are you really here?"

"That is the reason. It is my shoulder and I have insomnia also. My friend Cuate said that you could cure me."

He scowled and harrumphed and opened the chain-link gate, as if bound against his will to the Hippocratic oath. Inside the compound there were a few low buildings and tin sheds, shy teenage girls walking past, grazing horses, dogs, cats, and chickens. Dragging his bad leg, Nachito limped over to a small brick building with a metal door. I left John waiting in the truck and followed him inside.

Crack Pipe Cuate had come here with a shoulder problem that sounded like my bursitis. He joined a line of people waiting outside the compound. They told him he would need an egg from a *gallina casada,* a married hen, which is a polite country term for a fertilized egg. Cuate asked where he could get one. They pointed to a man who was selling eggs and assuring his buyers that they came from married hens.

Nachito passed the egg over Cuate's body and then wrote him a prescription for various roots, herbs, and preparations to be filled at the local apothecary's shop in the village of La Pinta. "There is no charge," he said. "But if you want to leave something for the saints . . ."

Cuate left a hundred pesos (ten dollars) for the saints and swore his shoulder was cured even though it still gave him trouble from time to time.

I stepped into a small room with a pine wood fire burning in the fireplace and candles all over the floor. There were plaster effigies of the saints on a shelf mounted on the far wall, including Jesús

Malverde, the mustachioed, neckerchief-wearing bandit who is the patron saint of drug traffickers. A well-thumbed medical encyclopedia lay open on the cluttered desk and nailed to the wall behind it was a medical diagram of the human body without its skin.

Nachito gestured to a chair, opened a desk drawer, produced an old stethoscope, and fitted its horns into his ears. "Don't I need an egg?" I asked.

"Not you," he said. He listened to my lungs while I stared at the collection of "Magnetic Sand" arrayed in little glass tubes on his desk. "Do you smoke?" he said.

"Not anymore."

He took my left hand and examined the palm. "Are you married?"

"Divorced."

"You will be married again."

He sat down heavily behind the desk. I started crossing one leg over the other and he reached out with surprising speed and slapped down my foot. "No!" he barked. "Not this!"

I placed my feet parallel on the floor and rolled my right shoulder. It made its usual crunching and grinding noises. "I have pain here in my shoulder. It never goes away. And I have insomnia."

"And you eat a lot of red meat."

"Well, yes. I suppose I do."

"How often do you eat red meat?"

"What else is there in Chihuahua?"

"You must eat chicken. Chicken and fish."

"I don't eat fish. I have an allergy against fish."

"Then you must eat chicken."

Inadvertently I started to cross my legs again and he gave my foot another hard whack. "No red meat for two months! It releases a vitamin that gets into your shoulder and makes pain. And stop this with your legs. Don't make me hit you again."

His eyes were fierce and charismatic and when he locked them onto mine he seemed to see right through me. "You are carrying around many sorrows," he said.

"My divorce was recent. I have pain in my heart and money troubles." I listened to myself blurting it all out. "I left my wife because she was a drunk but I drink too much also. It is difficult to sleep without drinking."

"Why are you in Mexico? Are you looking for another wife?"

"No. I am a writer. I am traveling through the Sierra Madre and writing a book about it."

"But the Sierra is a dangerous place, especially for you. There are many *narcos* and killers here. Are you looking for your death?"

"No. I don't think so. I feel happier to be alive in the Sierra."

He grunted dismissively and pulled out a prescription pad. He filled the page with a looping blue illegible scrawl, ripped it off, and then filled up the page underneath. "There is no charge," he said, handing me the two pages.

"Perhaps I could leave something for the saints."

"If you wish."

I left ten *gringo* dollars on the shelf of saints and walked outside into the fading dusk, feeling dazed and numb. I showed John the prescription. "He says they will fill this in La Pinta."

"We'll have to see if it's still open although I imagine they'll open it up specially for you. Goodness gracious. What is all this?"

"I have no idea."

The pharmacy was open. An Indian-looking woman with no expression on her face took my prescription. She went into the back for fifteen minutes or so and then came up to the cash register with plastic bags full of herbs, roots, twigs and dried flowers, a box of "rattlesnake pills" with a picture of a coiled snake on the front, a packet of "Aztec energy tea," a packet of Celebrex arthritis pills, and three boxed syringes loaded with a cortisone steroid that had been banned in the United States and presumably dumped on the Mexican market. She wrote out all the instructions and a bill that totaled nearly a hundred American dollars. I handed over the money and said thank you.

That night I took my two prescribed rattlesnake pills and made myself two cups of the root, herb, and twig tea that Nachito had recommended for insomnia. I lay there in John's spare bedroom feeling drugged and immobilized but stubbornly awake for most of the night. When I did slip into sleep my dreams were the most vivid and horrific nightmares I have experienced since childhood.

By dawn I felt completely wrung out in mind, body, and spirit. "Fortitude, man," I told myself as I struggled into my clothes and inspected my gaunt, shattered-looking face in the mirror. "If you don't buck up, you're doomed."

WE SET OUT on a long looping drive through the eastern slopes of the Sierra Madre, which become more gradual south of Casas Grandes and flatten out in some places to form big windswept benches and plateaus. There were tumbleweeds caught on the fences and men on horseback wearing baseball caps and sandals, eyes narrowed against the wind and dust, herding bony-hipped cattle along the side of the road. We drove through gray sawmill towns and dusty *ejido* villages where only the old men and a few women and small children were left. Handwritten signs nailed to wooden posts advertised a direct bus service to Phoenix, Arizona.

The farmers here had been living above the subsistence level, selling off their surplus corn to buy farm equipment, pickup trucks, and construction materials for their houses. Then, in 1994, came the North American Free Trade Agreement (NAFTA), which put them in direct and hopelessly unfair competition with U.S. corporate agriculture, followed by ten years of drought. Occasionally a brand-new pickup truck with tinted windows would drive past and remind us that one export crop was doing just fine.

Deeper into the mountains, the roads turned to dirt and the landscape became steeper and pine-forested and slashed with canyons. We went to the cliff dwellings at Cuarenta Casas, which had been developed for tourism with trails, guards, fences, and fees. We struggled up a washed-out logging road into a grove of aspens where snow lay on the ground and one of the few remaining flocks of thick-billed parrots flashed green among the treetops. Then we descended to Bavícora, where William Randolph Hearst owned a million-acre cattle ranch that was disbanded during the revolution, and Gomez Farías, where we stopped for dinner in a big tiled barn of a restaurant on the edge of town.

"I thought you were giving up red meat," said John when I ordered a steak, a beer, and a shot of tequila.

"I'm giving up rattlesnake pills and herbal teas instead."

The steak was grilled over mesquite wood, thinner and chewier than an American steak but with a richer, meatier, moaningly delicious flavor. Vitamins in the shoulder? To hell with Nachito. He had made a fool out of me and fleeced my wallet and given me nightmares for good measure. Maybe I had asked for it, with my prurient tourist's curiosity, but he wasn't going to fool me into giving up the pleasures of red meat.

DRIVING BACK TO John's house that night, with the moon rising over the desert plains and no traffic on the highway, he started telling stories about his father and the old days in the Sierra, letting his mind unspool behind the wheel.

As the lone country doctor in an area that had always gotten by with *curanderos,* folk healers in the Nachito vein, John's father often found himself arguing against deeply entrenched beliefs. If a pregnant woman sees a toad, for example, her child will be a hunchback. If she sees a snake, it'll be a harelip. Never eat fresh fruits, juices, or vegetables when you have a cold. When a girl is suffering from *atiricia,* a condition characterized by loneliness, homesickness, and emotional gloom that doesn't appear in any dictionary, medical or otherwise, the only remedy is to give her a bright red dress. Dr. Hatch tried gallantly but he never found a way to win these arguments. If a pregnant woman saw a toad and didn't give birth to a hunchback, it simply meant the saints had answered her prayers and intervened.

Dr. Hatch, having qualified in Mexico City, began practicing medicine in Chuhuichupa in 1943. I asked John if the old mountain colony was still exclusively Mormon at that time. "No, no," he said. "There were some Mexicans living there. And there was a bandit from Tombstone, Arizona, called Loftus, although I don't think anyone believed that was his real name. He came down to the Sierra for his health and stayed for the rest of his life."

The retired bandit was a small man with penetrating yellow-green eyes, standing about five feet four and weighing no more than 115 pounds. He rode into Chuhuichupa in 1925 or thereabouts, tied up his horse outside the adobe general store, ordered his supplies— flour, beans, lard, coffee, salt, sugar, matches, tobacco, cartridges for his pistol and saddle rifle—and paid for it all with an old gold U.S. coin. The Mormons asked his name. "Loftus," he replied. And his first name? "Lofty," he said. "Yessir, that's my name. Mr. Lofty Loftus."

He took up residence in a cave near a place the Mormons called Possum Hollow and lived there with his horses for nearly thirty years. The Mormons grew fond of him and enjoyed having such a colorful character in their midst. Mr. Loftus was a well-spoken man, fluent in Spanish and French and able to recite Shakespeare and other poets. In the presence of women he bent at the waist, doffed his old shapeless Western hat, and showered them with compliments and fragments of poetry.

John's father once asked him about his upbringing and education. Loftus said he was born in France, brought over to the United States when he was a year old, and raised by two rich maiden aunts in New Orleans. They sent him to a good school and college but he got bored with education and the prospect of a bourgeois life and went out west to Tombstone, Arizona, to find some adventure. Then he told John's father that he asked too many questions and changed the subject.

Over the years he let slip a few wistful remarks about the old wild days in Tombstone when he was "full of vinegar and had a full set of tail feathers." He told a few stories about rustling cattle, robbing trains and stagecoaches, and shooting it out with rival bandits. The prevailing wisdom in Chuhuichupa was that Loftus had robbed a big bank shipment near Tucson or Tombstone and ridden the old outlaw trail down into the Sierra Madre with the loot. Apart from joining the occasional cattle drive as a cook, he was never seen to work and he always paid for everything with old gold and silver U.S. coins.

Loftus lived a frugal life in that cave but there were some things he couldn't do without. First and foremost was something to read. People knew never to throw out an old magazine or newspaper but save them all for Mr. Loftus. He was also fond of liquor and sporting women, neither of which were available among the wholesome, teetotal Mormons of Chuhuichupa. So he would ride over the mountains to the rough sawmill town of El Largo, where mescal flowed like springwater and Dr. Hatch was required to make weekly checkups on the prostitutes.

"Everyone always wondered where Loftus had his money hidden," said John. "People used to follow him, hoping he would lead them to his main cache. They would dig up the floor of his cave when he was gone."

John's father came to know Loftus as well as anyone and this was partly because Loftus was a hypochondriac. He would ride in to see Dr. Hatch convinced that he was about to die and asking for help in drawing up his will. Dr. Hatch would examine him, find nothing worse than some rheumatism and a slightly irregular heartbeat, and Loftus would ride off happily and postpone the writing of his will again.

By the 1950s Dr. Hatch had left Chuhuichupa and was practicing medicine down on the plains in Casas Grandes. One day he received a message that an old *gringo* staying in a cheap hotel wanted to see him urgently. He went over to the flophouse and found his Loftus in a severely wasted condition. He had gotten drunk, passed out in the snow, and nearly died. His most urgent medical problem was a severely frostbitten toe.

Dr. Hatch amputated the toe and put up Loftus in a friend's garage. The wound was slow to heal and the entire foot extremely painful. Dr. Hatch left three Nembutal capsules for the pain and told him not to take more than one at a time.

"Then my dad got a call that he was dying," said John. He had been telling Lofty's story for nearly an hour now and we were getting close to the lights of Casas Grandes and the turn-off to Colonia Juárez.

"Dad went over there and found that Loftus had taken all three Nembutals and was in a coma. Dad gave him a stimulant and some coffee and Loftus came around but I guess he was still pretty much out of it. He started talking about his will. He said he had some property in California and his horses and a large sum of money buried somewhere in the mountains and he wanted to leave it all to my dad and a young fellow in Chuhuichupa named Bill Judd."

The next day Dr. Hatch went back there with Bill Judd and Loftus started dictating his will. His property in California and his horses were to be divided between the two of them. "What about the money you buried?" asked Dr. Hatch. Loftus looked startled and said he didn't know anything about any buried money. Dr. Hatch said he had talked about it the day before under the influence of Nembutal. Loftus sighed and came out with the whole story.

"He and some other fellows had robbed a bank shipment outside Tucson," said John. "Loftus and a fellow called the Black Giant had double-crossed the rest of the gang and slipped down across the border and up into the Sierra on the old outlaw trail. They were camped one night on this particular mountain and they started getting suspicious of each other to the point where neither one of them wanted to fall asleep. Loftus ended up shooting the Black Giant and burying him up there. He also buried three bags full of silver and gold coins on a ledge above a spring, putting them into some old Indian grinding holes and then covering them over with rocks.

"Well, when my father heard that, he more or less dragged Loftus off his sickbed and went up there to dig up the money. But a forest fire had come through the area and it looked different to how Loftus remembered it, and then Loftus started getting sick and delirious, raving about the Black Giant, and my dad couldn't get any sense out of him. Dad dug a few holes but his hands got blistered up and he was worried about Loftus and they came down out of the mountains without finding it. Dad always swore he was going to go back there with a metal detector calibrated for gold and silver."

"And did he?" I asked.

"Well, in 1972 he went up there with my brother-in-law. They had rented a metal detector but they didn't know how to use it properly and they gave up without making a concerted effort."

By now we were parked outside John's house in Colonia Juarez, sitting side by side in the dark.

"Who else knows about it?"

"I don't think anyone knows the location outside my family. I've been meaning to go up there myself for years. There's a fellow I know here who's pretty good with a metal detector and I keep meaning—"

"John," I interrupted. "You've got to do it and take me with you. I'll pay your guiding fee. I don't even want any of the money if we find it."

WHEN I TOLD my friend Tom Vaught that I was going to dig for an outlaw's buried treasure in the Sierra Madre, he came close to begging and pleading for an invitation. Tom is an actor and bartender who lives in downtown Manhattan and thinks the world has been going to hell since 1974, at which time he was seven years old. He refuses to own or even touch a computer—"They're a fad," he likes to say—and seldom wears an item of clothing that would look out of place in 1938. He's built like a barrel and he speaks with a deep, rasping, whiskey-cured growl that gets him a lot of work in television voiceovers and radio commercials. He also does a few plays, appears as Pirate Tom and Santa Claus in seasonal children's productions, and sings old blues and sea chanteys at parties and bars. He was a little disappointed to hear that we wouldn't be riding mules but otherwise the trip promised to fill all his criteria of nostalgic cool.

I went back to Tucson and picked him up at the airport. We stopped off at Arizona Hatters, where Tom outfitted himself with a silverbelly Pacific-brim Stetson for the trip, and then went to my house for a viewing of *The Treasure of the Sierra Madre,* which Tom raided for material. "I can smell gold like a jackass can smell water," he growled as I packed the truck with camping supplies. "Now gold's a devilish sort of thing and I know what it does to men's souls."

It was a long drive back to John's house and my mind kept running away with me. I knew from my research that buried treasure stories were a dime a dozen in the Sierra Madre and they nearly all had the same ending: the treasure wasn't where it was supposed to be. I thought we had no more than a 5 percent chance of finding Lofty's gold. But I couldn't stop thinking about what would happen if we did find it. I kept returning to one question in particular. Why had I made that blithe, idiotic remark about not wanting any of the money?

At the time I meant it but that was then and this was now. I was the one who had made this expedition happen, wasn't I? I had invested more of my time and money in it than anyone else and thanks to my ex-wife and the divorce settlement, I was in dire need of money to fund the rest of my travels in the Sierra Madre. Surely John would understand that I was entitled to my fair share. Surely he wouldn't try to hold me to some hasty, offhand remark I made on the spur of a moment when I was strung out on rattlesnake pills, severely sleep-deprived and riding out the last buzz of two beers, a big steak, and a shot of tequila?

Nor had I appreciated at the time how valuable those old coins might be. Lofty Loftus told Dr. Hatch (as a Tom Waits song might begin) that he'd buried "three stout bags full of gold and silver coins, a good load for a packhorse." Without knowing the dates on the coins it was hard to estimate how much they were worth, because some years were rarer and more valuable than others, but one Tucson coin collector made some calculations and told me they might bring two million dollars if we managed to smuggle them through the army and police checkpoints in Mexico, across the border past U.S. Customs, and sell them off discreetly in small batches to avoid flooding the market and paying any taxes.

That was half a million dollars each, if you split it between John, the metal detector man, Tom, and me. Or was John planning to cut Tom out of the deal as well? He had agreed to Tom's coming along and digging but we hadn't discussed Tom's potential share of the goods. And when I brought up my share, John reminded me in a half-joking sort of way that I'd said I didn't want any of the money. I half-joked back that we'd have to see about that. It was true. I didn't know what I might do if I found myself standing over a two-million-dollar pile of gold with a shovel in my hand and John tried to tell me that I wasn't getting any of it.

In a different part of my consciousness, I was shocked to see these nasty, greedy, suspicious thoughts bubbling and backfiring through my brain. It seemed so unlike me. My attitude toward money has always been a kind of wary disdain, a determination not to let it get too much power over me. I've been known to get tightfisted with money and I hate being ripped off but this was something else. This was something new and it bore all the signs and symptoms of gold fever.

AT DAWN JOHN Hatch had his maps out on the kitchen table. The side of his neck was flushed and he was trembling with excitement. Or was that greed? His fingertip jerked and quivered as it traced the thin dirt roads that would take us through the Sierra and he jabbed seven or eight times at the spot where the treasure was supposed to be buried. "This is the mountain, this is the west-facing slope, this is the place my father always pointed out to me."

I had his father's memoirs open on the table. The family had published them privately in an obscure green hardback called *Médico, My Life As a Country Doctor in Mexico* by E. LeRoy Hatch, M.D., and they contained nearly two chapters about his friend Lofty Loftus and a detailed description of where his money was supposed to be buried—in an Indian grinding hole above a spring high on the west-facing slope of Devil's Peak.

"It's really Bull's Peak," said John. "Dad changed the name of the mountain to keep people away from it. He told us there was a series of ledges at the base of the west-facing cliffs, right above the spring, and that's where it was supposed to be."

Tom stood over the table leaning on his knuckles, pretending to study the maps while studying John and shooting me significant glances. "At first I was in it for the journey, the once-in-a-lifetime opportunity," Tom told me later. "Then I saw John trembling that morning and that's when I started thinking we might actually find it."

There were three other people in the kitchen. John's wife, Sandra, leaned back against the sink, arms crossed, eyebrows arched in amusement at her husband's condition and perhaps the general solemnity of men and their maps. The other two were local Mormons. Todd Romney was the metal detector man, a solid, serious, slow-talking fruit farmer and volunteer policeman in his early thirties. Lee Robinson was in his midforties, a cowboy with a horse business and a much-repaired straw hat. He seemed like a nice guy but John hadn't told us he would be coming along and presumably claiming a share of the goods.

So now it would be a five-way split, would it? And it better get split five ways. The rational part of my brain told me to get a grip, man, for God's sake. We weren't going to find any buried treasure. We were going to have a pleasant weekend in the mountains with our new Mormon friends.

On the way out of Colonia Juárez we stopped at the cemetery. After twenty minutes of hunting around in the weeds we found a tombstone that wasted no words: LOFTY LOFTUS 1955. Ever alert to theatrical possibilities, Tom produced some turkey feathers that he'd found and a jar of vinegar siphoned from John and Sandra's kitchen and placed them reverentially on the grave, to honor a man who had once been full of vinegar with a full set of tail feathers. He stood there with his new Stetson over his heart and made a speech asking Lofty for his blessing. He threw in some half-remembered Shakespeare for good measure and apologized for not having any liquor to pour on the grave. "And as for us," he concluded, setting his hat back on his head, "where once was famine will now be feast."

We set off in two pickup trucks heavily laden with picks, shovels, camping gear, water, spare tires, and supplies. We had two-way radios, topographical maps, GPS finders, a combined Mormon experience of about ninety years on those confusing, interbraiding mountain back roads, and we still managed to get lost a few times. After seven hours we reached the base of a mountain that John was sure was Bull's Peak. He unloaded his ATV and zoomed up an old logging road that climbed its western flanks. The rest of us stood around, peed in silence, munched on snacks, and made some low-energy masculine small talk. Twenty minutes later John came back all breathless and excited.

"This is it," he said. "It's exactly how Dad described it and this road'll take us right up there." We had to clear some fallen trees off the road and stand on the back bumper of John's truck to get it up the steep slope and then we reached a small clearing of level ground at the end of the road and it did indeed look perfect. The spring had gone dry but you could tell from the black irrigation pipe, discarded tin cans, and plastic seedling pots that it used to irrigate a good-sized marijuana camp. And if you looked uphill from where the spring used to be, there was a series of ledges at the base of the west-facing cliffs that soared up to the peak.

Todd fitted together his metal detector. The rest of us grabbed shovels and picks. We clambered up a loose, steep rocky slope to the ledges and Todd started wanding his machine back and forth. Almost immediately there was an urgent, high-pitched electronic whine. My heart leaped into my throat and I charged over there. We all did.

Todd twisted down one of the dials and passed the metal detector over the spot again. This time it made a feeble bleat. "Probably ore in the rock," he said.

"Probably?" I said. "Shouldn't we dig to make sure?"

"It's not worth it. Signal's pretty weak."

We fanned out across the ledges. They were covered in rockfall from the cliffs above them and it soon became apparent that three stout canvas bags buried in an Indian grinding hole eighty years ago might be four or five feet under the surface by now.

"How far down can that thing detect metal?" I asked Todd.

"Depends on the ground."

"Well, what about ground like this?"

"A foot. Eighteen inches maybe."

This was disheartening to say the least but we weren't about to give up. We consulted Dr. Hatch's memoir again, which had come to resemble a sacred text, made our triangulations and dug holes in the likely spots. It was lung-heaving, back-aching, sweat-drenching labor. We must have been at nearly nine thousand feet and the ground was made of big, loosely compacted rocks and small, tightly compacted rocks. When you got down to three feet you would call for Todd, who would amble over and dip his metal detector into the hole. Half the time he would get an excited beep on the first pass and your heart would leap. Then he would turn down the dial, get nothing and say, "Nope," with no hint of sympathy for your crushed hopes.

"How do we know he's not marking out the best spots for himself?" hissed Tom. "How do we know he's not going to come back here next week and dig it up on his own?"

"I was wondering that too."

"You dig and dig and all you get is '*Wheep-wheep*. Nope.' Then he goes off on his own and that's when you hear '*Wheep-wheep. Wheep-wheep-wheeep. Wheep-wheep-wheep-wheep*. But he never calls anyone over to dig there. I mean, what the fuck?"

The next morning our suspicions were confirmed to be false and paranoid. We buried the head of a pickax under twelve inches of loose rock and called Todd over. He waved the metal detector over the spot and got no sound at all. Even if he wanted to cheat us out of our gold, his machine wasn't going to help him.

We dug holes all morning, deeper holes to compensate for the shortcomings of the metal detector. "We need a gold-sniffin' badger," panted Tom, leaning on his shovel. I toiled on one particular hole for more than an hour. I poured all my hopes and energy into it and grew resentful that no one would help me dig. My hole was directly in line with where the spring used to be and the fire-blackened center of the cliffs, exactly where the grinding hole was supposed to be, so why were they all clustered around another hole, taking turns to dig in what was clearly the wrong place?

Sure enough they came up with nothing. I was down to four and a half feet and with every scrape of the shovel I imagined uncovering the frayed top of an old canvas bag. I called for Todd. He came over with the others and we all stood around the hole. Todd lowered the metal detector into the hole, waved it back and forth, got nothing and said, "Nope." I hated him in that moment. I wanted to grab that worthless metal detector and pound him over the head with it. I was learning what gold does to men's souls, even when its presence is entirely theoretical and based on fifty-year-old hearsay.

ON THE WAY out of the mountains, our passage was blocked by two black trucks with no markings or license plates. They saw us coming and pulled across the road in a V-shaped barricade. Three men with pistols on their belts jumped out. One was wearing a bandanna tied over his head and a T-shirt with a dancing skeleton on the front. The second had slicked-back hair, jeans, and a polo shirt. The third man was older and craggier with a shock of pepper-and-salt hair and a big push-broom mustache.

They said they were *federales*, Mexican federal police officers. Having just seen *The Treasure of the Sierra Madre*, I was briefly tempted to ask them for their badges but they were rude, aggressive, and threatening and I had heard so many horror stories about predatory *federales*. What were we doing in the mountains? Illegal hunting? Buying drugs? Didn't we know the Sierra was full of bad men and *narcotraficantes*?

The one with the push-broom mustache started questioning Tom.

"*De donde es?*" he asked.

"No *español*," said Tom.

"Where you from?" said the *federal* in heavily accented English.

"New York City."

"Are you Italian?"

"No. Dutch, Polish."

"You look Italian. Where is your *pasaporte*?"

Tom dug out his passport and handed it over. The *federal* looked at it suspiciously and then looked up at Tom. "Are you sure you're not Italian?"

"I like Italian food," offered Tom.

"Hah! So do I!" said the *federal*. "Get out of the truck."

Tom stepped out of the truck. Meanwhile the other *federales* were rifling through our gear. If we had dug up Lofty's treasure there was no question they would have confiscated it. Then one of them found a loaded nine-millimeter pistol under Todd's seat and held it up triumphantly. Todd explained that he was a volunteer police officer in Colonia Juárez and licensed to carry the pistol. The *federal* with slicked-back hair jacked out the magazine, pulled out a bullet, and held it up. "But these are hollow points," he said. "Illegal bullets. What is the name of your commanding officer?"

John got angry and asked them why they were being so rude and what was the name of their commanding officer, and how was it going to look when he found out that they had been harassing innocent tourists and fellow officers of the law, and why hadn't they shown us any identification, and what exactly were they looking for? It was an impressive bluster and it put them on the defensive. They said there was a lot of drug activity in the area.

"Then why are you wasting time with us?" asked John. "Illegal bullets," they countered. "This is a very serious matter." But the momentum had turned and soon afterward they let us go.

John fumed for the next half hour, sounding very much like a man of the Sierra Madre in the way he sided with the outlaws against the authorities. "I've never had any trouble with the drug people, just the ones pretending to put a stop to it. If they're up here looking for drugs, why don't they ask me for help? I can take them right to a couple of the big *narcos* around here and then we'll see if they still feel like throwing their weight around. Those *federales* will be out of the mountains right behind us. They'd never stop a vehicle after dark in the Sierra Madre. Then they might be forced to do what they're pretending to do and they'd be in real trouble."

I TOLD MYSELF that it wasn't greed that brought me back to Bull's Peak. It was the inconclusiveness of the first trip, the crappiness of Todd's metal detector, and the nagging uncertainty it left. This time there were three of us: me, John, and a professional treasure hunter with a metal detector called the Bloodhound, capable of beaming its signals through rocky ground to a depth of thirty feet.

The treasure hunter was a tall, bearded, muscular man in his early fifties. He wore a NASCAR T-shirt and a canvas camouflage hat and spoke with a voice that made Tom Vaught sound like a mezzo-soprano. He used to be a rodeo cowboy and a bull had kicked him in the throat and destroyed his voice box. The doctors implanted a set of Teflon vocal cords, which made his voice so deep that neither telephone answering machines nor my digital voice recorder could pick it up properly. "My frequency's too low," he explained. "The middle and bottom register don't record."

He doesn't want his real name in print because his life requires a certain amount of illegal activity, such as failing to report treasure finds to the authorities, dodging taxes, and smuggling antiquities across the border. For the sake of convenience I'll call him Bill. He lives in a small house in Tucson crammed to the rafters with arrowheads, bones, Indian artifacts, nuggets of gold, chunks of precious gems and minerals, complete sets of five different treasure-hunting magazines dating back to the nineteenth century, and lots of old gold and silver coins. "The mistake a lot of treasure hunters make is they get fixated on gold. When I'm hunting treasure, I'm looking for shapes, forms, colors, a glint, anything that breaks the pattern of how that land would look undisturbed. A linear depression in the ground, a game trail. My eyes are going crazy trying to take it all in and my brain is whirling trying to categorize it all. I tell you, man, it'll take your mind into a different dimension."

I told him the story of Lofty Loftus and our efforts to date. He asked a lot of questions and then agreed to come with us on the final dig. It would be a three-way split. We would divide up the coins once we had gotten them out of the mountains. Then it was every man for himself.

There were no signs that anyone else had been to Bull's Peak in our absence. Back we clambered to the ledges and Bill went all over them with the Bloodhound. He got nothing and then went over them again to make absolutely sure. Finally we knew for certain that the treasure wasn't there but the story still worried away at us.

We sat down on a slope carpeted with pine needles and talked it over. "Three stout canvas bags," said Bill. "A good load for a pack-horse. And he was up here for what, thirty years? He spent it all."

"What do you mean?" I said. "How's he going to spend two million dollars' worth of coins living in a cave by himself?"

"Back then gold was worth its face value. A $20 double-eagle gold coin weighed one ounce. Today it might be worth $5,000. Some of the rare ones go for $100,000. But back then gold was worth $20 an ounce. People weren't collecting old coins and certainly not in the Sierra Madre."

He started doing the sums, a little chagrined that he hadn't thought to do them in Tucson. A pound of gold had been worth $320. A good load for a packhorse on steep Sierra Madre trails was probably a hundred pounds, which was worth $32,000. And that worked out to roughly a thousand dollars a year for the thirty years Lofty was in Mexico, or eighty dollars a month for all his supplies including ammunition, liquor, and sporting ladies. No wonder he lived in a cave. The stuff was too heavy for a bank robber to get rich.

"It never occurred to me that he spent it all," said John. "People always talked about Lofty's gold like it was a fortune. But why would he tell my dad that it was buried here and to come up here and look for it?"

"Maybe he'd lost his marbles," suggested Bill. "He was an old man with frostbite and he'd just had a toe amputated and taken all that Nembutal."

"I think Lofty was a trickster at heart," I said. "He knew how feverish people were about finding his money and he wanted to have a laugh after he was gone. He made a fool out of your father and now he's made a fool out of us fifty years later. I bet the little feather-tailed bastard is chuckling in his grave."

In the final scene of *The Treasure of the Sierra Madre,* when the treasure hunters realize the gold is gone and will never be found again, they fall into delirious, ecstatic laughter. Our laughter was quieter and more rueful but it carried a similar sense of release. Having finally debunked the legend of Lofty's gold we were free of it and I felt somehow cured and whole again. The fever was gone and it was time to see what lay in store farther south.

8

Blasting Parakeet with The Pelican

I REACHED THE GRITTY little town of Tomochic in a screaming wind and ducked into a restaurant called the Fat Little Chicken. There were two enormously fat Indian women behind the counter who ignored me for a long time until the owner came out of a back room and told them to serve me. I sat down with half a grilled chicken, tortillas, salsa, and limes. Pictures of *The Last Supper* were hanging all around the walls. The one opposite me was etched into a mirror. The only sound was the tink of knives and forks against plates.

The door opened and out of the wind came three hard-eyed men who were unmistakably *narcos*. They were wearing ostrich-skin cowboy boots with matching belts, black leather jackets, silk shirts open to the sternum, gold chains, gold watches, and expensive white cowboy hats. The tinking stopped. I hunched down a little lower over my plate.

The *narcos* ordered beer and joked loudly that a chicken was hardly worth fucking, let alone eating. The two Indian women moved at a rapid waddle to serve them. The *narcos* downed their beers and ordered more and then chopped out lines of cocaine on the table and snorted them up. I was sneaking glances at them in *The Last Supper* mirror and one of them sensed it. Our eyes met briefly in the mirror and then he turned around in his seat and looked directly at me.

"*Que hay?*" he said. What is there?

"Nothing," I said. "Just eating lunch."

"What are you doing here?"

"Passing through, no more."

"Do you want a *chirrisquin*?" The others laughed.

"A what?"

He mimed the action of snorting coke. They all stared at me glittery-eyed and expectant.

"No thank you," I said. "Thank you for the offer but I must be going." I got up, left far too many pesos on the table for the bill, wished them an enjoyable lunch—*"Provecho, señores"*—and walked out into that evil wind, feeling thoroughly scared and rattled.

Tomochic lies on one of the two paved highways that cross the Sierra Madre. That's why I thought it would be safe to come here alone and without an introduction or even a name to drop. Now I wasn't so sure. The whole town had an ominous feel. More *narcos* drove past in brand-new pickup trucks. Men with tough hostile faces walked down the side of the highway with their right hands on top of their cowboy hats in that wind that blew like a curse or a punishment. If I hadn't seen a sign for a museum, painted in red letters on a boulder, I would have left immediately.

SOMETIMES WHEN YOU'RE trying to make sense of a foreign country or culture you come across a story that rings a big brass gong in your head. The Tomochic rebellion of 1891 and 1892 is usually described as a precursor or a foreshadowing of the Mexican revolution, which I wouldn't disagree with, but for me it also resonated with that surreal, absurd, fantastical, and peculiarly Mexican quality that I found so puzzling and intriguing.

Like so many bloody sagas in the Sierra Madre, it began as a matter of honor. The two hundred villagers of Tomochic (sometimes spelled Tomóchi) were already unhappy with their new mayor. He was an outsider, appointed by the regional strongman of the day, and he grazed his cattle on their land without paying or asking permission, forced them to work for him at miserably low wages, and threatened them with military conscription if they sought better-paying work in the mines. When they protested, the mayor responded by changing the route of the annual silver shipment from the mines at Pinos Altos, which had traditionally passed through Tomochic on its way to Chihuahua City. The villagers were outraged. It was an insult to their honor, implying that they were thieves and bandits who couldn't be trusted, and they staged an angry, threatening demonstration outside the mayor's office.

The mayor was crafty. He sent a report to Mexico City saying the villagers were rebelling against the federal government and planning to steal the annual silver transport. It was a well-calculated lie, designed to make President Díaz nervous and bring down the wrath of the federal government on the villagers. Díaz took the bait and sent federal troops to Tomochic. After a brief skirmish, the villagers withdrew into the mountains and the governor of Chihuahua reported to Díaz that the rebellion had been quashed. In fact it was only just beginning and already it had taken on a supernatural component.

The villagers had fallen under the sway of a messianic cult focused on an eighteen-year-old girl called Teresita, who lived across the mountains in the village of Cabora, Sonora, received visions of Christ, and performed miracle healings. At that time she was preaching a simple, humanistic creed that made no mention of political rebellion but then as now information traveled across the Sierra by word of mouth, the truth was fluid, and people believed what they wanted to believe. The villagers of Tomochic, led by the handsome, charismatic, domineering Cruz Chavez, convinced themselves that Teresita had authorized their fight against the mayor and the federal troops. Just to make sure, they decided to make a pilgrimage over the mountains to receive the blessing of Teresita in person.

It was a difficult, grueling journey at the best of times but they were pursued and harried by three different companies of troops. The villagers, who had been fighting Apaches in these mountains for generations, managed to defeat the first set of troops, elude the other two, and make it through to Cabora only to find that Teresita wasn't there or expected back anytime soon. Undeterred, they celebrated mass in her chapel, filled themselves with holy fervor, and reinforced their convictions that Teresita and God were on their side. Then they went back over the Sierra, dodging and fighting troops all the way.

When they got back to Tomochic, the state governor offered them a deal. They could have amnesty if they recognized the authority of the mayor and the state and federal government. Cruz Chavez refused. Their numbers were modest, perhaps a hundred fighting men in total, but with God on their side, how could they lose?

General José Maria Rangel was given command of a full battalion of federal soldiers and a troop of reinforcements from Chihuahua. He had nothing but contempt for the upstart hillbilly peasants of Tomochic and marched straight into the village without waiting for his reinforcements or doing any preliminary scouting or planning. His soldiers were poorly motivated, inexperienced conscripts armed with one-shot rifles. The men of Tomochic were hardened Apache fighters armed with Winchester repeating rifles. They killed all Rangel's officers and shot down a great many of his soldiers as they fled. Naturally Cruz Chavez took the victory as further evidence of invincibility.

President Díaz relieved Rangel of his command and sent a cavalry detachment led by his personal friend General Felipe Cruz, who took the campaign against Tomochic into the far reaches of the absurd. He never even got to the village. After marching for two days and drinking bottle after bottle of brandy, he reached such an advanced stage of befuddlement that he mistook a cornfield for the rebel villagers and ordered a full cavalry charge. He led the charge himself, slashing at the cornstalks with his sword and since he was their commanding officer the men followed suit and cut that cornfield to pieces.

Then General Cruz returned to Chihuahua City and sent a report to his superiors saying he had crushed the rebels and won a famous victory. That was the clinching part of the story for me, the Don Quixote charge into the cornfield and the brazen claim of triumph. That sounded like the Mexico that kept me coming back and scratching my head. In a novel it would be called magical realism but what was it doing in a history book?

No one hates ridicule more than a dictator and when the news of General Cruz's victory over the cornstalks became public, Díaz sent twelve hundred battle-hardened federal troops and a cannon to Tomochic. For the villagers, the only logical course of action was to withdraw into the mountains and wage a guerrilla campaign. But who needs logic when you are invincible? When Cruz Chavez heard about the twelve hundred troops coming, he decided to stand and fight in the village with his hundred men.

The federal troops had heard all about the invincible holy warriors of Tomochic and they were filled with dread as they marched into battle. They told each other that each rebel fighter was worth ten of their own men. When they reached the village, thirty women dressed in black came out to meet them. The troops didn't know how to respond. There was no order from their commanding officer. The women kept advancing slowly toward them and then threw off their shawls, produced Winchester rifles from their dresses, and revealed themselves to be men. They shot down the front line of the federal troops and the rest fled in terror. Men in dresses with Winchester rifles—naturally I thought of Raúl Sala.

The officers forced the troops back into battle and two weeks of bloody horror ensued. Hundreds of federal troops were killed, villagers were massacred in the church. At the end only Cruz Chavez and six others were left alive. The federal commander offered to spare their lives if they surrendered. They refused. He said they could leave unharmed if they recognized the authority of the government. Again they refused.

The federal troops stormed the house where they were holed up and captured the seven men alive. They were given cigarettes to smoke and then executed by firing squad. So ended the Tomochic rebellion, on a blood-drenched note of heroism spun into tragedy, a note that sounds so frequently in Mexican history and Mexican song.

How courageous were the Tomochis
Who knew how to die in a hail of bullets
Defending their hearth and homeland.

This is the last verse of one of the *corridos,* the folk ballads of rural Mexico, that was composed and sung about the events at Tomochic. Its lyrics were on display at the small, two-room museum, which was opened up for me by a very nice woman named Maria Gardea. She wore a smart burgundy suit and had dyed her hair the color of eggplants.

There were a few old guns and papers but the display was dominated by paintings and drawings by a local artist, who appeared to believe that no visual statement could be too bold. The pre-rebellion feudal regime was represented by a sneering overlord whipping a cowering peasant, and a terrified kneeling woman, seen between the colossus legs of the man about to rape her. Then came battle scenes. Women wept over hideously mangled corpses. Men writhed in their death agonies. For the church massacre, he had painted a brimming lake of blood and the Grim Reaper at the altar.

"Many people don't realize how hard the women of Tomochic fought," said Maria. "They had guns and their courage was equal to that of the men. The whole rebellion was an event of truly extraordinary courage and faith in God."

"What about Tomochic today?" I asked. "Is the story of the rebellion well known? Is it important to people?"

"No," she said sadly. "No one cares. Unfortunately, Tomochic today is in a very bad way. It is all drugs, alcoholism, prostitution, and a lot of killing and robbing. It's very unsafe here. They grow a lot right outside town and in the canyons higher in the mountains."

"Are there soldiers here?"

"No, the nearest ones are in Cuahtemoc and they don't come here much. There are state police but of course they are partners with the *narcos.* If I was younger I would leave this place. It's a shame because this was a nice town before the drugs came in, a close community."

I thanked her and said good-bye. "Thank you for being interested in our history," she said. "No one here gives a damn."

• • •

I GOT BACK in my truck and was overcome by a feeling of deep unease and sinking confidence. This was supposed to be a safe highway and I was intending to follow it all the way over the Sierra Madre and then go south to Álamos, where things had supposedly cooled off between the army and the drug growers. But now the highway didn't feel safe at all and neither did I.

"Don't worry," I had told my friends and parents. "I'll be extremely careful. The main thing is to never go up there alone." Now I was about to cross the whole mountain range alone and I couldn't decide if I was being reckless or paranoid.

It was a paved and well-traveled highway in good condition. Mexican tourists from Chihuahua City drove it to get to the beaches in Sonora, didn't they? A few *gringo* tourists on the way back from Copper Canyon probably drove it, too, and I hadn't heard about any of them getting killed or kidnapped. So take a deep breath and buck up, man, for God's sake. And get over the Fat Little Chicken. Nothing happened except a few hard stares and an offer of free cocaine. If I couldn't handle that, it was time to get a straight job.

So up the road I went, telling myself I would be careful and wondering what that meant now. And then telling myself to relax and have fun. Next time snort the coke, buy a round of beers, and see what happened. Then I realized that I was second-guessing my instincts to the point where I couldn't tell what they were anymore. And this was bad because the only rule I had about dangerous situations was to trust my instincts.

Finally I told myself to shut up and start paying attention to the scenery. There were big mountain views opening up to the north, range after pine-forested range, each one a paler shade of blue than the last, all the way up to where Lofty's gold wasn't buried some seventy miles away. It was hard to believe that nearly all of it was second-growth forest or that people actually lived out there in *ejidos* and ranches and they had wiped out all the wolves and grizzly bears. It looked so wild and primordial but this was an illusion, the same one that the Apaches from Oklahoma projected onto the Sierra

Madre. The mountains were firmly under the hand of man, if not the rule of law.

I crossed the line into Sonora and made my first stop in the town of Yécora. A three-piece *norteño* band was playing on the bed of a flatbed truck and a crowd of thirty or forty people had gathered. I love *norteño* music. It's the most Mexican thing about me. When I hear those mutant polkas and waltzes, the driving accordions, the wailing florid vocals, it makes me want to yelp and howl, get drunk, and lean up against a wall crying.

I parked and rolled the window down. It was good, raw, soulful, caterwauling *norteño* just like I like it. I got out of my truck and walked over to the back of the crowd, wishing I was shorter and browner and wearing a white straw cowboy hat. The band was singing a *narcocorrido* about some drug lord who was the king of the Sierra, with many houses, fine women, and impressive machine guns.

A hundred years ago they sang *corridos* in the Sierra about famous bandits, outlaws, revolutionaries, current events like the Tomochic rebellion or a particularly bloody feud or heroic-tragic death. Now they sing *narcocorridos* about the drug lords, who sometimes commission the songs out of vanity, and events both real and imagined from the lives of drug growers, local bosses, regional traffickers, smugglers, dealers, pilots, assassins. There's a great deal of macho bragging and stancing involved and, despite the accordions and polkas, the music form it most resembles is gangsta rap.

The next song had hardly begun when three drunk men with twitching lips came up to me. They offered to sell me marijuana at a hundred dollars a kilo, premium quality, Yecora's finest, good price, special for you. When I said I had just pulled over to hear the music they got very suspicious and accused me of working for the DEA (the U.S. Drug Enforcement Agency), which is something you never want to hear in the Sierra Madre. I laughed it off with as much casual disdain as I could muster, said that I was a British tourist, bid them a sudden farewell, and concentrated on maintaining a relaxed and deceptively speedy gait as I walked back to my truck.

I drove all the way out of the mountains without stopping again. Late that night, with enormous relief, I collapsed into a motel on flat desert ground. Now I was safe, at least for a few days. It was an easy drive to Álamos tomorrow and it would take a while to find someone willing and able to take me deeper into the mountains from there. Crossing the Sierra on a paved and well-traveled highway was one thing but I would fornicate with a goat before going into the mountains above Álamos by myself.

THE NEXT DAY I stopped off in Navojoa and wandered through its central market looking for a saddlemaker called Pepe Delgadillo. Joe Brown had asked me to look him up. Joe had also advised me to buy a saddle from him but pickup trucks were clearly taking over from horses and mules in the Sierra and after seeing Ruben nearly get wishboned that was fine by me.

Pepe was a balding, good-humored, highly animated man who seemed to have a natural gift for happiness. He was absolutely ecstatic to meet a friend of Joe Brown's. Did Joe still ride that big horse Pajaro and no, no, no, of course not. It had been so long!

"There are so many stories about Joe Brown," he said. "That little plane he used to fly. He would fly it low to the ground—low, low, low!—and throw out cans of beer for people to catch. And he would come low over the whorehouse and one time he knocked the TV antenna right off it. Hah! No one can fly drunk like Joe Brown. And what a horseman! And a boxer, too, no? When is he going to come back to see all his good friends in Mexico?"

Joe had just written a book in three months, living on coffee and working eighteen to twenty hours a day. Then he had gone rounding up cattle on horseback for a week, at the age of seventy-four, and suffered the sixth and seventh heart attacks of his life. He was making a strong recovery but I doubted that Joe would be coming down to Navojoa anytime soon. "That's too bad," said Pepe. "There are so many people who would love to see him again."

It occurred to me that "friend of Joe Brown" was all I needed to justify my presence in his old haunts in the Sierra. People would want to know what I was doing there and it would sound more suspicious to say that I was a writer interested in the history of the Sierra Madre. If and when I got up to places like Chinipas and Guasaremos, where Joe had his ranch and is now heavy *narco* country, I would tell people that I was the trusted friend of Yo Bron, dispatched by Yo himself to find out how his old friends were doing in the Sierra. If that went down okay, then I might mention something about being a writer. Of course I hadn't cleared any of this with Joe but he had given me the names of some people to look up and it was only a mild stretching of the truth.

I RUMBLED OVER the cobblestoned streets into Álamos and parked on the alameda, a rectangular plaza with a market at one end where the Mexican community of Álamos conducts most of its social activity. Everything looked as I remembered it: mustachioed men in white straw cowboy hats, *norteño* music blasting and wailing from big, slow-cruising American pickup trucks, the occasional horseman clopping over the cobblestones, promenading teenagers, old women observing from doorways, wandering dogs, the smell of roasting meat from the taco vendors beneath the huge cottonwood or *álamo* trees that give the town its name.

I bought myself three tacos of *carne asada,* grilled steak cut up into tiny cubes and wrapped in a tortilla. I squeezed a lime over the meat and heaped up the tacos with strips of pickled red onion, a creamy avocado sauce that was simpler than guacamole, and a salsa made of roasted chilies and tomatoes. I ate them with salted radishes, cucumber rounds, and a cup of beans cooked with bacon and beer. Anyone who tells you not to eat street food in Mexico because you'll get sick is denying you too much pleasure, and it is my firm unproven belief that lime juice kills all the bacteria that need killing.

I got my boots expertly shined by a somber-faced boy of nine or ten. Grackles squawked in the trees, teenagers laughed and held hands, an overweight woman in her late forties smoldered her eyes at me and sashayed past, swinging her hips. There was no doubt in her mind that men were struck helpless with lust in her presence and I loved this about the women in Álamos, how confident they were of their sex appeal, how free they were of the perfectionist neuroses that bedeviled Anglo women.

Then I walked up through a narrow stone alley to the Plaza de Armas and suddenly there was no music to be heard, no smell of roasting meat, no charge of sexuality in the air. Gray- and white-haired American couples sipped margaritas on elegant colonial patios, opposite the Church of the Very Pure Conception, completed in 1786, and pecked away at keyboards in the new Internet café.

For decades now Americans had been buying up and renovating the old mansions erected here by the Spanish silver barons in the eighteenth and nineteenth centuries. They revere Mexican colonial architecture, adore traditional Mexican art and handicrafts, employ Mexican servants and gardeners, but very few of them speak Spanish and they keep themselves largely separate from the local Mexican community, staying away from the market, the alameda, and the *cantinas,* and leaving Álamos altogether from March to November. Most of them had no idea that huge quantities of marijuana were moving through Álamos. The two pillars of the local economy, drug trafficking and the American colony, were kept entirely separate.

I got to know only one American when I lived here and he was a mutant, associating almost entirely with Mexicans and staying in Álamos through the furnace of summer, when the town has to ration its water supply. His name was Mervin Larson and he was a construction wizard, botanical expert, former herpetologist, and semi-retired zoo builder, one of the first in his field to create simulated habitats for the animals rather than cages. He had turned the old, ruined colonial hospital into a hotel, with a small aviary against one ruined wall and an enclosure for snakes. He was living there with his Mexican mistress, Alicia, drinking beer by the case and sometimes harassing or throwing out the rare and occasional hotel guests.

A Mexican couple were staying there and found a snake that had gotten loose. The man killed it and set the dead reptile on Merv's doorstep. Sometime close to midnight Merv found it and came storming into the couple's room, "Get out! What kind of people are you to kill this beautiful snake?"

Suffice to say that Merv Larson was not put on this earth to be a hotel keeper and sure enough he went broke and had to sell the place. He was back in Tucson now living with his wife and trying to make enough money to keep supporting Alicia and his three Mexican employees, and finish renovating another property he had bought in Álamos. I would be staying there with Alicia, and one of those employees, Gustavo Aragon, who advised Merv on matters relating to property law, permits, and taxes, and cheerfully admitted to swindling him blind on occasion, was my best hope of a guide into the Sierra Madre. He was born in a village up there somewhere and spoke perfect English to boot.

It took a series of telephone calls and visits to her relatives but eventually I found Alicia in a big, half-built house on the Mexican side of town. She was in her late forties now, gratifyingly pleased by my new improved Spanish and full of sympathy about my divorce. She showed me to an adjoining guesthouse where I would be staying and gave me the news of people I used to know.

Her younger sister now had a daughter named Mervina in honor of Mervin. Mervina's father was in the drug business and unfortunately he had shot a policeman and had to leave town. My old drinking buddy Martín Calderon, a flamboyant drug trafficker who used to ride a black stallion around town and keep an old conquistador's sword in a scabbard attached to his saddle (inscribed on the blade of the sword were the words, "When the owl sings, the Indian dies"), had got into some trouble with an underage girl and gone north for his health.

You could see the first great ridge of the Sierra Madre rising up above the town to the east. I said that I wanted to go up there and I was hoping Gustavo could take me. She was horrified. "Why, Ricardo? There is nothing up there but poverty, drugs, and killing. Why don't you stay here and find yourself a nice Mexican girl? Mexican women are not crazy like the *gringas*."

THE NEXT DAY I walked into town feeling naked and unmanly without a white straw cowboy hat and determined to rectify this situation. I crossed the dry riverbed and entered a thick crowd lining the alameda. It was November 20, the anniversary of the outbreak of the Mexican revolution, and a parade was in progress.

A platoon of small boys marched past with outsized sombreros, painted-on mustaches and fake bandoliers across their chests, followed by a chubby girl plodding along disconsolately in a tiger suit. Then came a teenage boy in his briefs, sprayed gold from head to toe and standing in the bed of a slow-moving livestock truck. Then a man in a green parrot suit dancing in a pair of giant orange plaid carpet slippers. Then a cattle truck blaring Mexican pop music and trailed by a dancing, capering man dressed as a big blue egg.

"Our art movement is not needed in this country," said the French surrealist André Breton after visiting Mexico. I take his point but it's also true that surrealism is in the eye of the beholder. I studied the calm, impassive expressions on the faces of the grandmothers sitting in their doorways, the young couples arm-in-arm, the off-duty drug dealers standing outside the *cantina,* wearing silk shirts decorated with pictures of roosters, scorpions, pickup trucks, AK-47s, and the Virgin of Guadalupe. To them I'm sure that none of it seemed bizarre or incongruous or anything more than festive.

When I lived in Álamos in the early 1990s there was a certain mailman that you would hear stories about and sometimes encounter if you happened to be in the *cantina* in the mid-afternoon. He was always drunk and often belligerent, with a sack of undelivered mail at his feet. Finally, in the late afternoon, duty would call. He would pick up the mail sack and stagger out of the back door of the *cantina* and empty the mail sack into the dry riverbed. There he would stand unsteadily, shooing away the pigs with drunken curses and fumbling with his matches. Then he would set fire to the mail, in full view of the locals watching from the bridge. They didn't care or even pay much attention to it but I took it as proof that life in Mexico was surreal and upside down. The cops were criminals, the politicians were thieves, hit men went to a saint to get their bullets blessed, and it was considered perfectly normal for the mailman to set fire to the mail.

AFTER THE PARADE I bought myself a good fifty-dollar hat with a card inside the brim that was translated into English: "Applied with today's cowboy fashion, for your many times of appreciation and lucidity."

I put it on and worked the brim a little and went into a *cantina* called Casino Señorial, a big concrete barn with the walls painted Tecate red and gold, white plastic tables and chairs, and a giant, pulsating, multicolored jukebox in the corner. The place was three-quarters full and it was all men and I could tell from the hard faces, lean shanks, and tire-tread sandals that most of them had come down from the Sierra.

On the wall behind the bar was a stuffed mountain lion, caught in the act of tearing the throat out of a stuffed deer. Fake blood was smeared around the wound and splattered down the wall. Next to the lion and the deer was an ocelot chomping the bloody neck of a squirrel. I sat down at the bar and ordered a *caguama,* a giant sea-turtle, or in this case a big, quarter-gallon bottle of Tecate beer. A quart of Pacifico beer is a *ballena,* a whale.

It came with a small plastic cup perched on top. I offered a pour to the man sitting next to me and discovered that he and many others had come from the Sierra to attend a religious fiesta in the village of Aduana, ten kilometers south of Álamos.

"How are things in the Sierra?" I asked.

"Bad," he said. "Soldiers killed. Mafiosos killing each other. Bandits robbing people on the roads. But now many people are down at Aduana for the fiesta."

He was a bootlegger by profession and had brought down two cases of *lechuguilla* to sell in Aduana and was thinking about going north with the proceeds and walking across the desert to the United States. He had gone there when he was younger, fifteen years previously. He dyed his hair blond, learned a few words of English, bluffed his way past the border guards in Nogales, Arizona, and ended up working at Disneyland in Anaheim, Cailfornia. "I love the United States," he said. "I got drunk all the time on Budweiser. People treated me good."

THREE WOMEN APPEARED and paraded up and down the concrete floor on stiletto heels. One was enormously fat, the second was young, plump, and pretty, and the third, I noticed on closer inspection, was a drag queen, tall and skinny with dyed blond curls. "How much do they charge?" I asked the bootlegger. He named a sum equivalent to twenty dollars and maybe a little less for the *joto,* the gay female impersonator. "He will end up with some cattle rancher who is too drunk to care and both of them will be happy."

He admired the fat one. *"Mucha carne,"* he leered. Lots of meat.

The whores collected money from the bartender and fed it into the jukebox. The music was all *narcocorridos.* The lyrics were slangy and hard to understand but I caught snatches—"I'm one of the players in the Sierra where the opium poppy grows . . . I like risky action, I like to do cocaine, I walk right behind death with a beautiful woman on each arm . . . I've got an AK-47 for anyone who wants to try me."

Some of the *narco* slang I knew. An AK-47 was a *cuerno de chivo,* a goat's horn, a reference to its curved ammunition clip. *Colas de borrego,* sheep's tails, were big, fluffy buds of marijuana. *Ganado sin garrapatas,* cattle without ticks, was marijuana without seeds. Cocaine was *perico,* parakeet, because it made you chatter without knowing what you were saying. Marijuana, especially in joint form, was *gallo,* the rooster, and heroin was *chivo,* the goat. All these terms, now in general use throughout Mexico, reflect the origins of the Mexican drug-smuggling business in the rural backcountry of the Sierra Madre.

The bootlegger left to go to Aduana and a group of men beckoned me over to their table. One of them was clearly in charge, a big paunchy man with a glassy-eyed smile and a magnificent Roman nose. The others called him El Pelícano, The Pelican, and warned me that he and the younger man next to him were cops from Navojoa. I pulled up a chair and sat down and The Pelican thumped his empty *caguama* on the plastic table. The bartender scurried over with a fresh one and The Pelican looked at me to pay.

They all looked ripped on cocaine, including the two cops. Their lips were writhing and they were chewing at their tongues and guzzling down beer at a crazy pace. Five minutes after it arrived the *caguama* was empty and The Pelican thumped it down on the table. Again I paid and five minutes later I paid again and so on for the next twenty minutes.

They started making motions, as if lifting a key or a spoon to their nostrils. "Do you like parakeet?" asked the younger cop.

"Sometimes but not now thank you," I said. Call me paranoid but the idea of doing cocaine with Mexican cops made me nervous. I bought more *caguamas* and we drank them at top speed and then The Pelican leaned over the arm of his plastic chair and vomited on the concrete floor. It was the most casual puking I have ever seen. Then he smiled and thumped the empty *caguama* on the table. The bartender brought a fresh one, I paid, and a young teenage boy appeared with a mop.

The beer was getting to my brain and my bladder. I got up to go to the bathroom and the two cops followed me in there. We stood there at the trough in that slightly awkward male silence, waggled, and zipped up. Then The Pelican raised his forefinger to stop me leaving, took out a plastic bag of cocaine, scooped a little mound on the end of his pocketknife and offered me a *pericazo,* literally a parakeet-blast.

"*Gracias, amigo,*" I said, snorting it up my right nostril and turning to leave. "No, no, no!" chorused the two police officers. "You must do the other nostril. It is very important."

"But of course."

I was too drunk for the cocaine to do much more than halfway sober me up. Either that or it wasn't very good cocaine. We sat back down at the table and drank more *caguamas*. The Pelican saw the notebook in my shirt pocket and demanded that I give it to him. He leafed through it and then asked for my pen. He wrote his name, rank, address, and telephone number and said, "If you're ever in Navojoa and you have problems, you call this number. We are friends. Let us do another parakeet-blast."

This time he didn't bother going to the bathroom. We snorted it off his pocketknife at the table and the bartender came over and waved his forefinger from side to side and pointed to the bathroom. It was a simple system and we had abused it. The Pelican apologized, motioned us to our feet, and we went single file to the bathroom and snorted up the last of the cocaine.

Now they wanted me to buy more, which looked like a classic Mexican setup: I would buy the cocaine, the cops would bust me and extort a large bribe, which they would then spend on cocaine. My instincts were telling me to leave but I didn't know how. To leave a Mexican drinking session before it reaches its natural conclusion, which is absolute drunkenness, is considered rude and disrespectful and in the rougher parts of the Sierra it is a frequent cause of homicide.

The Pelican thumped down another empty *caguama* and I pulled out my wallet again and found that it was empty. A godsend! I showed it to everyone around the table and thanked them for their fine company and outstanding hospitality and assured them that my house was at their orders if they were ever in Tucson, Arizona. I got up to leave and The Pelican said, "No, we need more *perico*. We need more beer. You can get more money from the wall of the bank. We are friends. Or are you too proud to drink with Mexicans?"

"We are friends without doubt," I said. "And there are no better people in all the world to drink with than Mexicans. I will go to the bank and get money from the wall. And we will finish what we have started because I do not do halfway things. Because that is the way of the coward!"

I made my reeling exit, weaved around two corners into the welcoming darkness of the dry riverbed, and lurched back to Alicia's guesthouse. What if I ran into the two cops again? I passed out serenely, confident that my departure would be fuzzily remembered at best.

9

Hat Talk

IN 1683 MAYO INDIANS in the thorn forest outside Álamos saw a virgin perched on top of a tall, prickly *pitahaya* cactus. She was wearing white robes and a blue shawl, which was how they knew she was a virgin. They piled up rocks against the cactus so she could climb down but instead she flew away. They followed her and a short distance away they found a fantastically rich vein of silver in the ground. A mining town sprang up called La Aduana, now colloquially shortened to Aduana, and a church was built at the site where the virgin first appeared. She was given the name of Our Virgin of Balvanera and now, during the last ten days of November, people come from all over southern Sonora and parts of Sinaloa and Chihuahua to celebrate her annual fiesta. Some of them walk forty miles or more to get here and a few crawl on their bleeding hands and knees in accordance with the *mandas* or promises they made to the Virgin last year. If you heal my sick child, a mother might promise, I will crawl twenty miles on my hands and knees to your fiesta next year to show my adoration and gratitude.

When I arrived, hoping to meet Sierra people on safe neutral ground and wrangle some invitations up to their villages, a soft winter rain had been falling for two days and the makeshift parking lot at Aduana was a slithering shambles of mud, spinning wheels, gridlock, and confusion. According to the newspapers, ten thousand pilgrims were in Aduana this year, which was about half the normal turnout. The newspapers weren't saying why but my bootlegger friend had explained it to me. It was all the army's fault. The soldiers had seized or burned nearly all of the fall marijuana harvest in the nearest ranges of the Sierra Madre and many of the faithful couldn't afford to come to Aduana this year, or pay the bribes on their next crop.

Nonetheless, ten thousand people in an abandoned mining town with fifteen buildings still standing, no toilet facilities, and no trash collection plan, made for an impressive throng and over the last eight days they had created an impressive amount of chaos, including many thousands of empty beer cans. Being accustomed to Anglo Protestant cultures, which like to keep life neatly divided in separate compartments, I found it difficult to keep the idea straight that this was a solemn religious festival, a drunken party, a social occasion, and a flea market, all rolled into one.

From the parking lot I shuffled along with the crowd through a long, cacophonous avenue of dry-goods vendors. They had tied pieces of elastic around their heads, mounted tiny microphones just under their noses, and the elastic was pulled so tight that their facial features were distorted and grotesque. They banged on pots and frying pans, unfurled blankets and velvet paintings, held aloft packets of women's underwear, and kept up a continuous stream of sales patter that was ear-splittingly amplified through huge stacks of speakers sometimes ten feet high and often blown out to a distorted fuzz. The little microphones bobbed and quivered under their noses with every syllable and everything was a special one-time-only price, ladies and gentlemen, special for you, only fifty pesos for this entire set of kitchenware and would you look at the outstanding quality of this fine acrylic blanket and admire the radiant beauty of this unicorn prancing across a velvet beach in the moonlight.

Behind his tented stall I saw one of the vendors dip a long thin knife into a plastic bag full of white powder, administer a parakeet-blast to both nostrils and then step up to relieve his partner. *"Señores y señoras!"* he bellowed. "I now present to you a most exquisite item of the finest quality at a price that is not to be believed! I have no boss, I have no wife, I have no children, my friends say I have lost my mind! Maybe that is why I can offer you a price of one hundred—NO! Eighty!—NO! Seventy!—NO! Fifty pesos is all I ask for this beautiful, hard-wearing set of saucepans."

He clanged them together and beat on one of them with the palm of the hand. "Listen to that! Pure quality, nothing but the best for my customers. *Señores y señoras!* Fifty pesos, fifty pesos, fifty pesos . . ."

I reached an open area filled with food stands, roofed over with a leaky patchwork of tarps, and floored with mud-trampled paper plates and beer cans. Men sliced off slivers of cheek meat from roasting cow heads and ladled out bowls of goat stew and *menudo*, a spicy cow tripe soup. Thin sheets of marinated steak sizzled over charcoal fires, and to make yourself heard you had to yell your order directly into the ear of the food vendor or his assistant.

Everywhere the crowd was packed and seething. There were cowboys, drug dealers, peasant farmers, truck drivers, well-dressed young men and women from Álamos and Navojoa, a pair of old cattle ranchers sitting on their horses and serenely passing a plastic bottle of *lechuguilla,* old Yaqui women in homespun red dresses, Guarijío Indians down from the Sierra, and an old Tarahumara man I recognized from a trip to the small village of Tatahuiche, Chihuahua, ten years before.

I cupped my hands and bellowed words to this effect into his ear. He made no reply and started walking away and motioned with his chin that I should follow. We found a quieter section where vendors were selling religious articles and baseball caps with marijuana leaves and AK-47s on the front. I said again that I had been to Tatahuiche and seen a footrace there and he nodded politely and clearly didn't remember me. I asked him how he had traveled to Aduana. *"Por pata,"* he said, by foot or literally by paw, which meant that he had walked nearly a hundred miles across some of the most rugged country on earth. It had taken him three days and he had drunk from the streams and rivers and eaten nothing but a little of the toasted, ground corn called *pinole* along the way. I asked him how old he was.

"Seventy, more or less," he said. Why had he come here? Did he need a favor or a miracle from the Virgin?

"I am here because it is my custom to come here," he said and shook hands good-bye in the Tarahumara way, a soft grazing of the fingertips across the palm.

As usual, the *narcos* advertised their profession as flagrantly as they could afford to, with gold accessories and expensive cowboy hats distinguishing them from the wannabes, and many of them wore scapulars around their neck containing the image of the narco-saint Jesús Malverde. The young ones wore their hats with the sides curved up so high and tight that they pressed in against the crown—a style known as *cinco en troka,* five in the truck, meaning the crown of the hat is squeezed in as tightly as five people sitting across the bench seat of a pickup truck. They stood around with beers in their hands looking twitchy and wired. Their girlfriends were on the short and chubby side with almost invariable miniskirts, muddy stilettos, tight low-cut tops, and dyed, curled, elaborate hairstyles.

I shuffled along with the crowd and finally the old church came into view with its astonishing cactus. After producing many fortunes the silver mine finally ran dry and the miners drifted away from Aduana. Then a cactus started growing out of the vertical stone wall of the church, apparently nourished by nothing but stone, mortar, air, and rain. Its roots are about eight feet off the ground, tethered somehow into a chink of mortar. It grows up in a tall column with several arms and its shadow is said to look like the Virgin Mary. It was a cloudy, rainy day so I can't pronounce on its shadow but its existence certainly seems miraculous. Are there plant nutrients in mortar?

All around the church were groups of uniformed musicians with trumpets, guitars, accordions, and saxophones, all of them playing different songs at the same time and trying to drown each other out. It may be that I was still slightly hung over but like the avenue of vendors it seemed fantastically loud, chaotic, and painful to listen to. It took all my forbearance not to clamp my hands over my ears but on the flagstones around the church, surrounded by dueling musicians, Mayo Indian families slept peacefully on checkered acrylic blankets.

I joined the line of people moving slowly toward the church entrance, where three old men with screwed-up, contorted faces were singing *corridos* about the revolution and trying to make themselves heard over a younger trio singing *corridos* about the drug life. I ducked inside, the music faded, and my eyes slowly grew accustomed to the gloomy light coming through the high windows. At the nave of the church, surrounded by a warm glow of candles, was a tiny doll-like figure no more than a foot high in a glass box. Her face was white (the only other white face in Aduana that day was mine) and in her arms she held a baby.

Around her shoulders she wore a red cloak festooned with the tiny gold symbols called *milagros,* each representing a different type of miracle. There were *milagros* in the shape of babies, hearts, legs, arms, and VW Beetles. People filed past, touched the glass with their fingertips, crossed themselves, and dropped coins into an old wooden box. I did the same and asked for the miracle of understanding Mexico.

Outside the church, moving away from the noise and the crowd, looking for somewhere to pee, I climbed up a muddy hillside and disturbed two fornicating couples. A drunk was passed out in the mud with the rain falling into his open mouth. I came down a different way and reached a wide sandy streambed with a trickle of water flowing through it, where Gypsies had set up three-card monte tables and other games of chance. Beyond the Gypsies a small crowd had gathered around two men on dancing horses, each man trying to outdance the other. *Narcocorridos* were blasting out of a green Chevy truck and the horses were picking up their hooves and setting them down in time with the music, encouraged by a light tapping on their flanks from the men's bootheels.

I got talking to two brothers in their late twenties who explained how you train a horse to dance, "You tie him up and get on his back and keep kicking your heels into his ribs. He tries to go forward but the rope catches him and makes him step. Then you make him step in time to the music and he learns to listen to the music and do this by himself."

The brothers were wearing gold jewelry, ostrich-skin boots, and good hats and said they had come here from a village in the Sierra Madre called Guirocoba. They had arrived yesterday morning and had been drinking ever since. Guirocoba? I thought. Wasn't that the village where Gustavo was from?

"Do you know my friend Gustavo Aragon?" I said. "I think he was born in Guirocoba."

They didn't know Gustavo but they recognized the family name and this made them nod and relax. I offered to buy them a beer and they looked at each other and said let's go. I bought a round, they bought one back, I bought another and told them that I wrote history books and was interested in the area around Guirocoba and was hoping to pay a visit there with my good friend Gustavo Aragon and did they think that was a good idea?

"We are good people in Guirocoba but we have big problems with the fucking army right now," said Jaime, the older brother. "If anyone gives you problems there, tell them you're a friend of Jaime B and that he speaks for you."

This was no small matter. If my visit was connected rightly or wrongly in the suspicious minds of the outlaw clanfolk with some future bust or raid, Jaime would be held responsible and he could be killed for it. When you vouch for someone in a Sierra Madre drug village, you vouch for them with your life. So why did he do it, on such a casual acquaintance? Maybe because I knew a family name in his village. Maybe because he was feeling in an airy, expansive mood after drinking for thirty hours. There is always this tension in the Sierra between suspicion of outsiders and the urge to show hospitality toward strangers, and I seemed to have tapped into the latter. It was the opportunity I had been waiting for: safe passage into a notorious Sierra Madre drug-growing village.

> *Federal police say it feels spooky to go through these places*
> *That it brings goosebumps to the skin . . .*
> *I dedicate this corrido with pleasure*
> *To the famous opium growers of Guirocoba*
>
> —Numen Navarro Rubio, *Corrido Del Cajón y Guirocoba*

• • •

Back in Álamos I finally caught up with Gustavo. He was a small, stocky man with blue eyes and fair skin, bequeathed to him by his German-American grandfather, who had gone south to avoid the draft for the First World War and ended up settling in Guirocoba with a Mexican woman. Gustavo was wearing trifocals now, bald under his cowboy hat and a little paunchier than I remembered him.

"Ricardo, I hear you got divorced," he said. "What was it? *We were so happy together until I got to know you.* That's what my ex-wife said to me."

We laughed at that and I said no, it was more a question of whether she went crazy or I drove her nuts. "You should get a Mexican woman," he said. "They're less trouble and it's the best way to learn the language, with a horizontal teacher."

"And then all her relatives and second cousins come around wanting money all the time, right?"

"Of course. You may be British but to us you're still a *gringo* and everyone knows the *gringos* have far too much money for their own good. It is our duty as good patriotic Mexicans to part you from that money and we can't respect ourselves if we don't try."

That was certainly Gustavo's operating principle ten years ago, although he had never bothered trying to swindle me, mainly because I was always scrimping along on a shoestring. Now I offered him forty dollars a day to guide me around whatever parts of the Sierra Madre he thought safe to visit and he said that was too much. Twenty or twenty-five a day would be fine. "Gustavo," I said. "Are you feeling unwell? Where is your pride as a Mexican?"

He turned up his hands and said he was resigned now to never being a rich man. Whenever he made any real money, a family member would get sick or fall off a horse and the hospital bills would clean him out. Or his truck would break down, or the roof of his house would cave in, or some official would need bribing, and one way or another he always ended up back where he started. He had come to the old man's conclusion that his family, his friends, and his little ranch by the Cuchujaqui River with its few cows and horses were more reliable at making him happy than his brief glimpses of wealth. He sounded convincing but I couldn't help wondering if it was the opening gambit of some cunning plan to strip me of everything I had.

When I told Gustavo about my invitation to Guirocoba he winced and inhaled sharply through his teeth, "Let's hope they aren't inviting you there to rob you and steal your truck. It's not worth much but it will look good to them. Your watch is cheap but they'll be happy to steal it. This is a bad time to go into the Sierra. A lot of people have lost their crops this year and those with money have spent it all at Aduana and so there are a lot of hold ups and killings going on. I think it's better if we wait a week or two. Right now there's a little too much lead in the air."

One of Gustavo's jobs in Álamos was doing clerical and translating work for the *municipio* or county police department and this gave him access to the murder reports and crime statistics from the area. I started looking into the numbers. The population of the *municipio* was approximately 23,000, with 9,000 in Álamos, 3,000 in San Bernardo, and the rest scattered in small mountain villages and ranches. Gustavo said they were averaging ninety reported murders a year and that it was safe to add at least another twenty unreported murders to that figure. Murders went unreported if they pointed toward a powerful, well-connected mafioso, for example, or if they occurred in a place where no one wanted the authorities involved. Let's call it a hundred murders a year, committed by a population of 23,000. I knew that Mexico's overall murder rate was twice that of the United States but here was a rural county with a murder rate eight times higher than the most homicidal U.S. cities. And Gustavo said things had calmed down considerably from the 1980s and 1990s, when the drugs first came in and the mafias fought to establish their territories.

"What about before the drugs?"

"There was a lot of killing back then, too," he said.

"For what reasons?"

"Matters of honor. Someone would do something disrespectful

while courting your sister or your daughter, for example, and you'd have to kill him or be dishonored. There were a lot of feuds over money and land. There's hardly any law up there now but back then there was no law at all. So people would settle their differences with bullets."

What you had now, in other words, was a hillbilly vendetta culture that was up to its eyeballs in the world's most murderous business enterprise: illegal narcotics. Its existing tendencies toward violence, vengeance, and ruthlessness had become supercharged. Homicide was now the leading cause of death for men in the mountains of southern Sonora and the entire state of Sinaloa.

From time to time I would see small items in the newspaper about the army killing drug growers in the Sierra. Were the growers shooting back or resisting arrest? Or was the army just executing people up there?

"Not exactly," said Gustavo. "If they catch you with your crop and you haven't fixed them with a bribe, they sometimes give you a choice between *bote, leña,* or *plomo. Bote* is the can—prison—and for any kind of crop at all you're looking at ten years and these are not nice, clean *gringo* prisons where they give you food. *Leña* is firewood and what this means is they will take a piece of wood and beat you half to death with it. In three days you might be able to walk. You might be lying down on the one little piece of your body that isn't broken and drinking through a straw but you'll be alive. *Leña* is the smart choice but it's a very hard choice to make.

"The third choice is *plomo,* or lead. They take you into a clearing and the captain says, 'Start running and we won't start shooting until you reach the brush.' Then they open up with automatic rifles. When you hear the army killed a grower in the Sierra, it usually means the grower chose *plomo.* Most of them do. Their pride won't allow them to stand there and be beaten or taken off to jail. *Plomo* is the brave, macho, *valiente* choice and you might live and get away with it. And if not, well, we Mexicans are a fatalistic people and all it means is that your number came up and it was your time to die."

• • •

A WHOLE WEEK went by with only one reported murder. On the road between Álamos and San Bernardo someone with an AR-15 automatic rifle fired thirty-eight rounds at a pickup truck and thirty-two of them hit the victim, which Gustavo said was good close-range shooting and nothing for us to worry about. It was just *narcos* assassinating another *narco* and time for us to go to Guirocoba.

"Put on your hat to look more like a Mexican and leave your watch and sunglasses behind," he said. "We'll say we're researching the history of the area. My grandfather wasn't the only American who went down there to avoid the draft for the First World War. There was a Clay Montgomery and Sam McCarthy who settled there, too. We'll look for their graves and ask about their descendants and call in on your friend Jaime and see if he wants to steal your truck."

We took a bumpy, rattling, potholed dirt road that crossed the Cuchujaqui River and then was suddenly graded and improved as it reached the huge country estate of a local drug lord. Gustavo said he was untouchable and marveled at the opulence of his fences. "Look at that. He's got eight strands of wire on *palo colorado* fence posts. Those fence posts are thirty pesos [nearly three dollars] each and they go on for miles and miles."

Then the potholes deepened again and became more numerous and the ground was grazed down to dust. This I recognized as *ejido* land. We wound through the foothills in first gear, dropping down into gullies and ravines and struggling up the far banks, our progress marked by a tall plume of dust. Guirocoba was situated on an area of flat ground surrounded by hills and ridges with the high Sierra rising up behind in a broken wall. The name of the village was almost illegible on an old rusty sign riddled with bullet holes.

Just past the sign and a few hundred yards short of the village was a rocky cemetery adorned with ribbons and plastic flowers. We spent twenty minutes there hunting for the graves of the American draft dodgers. Clay Montgomery set himself up here as a doctor and Sam

McCarthy mined for placer gold and planted an orange grove but there was no trace of either of them in the cemetery. The tombstones were poorly made and falling apart. Lizards used them for sunning platforms. Gustavo found a marker for one Bartolo Rabago and said he was the first man to introduce marijuana to the area. He wasn't sure who first planted the famous Guirocoba opium but the first opium seeds were brought to the Sierra Madre by Chinese immigrants and traders in the 1930s.

We got back in the truck and rolled slowly into the village. There were about two dozen shacks, most of them built out of crudely woven sticks and dried mud with palm-thatch or corrugated tin roofs. More often than not, they also had a solar panel, a TV satellite dish, and a big American pickup truck parked out front.

"With the money from your first crop you buy clothes, jewelry, and guns," said Gustavo. "It's illegal to own a firearm in Mexico but I can assure you that every one of these huts has at least one pistol and one rifle inside. Then you buy your truck, your solar, your satellite, and TV. The last thing you spend money on is the house. Look at that: he didn't even buy a tin roof to keep the rain out but he's got a thirty-thousand-dollar Dodge Ram parked out front."

The village looked deserted and it was eerily still and silent in the bright glare of midday sunshine. Gustavo thought the men were probably out in their illegal fields and the women watching us through chinks in their wattle-and-daub. We found one hut with chickens pecking around it and a sun-faded Fanta sign. We waited outside a fence of planted sticks until a woman appeared and said, *"Pásale,"* come inside. This was the local store. It was stocked with sodas, chips, eggs, canned beans, canned chilies, and tortillas.

We ordered two Cokes and drank them while Gustavo established his clan credentials. He told the woman that he was born in Guirocoba to the Aragon family, then he asked after various other families and if they were still living in the area. The woman smiled politely and gave very brief answers. I said I was a friend of Jaime B and that he had invited me here and did she know where I could find him?

She pointed to his house and said he would be back later in the afternoon.

We drove on to the next village, passing a rock formation known locally as the Devil's Ass and a spire called Cerro de Verga, Hard Dick Peak. Beneath it were the ruins of Jesús Miranda, a village that had wiped itself out completely in feuds. A few low adobe walls were all that remained of that experiment in civilization. We drove on, skidded through a big brown mud puddle and soon afterward we saw a stream lined with cypress trees and the equally notorious drug village of Aguacaliente. Again it looked deserted.

We walked along the stream looking for the hot springs that gave the village its name. A middle-aged man appeared in a blue shirt and white hat and walked down the banks holding a tin laundry pail. "That's a woman's job," said Gustavo. "He was sent down here to see what we're doing."

The man had a quiet country dignity about him and introduced himself as Señor Espinoza. We all shook hands, said it was a great pleasure, inquired after each other's health and agreed that it had indeed been a fortunate season for rain. Then Gustavo ran through his clan credentials and said we were researching the stories of Clay Montgomery, Sam McCarthy, and the other *gringos* who used to live in the area. Señor Espinoza nodded and said there were descendants of Don Clay living in Aguacaliente today. Then, without any prompting, he started talking about the soldiers.

"*Nos rasparon,*" he said, they scraped us down to nothing. "We had a nice crop growing in the hills and we were getting ready to pick it when the army came with planes and helicopters and a captain that could not be fixed."

"It is these new college-educated army officers," said Gustavo. "There are a couple of them near Álamos who can't be fixed."

"They are not reasonable men," said Espinoza. "We used to grow a lot of opium here and the army have stopped that, too. It makes no sense. The army and the *federales* were getting their share, the politicians were getting their share from the mafia, the *gringos* were getting their drugs, and the people here were able to make a living. It was a good system for everybody and now it is broken. Even if we get a reasonable captain during the next harvest, we have no money now and will not be able to fix things with him."

He bade us a courteous farewell, apparently satisfied that we were harmless, and then walked up the bank of the stream into the village with his empty laundry pail. We walked back to the truck and sat in the cab making peanut butter sandwiches. "Did you notice the way he didn't use any cuss words?" said Gustavo. "Normally when two Mexican men meet each other we will throw in some cuss words but he was very formal and—"

"Gustavo," I interrupted. I was looking in the rearview mirror and it didn't look good. There were two young men leading horses directly toward us and they had very hard stares on their faces. Gustavo looked over his shoulder. Two more men appeared and then all four men pulled down their hats and when Gustavo saw that, with a piece of bread half-smeared with peanut butter on his knee, he said, "Go, go, go! Go now! Go!"

I started the engine and slewed out of there fishtailing in the riverbank sand. Gustavo was worried that more men would be waiting to ambush us at the mud puddle and it wasn't until we sloshed through it that he started to puff and blow and relax. "Son of a bitch!" he said. "Did you see that hat talk? Do you know what that means? That means get out right now or else. Did you feel what happened to the air? It got so thick you could have cut it into slices."

"What would have happened if we had tried to stay and talk to them?"

"They have many ways of telling you that you have overstayed your welcome. They might light a fire right next to your truck or step on your foot and say, 'Excuse me, did I just step on your foot?' and then step on it again. They might say, *'Buenas tardes,* would you mind lying down on the ground with your ass in the air so you can't see us anymore?'"

"Mexicans like to go through these rituals before violence."

"That's right. You get a little courting before you get fucked."

"Why were they so hostile?"

"They have an expression in these villages. It's a little hard to translate but it means don't come in my corral and roar like a bull claiming territory and heifers. That was our mistake, I think. We just walked in there and started looking around without introducing ourselves and showing the proper respect. While we were talking to Espinoza, those young guys were getting pissed off about it. They are very territorial people and they have already been invaded by the army."

It was late afternoon now and I drove back to Guirocoba and parked outside Jaime's house. It was a little bigger and more solidly built than most of them, with adobe mud walls and a poured-concrete porch. Hanging from a nail on the outside wall was one of the plastic pesticide sprayers that marijuana growers use for the *mochomos,* the voracious ants of the region, which are as much of a menace to the plants as the police or the soldiers.

A young, tired-looking woman came out of the house, listened to us without saying anything and went back inside. A few minutes later Jaime emerged looking rumpled and freshly awoken, wearing a ratty old pair of jeans and a frayed tank top and looking embarrassed to be caught without his finery. He said someone had killed a mountain lion and would we like to eat the leg? Alas we had just eaten. Then he moved straight on to the subject of the soldiers, who he said were still camped nearby. They had ruined the only way for a man to make a living in these unforgiving mountains and now he was thinking about going north and walking across the desert into the United States. "I am a proud Mexican and I love my country but everything in Mexico always turns to shit," he said.

Men were going north from these mountains every day, he said. If you factored in the killings and the arrests, there were hardly any men left, one for every six or seven women in Guirocoba. This, we realized, was why the villages all looked deserted.

"Fuck the army, fuck the *federales,* fuck the *mochomos* and the mafia and fuck President Fox with a great big donkey *verga,*" he said. "I have a cousin in Los Angeles and friends in Phoenix. I am strong

and hardworking and I will make a new life up there with the fucking *gringos*."

He invited us to stay for supper but Gustavo didn't want to be there
after dark so we wished him luck and headed back toward Álamos.
On the long bumpy road back we ruminated on the woes of the drug
growers and the suffering created by the army crackdown. Gustavo
thought President Fox was too eager to impress President Bush with
his commitment to the war on drugs. And in return for Fox's efforts,
President Bush was only pretending to do something about the estimated 1.5 million Mexicans who were crossing the border illegally
every year, as part of the largest unforced folk migration in human
history. Fox needed the migrants left alone because the money they
sent back to their relatives was now the second largest component of
Mexico's economy, estimated at ten billion dollars a year.

But the largest component of Mexico's economy was still drug trafficking, estimated at fifty billion dollars a year, and here was Fox's
dilemma. He needed to do something for Bush and he wanted to as-
sert his authority against the cartels but the unfortunate fact was that
his country was hooked on drug money. Without it there would be
economic collapse. According to a leaked study conducted in 2001
by Mexico's internal security agency CISEN, and quoted in Charles
Bowden's *Down by the River*, if the drug business was somehow wiped
out Mexico's economy would shrink by 63 percent. That was never
going to happen, of course. Even if Fox had the will to stamp out the
narcotics industry in Mexico, he didn't have the power. The institutions of government were too weak and corrupt and the market forces
were too strong. There was a demand just across the border that created fifty billion dollars in profit every year. Illegal narcotics was the
third-biggest industry in the world (after arms and oil) and the only
conceivable obstacle to its profits—America legalizing drugs—was a
political impossibility.

Fox was cracking down on the growers and smugglers in certain
areas, arresting some cartel bosses and a few crooked governors,
generally making things more difficult. The street price of Mexican
marijuana had risen slightly in the United States, reflecting these new

difficulties and also the higher profits to be made by overcoming them. Cocaine, the most profitable drug of all, was holding steady in price and during Fox's administration Mexican traffickers had increased their share of the American market from 75 percent to 90 percent.

The most dramatic change wrought by Fox's initiatives was unintended: a surge in murders, executions, kidnappings, and gun battles all across northern Mexico and the border. The big cartels were losing control of their monopolies. They were splintering into microcartels and gangs, warring against each other for control. Northern Mexico was now averaging one hundred reported murders a month, according to the *New York Times,* and the new weapon of choice for the mafiosos, replacing the AK-47, was the rocket-propelled grenade.

"Everything in Mexico turns to shit," I said, quoting back Jaime's remark to Gustavo. "Do you think that's true?"

"Absolutely," said Gustavo. "That's why we don't believe in the future. We don't plan and build to make a better future for ourselves because our history and experience teaches us that everything always turns to shit."

It seemed to me that the surest way to make things worse in Mexico was to try to improve them. For example, there had been a recent campaign to curb the endemic criminality among Mexico's police officers. In Mexico City, Ciudad Juárez, and elsewhere, hundreds of police officers had been fired for corrupt and criminal behavior. It sounds like a sensible idea but it had created a crime wave. Shorn of their badges and released from the web of patronage that kept them answerable for their actions, the corrupt, predatory cops were not enrolling in architecture schools or starting up Internet cafés. They were plying the only trades they knew—extortion, theft, assassination, kidnapping, drug trafficking—with an even greater ferocity and ruthlessness than before.

The Zetas were another example, although this one couldn't be blamed on the Mexican authorities. This was the U.S. government's doing. At the School of the Americas in Fort Benning, Georgia, the U.S. Army trained an elite unit of Mexican paramilitaries called the Airborne Special Forces Group and gave them the firepower, helicopters, and other equipment to go up against the heavily armed and defended drug cartels. In the late 1990s they switched sides and started working for the Gulf cartel, using all their training and equipment to break drug lords out of high-security prisons, guard and transport drug shipments, and assassinate their rivals, along with various troublesome police chiefs and journalists.

Now the Zetas, as they had dubbed themselves, were carrying out hits in Dallas and had effected a complete breakdown of law and order in the Mexican border town of Nuevo Laredo. The warring drug groups were fighting gun and grenade battles on the downtown streets in broad daylight. Twenty-eight visiting U.S citizens had been kidnapped, killed, or otherwise disappeared in the twelve months. A new police chief was appointed to take back control of the town and he lasted only eight hours in office before he was killed. In response to this and the other violence the U.S. State Department had issued a warning to American citizens against traveling anywhere in northern Mexico.

Here in this one small area of the Sierra Madre, the army campaign against drug growers had wrecked the local economy, caused an outbreak of holdups and burglaries, and convinced a significant portion of the male population to leave Mexico for good. On the other hand, as Gustavo pointed out, the drug business was not a healthy occupation or a good influence on society. It makes boys neglect their schooling and any other ambitions they might have harbored. It causes men to die young and violently and worsens corruption. It exaggerates the worst tendencies in Mexican society, most of which are contained in the verb *chingar*.

Its closest translation is "to fuck," but as Octavio Paz writes in his essay on the verb in *The Labyrinth of Solitude,* it always denotes violence, "an emergence from oneself to penetrate another by force. It also means to injure, to lacerate, to violate—bodies, souls, objects—and to destroy. . . . To the Mexican there are only two possibilities in life: either he inflicts the actions implied by *chingar* on others, or else he suffers them himself at the hands of others. This conception of social life as combat fatally divides society into the strong and the weak."

We were coming back across the Cuchajaqui River in the gathering dark, tired and beaten-up from a long day on bad roads. "The thing about Mexico is that everyone is out to get everyone else, except within your family and your very closest friends," said Gustavo. "We live with our senses and suspicions on full alert because who knows where the next plot against you might come from? Maybe someone thinks your wife is prettier than his wife so he whispers something to the police, or the mafia, and the next thing you know the police are planting drugs in your truck and you're going to jail for ten years or there's a bullet in your head and you may never know why."

He paused for a moment and let out a long sigh, "I don't know if you can understand what it is like to live this way."

10

A Girl Needs a Pistol

GUSTAVO HAD FOUND SOMEONE that he thought could get me safely into the mafia stronghold of San Bernardo and the Guarijio Indian country beyond it. The man in question was standing on the sidelines of a soccer game in Álamos, wearing denim shorts and shouting the occasional command at a team of Guarijia schoolgirls that he'd brought down from the Sierra. He was tall and solidly built with a gray mustache and silvery brushed-back hair and he was the first Mexican man or boy I had ever seen wearing shorts in Álamos. "I know," said Gustavo. "We wear jeans and shirts to go swimming at the beach. But Angel is a little different, more of the cosmopolitan type."

We stood there leaning against my truck, waiting for the game to end. "How much money does he want?" I asked.

"Nothing. Maybe you could give him something for gas."

"Are you sure he's trustworthy?"

"Absolutely. He's a schoolteacher, a bohemian interested in art and culture and all of that. He likes *gringos*. He has taken American scientists into the Guarijios before."

"He doesn't want money. You won't take what I offered. It makes me nervous, Gustavo. Why is no one trying to *chingar* me?"

"Ricardo, have you forgotten those guys in Aguacaliente already?

They would have loved to get you facedown with your ass in the air."

Gustavo seemed more shaken by our abrupt departure from Aguacaliente than I was, maybe because he understood hat talk better than I did and could visualize more clearly what might have happened next. For me it was a warning that we had successfully recognized and obeyed, like jumping back from a coiled buzzing rattlesnake. There was a fast heavy jolt of fear when the warning was given but I never really felt in danger for my life. At the crucial moment we were in a vehicle and they were on foot and if there were pistols in their waistbands I couldn't see them. Two days later Aguacaliente had settled into my brain as an adventurous lark but it had left me feeling uneasy about my cover story.

"Do you think it's going to work telling people I'm a writer researching the history of the area? Is the concept too foreign?"

"It would be better if you were a biologist or a botanist," said Gustavo. "People are used to *gringos* like that showing up in the Sierra. What you can't tell them is the truth, that you're a traveler who wants to see the country and write about it. In these remote areas people live outside the law. They kill their cows and make jerky out of the meat. They raise marijuana and kill each other. They might come to Álamos once or twice a year to sell their meat or marijuana, or party at Aduana, but they won't understand that someone might just be traveling to see the country. I would just say you're a friend of Angel Flores and leave it at that."

"Angel Flores? Like Angel Flowers?"

"That's it. It doesn't sound quite as precious in Spanish but it doesn't sound *muy macho* either."

He was the head of the school in Mesa Colorada, the biggest Guarijio village, and after the game he said it would be his pleasure to take me there for a week or so, with a stop-off to see his family in San Bernardo. He seemed calm, confident, good-humored, intelligent, and slightly ethereal, with none of the coarse swaggering machismo I had grown so used to. When he said he was unmarried I wondered if he was gay but he turned out to have an American girlfriend in Álamos.

"Tell me about the Guarijios," I said. "What should I expect?"

"They live in a different reality, close to nature," said Angel. "They have nothing and yet they are happy most of the time. They are very quiet, very shy, very suspicious of outsiders. I like them very much but they can get crazy when they're drunk, sometimes very aggressive."

"How do they make a living?"

"Well, growing marijuana is the main thing now, either for themselves or working in the fields of the local *narco*. Otherwise there is subsistence farming and a little cattle raising."

"Is it dangerous for me to go there?"

"No, no. There is no problem. Sometimes they get drunk and kill each other. There was a visitor last year who was robbed and killed but maybe he was coming to buy drugs. Maybe they will think that about you. Hah hah! But no, no, it will be fine. It is a beautiful place and for me very tranquil."

"What about San Bernardo?" I asked, ignoring his little joke about my safety. "I've heard that can be a dangerous place." That was where twenty-nine young men whom Joe Brown knew were killed in a single year. Now it was the home turf of a powerful drug mafia known as the Los Güeritos (The Little Blonds) or Los Números (The Numbers). A twenty-six-year-old reporter from *El Imparcial* newspaper in Hermosillo had just been kidnapped and tortured to death after writing about their activities.

Their leader was Raúl Enriquez Parra, aka "El Nueve" ("The Nine"). He had three brothers working under him, the most feared of whom was Wilfrido, known as "El Siete" ("The Seven") and also "The Terrible." They were allied to Joaquin "Chapo" ("Shorty") Guzman's mafia in Sinaloa, which was currently warring with the Gulf cartel, the Juárez cartel, and the Tijuana cartel and acquitting itself strongly, especially when you considered that Chapo Guzman was on the run, having bribed his way out of a maximum-security prison in a laundry basket.

Angel pooh-poohed the suggestion that San Bernardo might be considered a dangerous place. It was his hometown and he was a proud native son. "It is a very close community. I know all the mafiosos because we grew up together and with me they are very friendly and respectful. They are not bad people."

"But they do a lot of killing."

"It is the nature of the business, unfortunately. I feel compassion for them. They have made a bad choice and their only future now is to get killed or go to prison. It is sad when you see this happening to someone you have known all your life."

TWO DAYS LATER, heavily laden with supplies, we set off in Angel's battered red warhorse of a Chevy truck. The road was dusty, ribbed, and potholed, lined with thornbrush and cactus, and it passed through a number of small villages with strikingly large cemeteries. At Los Molinos there were three houses and at least a hundred tombstones.

At El Frijol (The Bean) people were still panning gold for a living. Outside Los Tanques we saw two men coming toward us in a horse-drawn cart and they looked so quaint and charming until we passed them and saw that one of the men had an AR-15 rifle resting across his lap. First you get your machine gun. Then you see about upgrading your transportation.

There were also a lot of dead cattle and feasting vultures by the side of the road and I wondered if drunken yahoos used cows for target practice, like they sometimes did in Arizona. "No," said Angel. "It is plastic bags. People throw their trash out of the window, the cattle try to eat it and choke to death on the plastic. It is so unnecessary. It makes me angry with my country. Are there things you don't like about Mexico?"

"I love Mexico but there is so much violence, so much machismo, especially in the Sierra," I said. I was only dimly aware at that stage of how much rape went along with that machismo.

"It is unfortunate," said Angel. "The people have good hearts and beautiful souls but they lack education, they lack culture, they are caught up in this lifestyle of machismo and status symbols. Also they need more law. It is so easy to kill someone and get away with it."

"How many friends of yours have been murdered?"

"Many," he said, shaking his head sadly. "Maybe twenty, twenty-five. But they were not all close friends. What about you?"

"None. I had one friend who was shot but he survived."

A moment of silence fell between us. I couldn't imagine twenty or twenty-five of my friends murdered and buried. He probably couldn't imagine my world, in which murder was such a marginal event.

THE DRAMATIC ROCK spires on the hills outside San Bernardo came into view—"The Pillars," as they were known locally—and then the town itself, a dusty, rumpled affair of adobe houses and dirt streets on the banks of the Mayo River, with the main cordillera of the Sierra Madre rising up behind it. Boys on horses trotted through the streets. Shiny pickup trucks with tinted windows drove around and around the bleak little plaza, blasting *narcocorridos* and bouncing up and down through the potholes.

"The *narcos* threw a big, big party in the plaza not long ago for the whole town," said Angel. "They hired a band from Jalisco. They had more meat, beer, whiskey, and tequila than you can believe. More than enough cocaine too. My sisters didn't want me to go but I had a good time. I drank a few beers, ate some tacos. The *narcos* all call me 'Maestro' ['Teacher'] and they were glad to see me."

I was thinking, did they really need to kill that young reporter from Hermosillo? Did they really need to torture him to death?

We went to his family's whitewashed house on the edge of town. Angel busied himself in the kitchen and I sat in the packed-dirt backyard under a shade tree with his older brother, Manuel, a scrawny, bright-eyed, highly animated man in his sixties with dyed black hair and an exuberant cackling laugh. He remembered Joe Brown very well and said he was always drinking, always wanting music because he loved to dance, and wasn't he flying out Rafael Russo's opium in that little plane of his? "I'll have to ask Joe about that,"* I said." I thought they were in the cattle business together."

"The cattle business!" chortled Manuel. "Those Russos must have been raising some very special cattle! No one else got that rich up there without growing opium or marijuana."

A sheet of raw beef hung on the laundry line buzzing with flies. Manuel had been drying it in the sun to make jerky. He took it down, folded it up into a leathery square, stuck it into a flimsy plastic bag, and then said that he was reading a very interesting book about Henri Christophe, the nineteenth-century slave king of Haiti. Had I heard of this man? I had indeed. I told Manuel I had been to Haiti and his face lit up and he started questioning me in detail about crime, poverty, voodoo, government corruption, what had become of Aristide. I was utterly charmed. This was what I loved about travel and what tourism so seldom delivered: something completely unexpected and improbable.

"Manuel, this is great," I said. "I never thought I would be discussing Haitian politics in San Bernardo, Sonora."

"Oh yes!" He laughed. "I love to read about the world and its history. I have too much curiosity! That's what people say around here. I would love to travel and see the world like you do but I never have the money. I have seen a lot of Mexico but that is all."

"Do you know the Sierra Madre well?"

"*Hombre!* I used to travel all over the Sierra selling livestock medicines. That was my job. Now I drive a school bus part-time."

I said I wanted to go up and over the cordillera to Chinipas, Chihuahua. There was a British connection in its history (true) and Joe Brown had asked me to go there and find out how his old friends were doing (almost true). Manuel said it was a very bad road and bandits had been a problem lately, although he probably knew most

---

*Joe Brown was convincingly scornful when I asked him: "Russo never grew any opium. Me and Russo were selling twenty-five hundred steers a year for $120 each. That's where the money came from."

of them. I had a twelve-year-old Toyota pickup in Álamos with four-wheel drive and off-road tires and he thought that would probably do. I offered him twenty dollars a day and he agreed to take me to Chinipas when I had had enough of the Guarijios. He described them with a wild cackle as pig-filthy *(muy cochino)* and belligerent assholes *(muy cabrón)* when drunk.

Angel brought out an excellent dish of pork stewed in oranges and limes, served with rice, tortillas, and the first salad I had seen since leaving Tucson. By the time we had eaten, cleared the table, washed the dishes, taken our siestas, picked up more supplies, said good-bye to Angel's relatives, filled up the tank with gasoline, exchanged pleasantries with various hard-eyed, cocaine-jangled characters who pulled up alongside us in their trucks, it was dark and I was itchy and impatient to leave, aware that I was exhibiting the classic behavioral signs of a *gringo* in Mexico but unable to stop myself.

The road to Mesa Colorada was a long, rocky, potholed son of its disgraced mother. For Angel, it was the road back to work, to his humdrum Monday morning. For me it led somewhere exotic and far-flung and I was eager as Lumholtz to fill my notebooks with the customs and beliefs of the reclusive tribal people who lived there. He had passed through the Sierra Madre without hearing a word of the Guarijios and their existence was unrecorded by the Mexican government until 1975, when President Echeverría announced that a lost tribe had been discovered in the remote canyons of the north-western Sierra Madre.

The Guarijios knew who they were, of course, and so did the local cowboys and cattlemen, a handful of foreign anthropologists, and Joe Brown, who remembered them as "about half wild, just as poor as they could be, wearing loincloths, clearing brush for the ranchers in exchange for a little salt and corn."

In 1981, after a long, bitter, and ultimately miraculous struggle, the government bought out the local cattlemen and gave the Guarijios ownership of their ancestral lands in the mountains and canyons along the Mayo River. The government had also built schools and a health clinic and now it was bringing electricity to Mesa Colorada.

The poles were already in the ground by the side of the road and the magic cables would be there soon. "They will use it for light, refrigeration, and television," predicted Angel. "And to save batteries in their boomboxes. They love *norteño* music, *narcocorridos*—music that sounds ugly to me."

The village was asleep when we arrived and barely visible in the starlight. Angel opened the gates to the secondary school compound, which consisted of three small buildings, a solar panel, a satellite dish, and a concrete volleyball court, all surrounded by a tall wire fence. My first impressions of Mesa Colorada were mostly auditory. I lay in the dark on a canvas fold-out cot in one of the school classrooms, listening to the sibilant flow of the Mayo River in the distance, dogs barking, a rooster crowing insistently six hours before dawn, a donkey braying, *norteño* music playing on a distant boombox, initially charmed by this rustic Mexican soundscape and then wishing I had brought some earplugs and finally hatching wild insomniac plans at three in the morning to wring that rooster's neck, hack him into pieces and put him in a pot with onions, garlic, carrot, celery, a little tomato, and a cup of wine.

THE TEACHERS ASSEMBLED in the gray light before dawn, stamping their feet against the cold, blowing on cups of instant coffee, and I greeted them with as much cheer as I could muster. Roque Rosas, a small, earnest, reliable-looking young man from Los Tanques, wearing cowboy boots and a straw hat, was looking for a horse or mule to ride up to the other school in the village of Guajaray. Normally he walked the trail in three hours or so but this time he had a stack of blankets for the children there.

"Are the Guarijios good students?" I asked him.

"No," he said matter-of-factly. "They are very shy and not very intelligent on the whole. They don't value education. It is a chore for them. They don't have ambition to get a nice house or a good job. If they can sell enough marijuana to get a good hat and a *cuerno de chivo*, a goat-horned AK-47, that is enough for them."

A few students were coming in the front gates now, fewer than normal because the river was high and some of them couldn't make it across. The boys were grubby and smelled as if they hadn't bathed in a while. They wore jeans, T-shirts, or western shirts and one of them had on a baseball cap with a picture of an AK-47 on the front and a Jesús Malverde scapular around his neck. The girls were immaculately clean and fresh-looking and this was a marvel because they all lived in dirt-floored huts with no running water. They wore the same print dresses as their mothers and grandmothers and their black hair was brushed to a sheen and pulled back in ponytails. A few of them had on bright pink fuzzy socks with their cowhide sandals.

Rocky Roses rode off on a horse to bring education and blankets to the children of Guajaray. Angel Flowers got his class of three teenage boys sat down at their desks with their textbooks open. Then he turned on the television and wandered over to the sink to wash up the coffee cups.

In small remote schools like this one, it would be almost impossible to hire enough teachers to teach all the subjects in the national curriculum. So the Mexican government has turned instead to the system of *telesecundaria*. The education ministry produces instructional television programs covering the whole curriculum and broadcasts them into the schools through solar-powered satellite dishes that also provide Internet access.

The programming moved fast with slick graphics and sound effects. The boys watched it for fifteen minutes, then Angel told them to complete the relevant exercises in their textbooks. They doodled, scrawled a few words, scratched themselves, fidgeted. Angel recapped the lesson with a question: "What were the causes of the barbarian invasions in ancient Rome?" The boys sniffed. One poked his neighbor in the back with a pencil. The third boy tried on his textbook for a hat. Angel gave up and turned the television back on for their math class.

In the adjoining classroom the girls were writing away. They were extremely reluctant to answer questions out loud but the teachers all agreed that they were better students, more industrious, and quicker to learn. The trouble was that the girls tended to get married, leave school, and start having babies when they were thirteen or fourteen.

When they broke for lunch I checked my email at one of the three working computer terminals, which had a faster connection than the Internet café in Álamos. A friend had sent me a *Washington Post* story for my narco-surrealism files. A delegation of drug traffickers' wives, "glowering behind designer sunglasses and clicking on their high heels," had gone to the Mexican Congress and angrily demanded that conjugal visits to their husbands be restored in the La Palma maximum-security prison. The government, which had already outlawed Jacuzzis in prisoners' cells during a previous crackdown, had banned conjugal visits because the drug lords were ordering executions both in and out of prison from their palatial cells.

From there the story took a Mexican leap deeper into the absurd. Congressman Gilberto Ensastiga agreed with the wives that conjugal visits were the legal right of every imprisoned Mexican citizen and the following morning he accompanied the wives to the national human rights commission and got the visits restored immediately.

Regarding Chapo Guzman's escape from a different prison in a laundry basket, the article noted that "to the dismay of many law enforcement officials," escaping from prison is not a crime in Mexico, so long as the escapee doesn't hurt anyone or steal anything in the course of escaping. A Mexican Supreme Court judge explained the court's position with immaculate Mexican logic: "The person who tries to escape is seeking liberty, and that is deeply respected in the law."

MY FIRST ATTEMPTS to communicate with the Guarijios were a comprehensive failure. The schoolchildren avoided my eyes and curled in on themselves with discomfort and embarrassment when I tried to talk to them. Sometimes I could raise a smile with a flippant comment but all my conversation-starters—what's your name? how old are you?—were met with cringing silence. Walking around the village, wending my way on dusty goat paths past their scattered huts, I greeted everyone with a polite nod and a *buenas tardes* and got nothing back except suspicious glances. Even the drunks wanted nothing to do with me.

On the banks of the river, women were digging holes and using gourds to scoop the sand-filtered water into ten gallon plastic paint buckets. When I approached, they all turned to give me their backs. I remembered Lumholtz's initial difficulties with the Tarahumara: "Wherever I came I was abhorred as the man who subsisted on babies and green corn, and the prospect of my ever gaining the confidence of the Indians was exceedingly discouraging."

Finally, toward the end of the second day, I managed a brief exchange with a young man called Juan, who was wearing a grubby AK-47 cap and had a sour boozy smell. He stood there staring at me by the school gates so I introduced myself and said I came from *Inglaterra*. He looked at me blankly.

"It's a country a long way away, across the sea in Europe," I said. No response. "Near Spain," I added hopefully.

"Do they smoke *mota* there?"

"Oh yes. I think they smoke *mota* in nearly all countries in the world."

"I don't smoke it. I only sell it. I like to get drunk."

"I like to get drunk also. It is a very popular custom in my country."

"Do you want to buy some *mota*? Eight hundred pesos [eighty U.S. dollars] a kilo."

"No thanks, I don't need any."

"Eight hundred. *Buena mota*. You want it?"

"No thank you."

He walked off without saying another word but it felt like a breakthrough. My first conversation with a Guarijio! I waited until he was gone and transcribed it eagerly into my notebook.

Walking around with Angel, who had lived and taught here five days a week for seven years, it was still astonishingly difficult to engage anyone in conversation, especially if they were female. Women whose sons he taught, whose husbands he counted as friends, would give us their backs when we approached their cookfires and Angel assured me that it wasn't my presence, that this was normal behavior. When we encountered his pupils on the trails, they would usually put their heads down and pass by without a word or glance of recognition. As one of them walked alongside us, Angel pointed to me and said, "Let's cut the balls off this filthy *gringo* pig. What do you say? Do you have a knife?" The boy cracked a sheepish smile but when Angel asked him if he was on the way home, his face turned into a mask and he veered away on another path.

Gradually I got on nodding terms with some of the men and that led to some exchanged greetings and soft monosyllabic small talk but it wasn't until the fourth day that I had a conversation with a Guarijio that actually interested me. Walking upriver on my own, maybe a mile past Mesa Colorada and looking for somewhere private to bathe, I encountered an old man dragging sticks and pieces of thornbrush across the riverbank. He was no more than five feet tall with his hat on and his eyes were partially clouded over. He wore a frayed pair of Levi's Dockers, rolled up at the cuffs, homemade sandals, and a faded blue workshirt. Normally when I was out walking people scurried to get away from me but I think he was just too old to move that fast.

I asked him what he was doing and he said a mountain lion had been coming down into the canyon and killing his donkeys. "He has killed two but he just ate the legs off one of them," he said in soft husky Spanish that was about as good as mine. "He's a young male but big."

He showed me the tracks in the sand. I could see they were lion tracks—like big dog tracks but with no claws showing—and since the front pawprints were spread farther apart than the rear pawprints, I could see that the shoulders were broader than the hips and therefore it was a male lion. "How do you know he is young and big for his age? Have you seen him?" I asked.

He shook his head and gave a little toothless smile and pointed down at the tracks again. I had read that expert trackers could tell these things and a lot more from an animal's footprints but I couldn't get him to explain how. He just kept pointing down. Maybe it was the depth of the tracks in the sand relative to their size. Maybe young lions walked with a different gait pattern than older lions.

"He also killed a calf," he said and led me upstream to the marks of the kill. This I could see clearly: the deep hind footprints that launched the lion's leap, the scuffling and thrashing, the dragmarks in the sand where the lion had hauled away the carcass.

I asked him if there were jaguars here and he said not anymore. What about *onzas*? "Yes there are," he said. I coaxed a few details out of him: "Dog meat is his favorite food. He keeps his tail tucked like a shamed dog. His ears are like a cat, smaller than the ears of a lion. He has a little tuft of fur here behind the elbows on his forelegs."

"Some people say the *onza* is a cross between a lion and a jaguar."

He shrugged and looked away. "I will continue my work now," he said.

"Are you building a corral to protect your donkeys?"

"No, I am making a field for tobacco. This brush will stop the animals from coming in and eating the plants."

I offered to help and he looked away to the side. Maybe we could talk later? Or tomorrow? *"¿Quién sabe?"* he shrugged and I knew what that meant.

The true folly of my hopes descended on me. It took Lumholtz four or five months of hanging around, being patient, refraining from asking questions, before the Tarahumara decided that he didn't eat babies and was actually a rain god and therefore worth confiding in. Here was I hoping to pluck the beliefs and customs of a related but even more reticent people in a week or so. Clearly, if I was going to get anywhere at all, I would have to stay here for months. And equally clearly I didn't have the patience for that. After four days in Mesa Colorada, I was already bored and restless, impatient to get deeper and higher into the mountains.

I SECURED AN interview with the tribal governor, a broad-faced muscular young man called Javier Zazueta, son of the late José Zazueta who was the leader and organizer of the Guarijios during their land struggle, although their main champion in those days had been an anthropologist from Mexico City called Teresa Valdivia Dounce who worked for the National Institute of Indigenous Peoples.

We sat down on cheap metal chairs under a palm frond ramada. He was wearing an old pair of slacks, an undershirt, and the traditional homemade sandals, exposing his broad callused toes. By Guarijio standards, he was lively and self-confident, with a leader's charisma and a ready smile, but there was a glint of something in his eyes that unsettled me.

"Now that we have our lands and are no longer working for the *yori* [a derogatory term for non-Indians], our priority is education," he said, sensibly enough. "We need doctors, lawyers, engineers, and teachers to make our life better here. At the same time we must keep our traditions and language alive. At the moment there are some old Guarijios who speak no Spanish and some young ones who speak no Guarijio. Most of us speak both languages and this is best. This is what we want."

"What traditions do you want to keep alive?"

"The *tuburada*," he said. "This is our ceremonial dance and feast where we all come together."

"What else?"

"The *tuburada* and our language are what makes us Guarijios," he said.

I said that I would like to go up to the other school in Guajaray to see my friend Roque Rosas and then maybe to the remote mountain village of Bavícora. "I am looking for a reliable, trustworthy guide to take me to these places. I can pay a hundred pesos a day."

He smiled and that glint sharpened in his eyes and he said, "No problem. I will find somebody to take you. But Bavícora is a long journey for a *yori*. First you go to Guajaray."

When I told Angel about my new plans, which I had made without consulting him, he started pacing up and down and shaking his head. "Ricardo, Ricardo," he said. "Javier is a friend of mine but you cannot trust him with your life. He doesn't care what guide you end up with. He will just say, 'Who wants to take a *gringo* up to Guajaray for one hundred pesos?' and bad people will jump at the chance. That visitor who came here last year? It was his guides who robbed and killed him. Those two men are still living here, smoking lots of marijuana, and they will be very happy to guide you."

"Well, maybe you know someone reliable who can guide me. I want to see some more of the country."

"Not now, Ricardo. There is lots of *mota* growing by the trail to Guajaray. The people there all have guns and they are very suspicious. It is too dangerous. They don't know you. In Guajaray itself, there are many drunks and much craziness. Someone was just killed there and there is a lot of tension."

"What about Bavícora?"

"Ricardo, please. Stay longer in Mesa Colorada. Then come back and spend a month here. Then everyone will know you're cool and we can find someone to guide you. Please, I ask you as a friend and my guest, don't make me worry about your safety."

As a sop to my restlessness Angel arranged to take me upriver to Huataturi. Our guide was a snot-plagued fifteen-year-old boy in yet another AK-47 baseball cap. We were many hours on steep trails made of loose rocks and he never once slipped or missed a step or broke his rhythm and despite my efforts and Angel's cajolings I doubt he said more than twelve words the entire time. When we reached a stream he would drop down into a push-up position, balancing on his hands and feet, and dip his mouth into the water to drink. Huataturi was another collection of Stone Age huts and awkward reticent people. There was nowhere to stay so we turned around and went back to Mesa Colorada, where I settled down and read my way through the thin library of books written about the Guarijios.

Javier Zazueta was right. Apart from the language, which was closely related to Tarahumara, and the *tuburada,* a two-day dance performed with a simple shuffling step to the rhythm of shaken gourd rattles, there didn't seem to be much else that was uniquely Guarijio. It may be that their culture was once a richer, deeper river but now it appeared to be a very thin trickle indeed. The elders had a

thorough knowledge of edible and medicinal plants but that was being lost. Younger Guarijios were more interested in clearing the forest
to plant marijuana. A few artisans, encouraged by the government,
carved harps and violins, although not as skillfully as the Tarahumaras. The women made pottery and wove baskets, hats, blankets, and
the sleeping mats called *petates*—all of them strictly functional with
no patterns or dyes.

Guarijio cuisine, as I sampled it at various cookfires, is the usual
Sierra Madre peasant fare: boiled squash, boiled beans, tamales, and
tortillas, supplemented by occasional deer meat, fish from the river,
and small game such as squirrels. Their music is equally rudimen-
tary: a shaken gourd rattle and a few repeated chants. "I sing *tuburi*
[a *tuburada* song]/Dance, little ones, dance." Or, "High on the moun-
tain/The morning sun is striking/Dance *tuburi*."

They have surprisingly little oral history or myths, legends, and
stories about themselves and this probably stems from their prefer-
ence for living apart from one another in dispersed huts with fences
of sticks around them. Within their families Guarijios are apparently
quite chatty but it's not their custom to get together with the neighbors and swap stories around a campfire. Howard Scott Gentry, an
ethnobotanist who made three trips among them in the 1930s and
wrote the first and most thorough ethnography, said they were the
most solitary and antisocial people he had ever heard of.

He also said they had no real tribal unity or consciousness of
themselves as a people. "They are just a group of people occupying a
certain geographical position, broken into many small groups but all
speaking variably the same tongue, living on about the same subsistence pattern and perpetuating similar customs. . . . Mainly through
tuwuri [tuburada] are they all held to something near a common consciousness and a general cultural pattern."

The two most remarkable things about the Guarijios are interre-
lated. One is their extraordinary reticence and suspicion of outsiders
and the second is their ability to disappear from the historical record.
In a mountain range whose history is entwined with legends and
false rumors of lost tribes—Lumholtz never found his cliff dwellers,

the Oklahoma Apaches never found their wild cousins—the Guari-jios actually did become a lost tribe, and not just once but twice.

The first reports come in the 1640s from Spanish explorers and Jesuits, who called them Varohios and found them to be fierce and warlike, qualities that are now long gone, and also "less communicative than the other nations of the region." After various rebellions and massacres they were subdued into the Jesuit mission system but after the Jesuits were expelled from Mexico by the Spanish crown in 1767, the Guarijios started drifting away into remote mountains and canyons, where they kept themselves very much to themselves. By the early twentieth century most anthropologists thought they had gone extinct or become unrecognizably assimilated into the surrounding populations.

They were located again in 1930 by two professors from the University of California, Carl Sauer and Alfred Kroeber, who were mapping the languages and distribution of indigenous people in Sonora. It was Sauer who encouraged Howard Scott Gentry to go into the mountains behind San Bernardo and document the existence of the Guarijios more fully.

Then the outside world forgot about them again until the mid-1970s, when a Canadian called Edward Faubert showed up in the Mayo River country, looking for native handicrafts to buy, and "discovered" the Guarijios yet again, living in the most abject poverty and virtual slavery to the local *mestizo* cattlemen. He started agitating on their behalf, President Echeverría announced their discovery from Mexico City, and so began the long tortuous struggle for Guarijio land rights. Ultimately it was Howard Scott Gentry's field notes from the 1930s that established their official existence as a tribe with a historic claim on these lands. What I was observing in Mesa Colorada and its environs was a happy ending of sorts, a life more pleasant and easy than the Guarijios had ever lived.

THE RIVER HAD subsided now and the number of schoolchildren had swelled. I stood up in front of fifteen boys and girls and announced in Spanish that I would be teaching them English. This was Angel's idea. All secondary school students in Mexico are required to learn some English but none of the teachers in Guarijio country could speak more than a few words of it. I had serious misgivings about my talents and qualifications as an English teacher but as Angel's guest, and the recipient all week of his excellent cooking, I was in no position to refuse.

"We will begin with greetings," I said in Spanish. On the blackboard I wrote in English, "Hello, my name is . . ." and under that I wrote, "How are you?" and, "I am fine."

I explained their Spanish equivalents and then asked them to say, "Hello," in English. The boys hunched over their desks. The girls sat up straight and stared devoutly at the floor. I singled out one boy who appeared to have a trace of nonchalance in his hunching slouch and asked his name in Spanish. He sat up and looked absolutely horrified. "What is your name?" I repeated. He ducked his head and slid his hands across his face, apparently willing himself to become invisible.

So it went with the next boy and the next two girls. "Come on, this is easy," I said. "All I am asking is for you to tell me your name in Spanish. Then I will tell you how to say this in English." Eventually I found a boy who had the wherewithal to tell me his name and undergo the hideous ordeal of being the first to say, "Hello, my name is . . ." in English. Once he had broken through that barrier, a few more followed him and some slow agonizing progress was made, although Javier Zazueta's vision of Guarijio doctors, lawyers, and engineers seemed very distant when that hour was up.

Then I went over to Angel's classroom and tried again with his three boys and two girls. I must have been doing something different, although I have no idea what it was, because we got through the conversational pleasantries and were reciting the names of animals by the end of the hour. For some reason the English word "chicken" amused them greatly, perhaps because it sounds more onomatopoeic than the Spanish *pollo*. The girls had to bring up their hands to cover their grins and one boy actually chuckled out loud.

My third class was all girls. There were four Guarijias in the traditional print dresses and Reyna Elena Félix Torres, who was the daughter of a *mestizo* family living in the nearby village of Burapaco. At fifteen she was the oldest girl in the school. She wore jeans, tennis shoes, and a striped sweater, answered every question I put to the class, made a solid attempt at speaking English, rolled her eyes at the reticence of her classmates, and so dominated the room that I had to think of some way of involving the other girls.

I came up with the idea of getting them to write a letter of friendship to high school students in Tucson. Each girl would contribute a sentence or two in Spanish describing their life in Mesa Colorada. When they were finished, I would translate the sentences into English, put them together into a letter, and, I hoped, teach them a few words of English along the way. This is what we ended up with:

Dear students,

   This is a letter of friendship from the students of Mesa Colorada, telling you something of our customs. In the afternoons in the days of cold it is our custom to make a fire on the ground and sit by it. At the time of Easter there are many burrs which get stuck on our heads. When the women leave for a place they wear a pistol and dress like cowboys. In my community there are many animals: goats, horses, dogs, donkeys, etc. In my community there are many people who grow marijuana. To make tortillas when there is no firewood we get some more from the *monte*. There are deer in the *monte* and also coyotes, squirrels, foxes, etc. In the month of June we grow corn, squash, watermelon and beans. We say good-bye to you and hope you reply soon to this letter.*

On my last day I went to Burapaco with Angel to visit Reyna. She lived in a small crumbling adobe with chickens pecking in the dirt

---

* I approached two high school teachers in Tucson, trying to set up a pen pal program, but they both balked at the references to marijuana-growing and pistols.

around it. She was making tortillas by an outdoor hearth, listening to schmaltzy romantic music on a boombox, and Angel snuck up behind her and surprised her. "Maestro, you scared me!" she exclaimed. "I could have shot you!"

"You see, Ricardo. They all have guns. Reyna, where is your pistol?"

"It's inside. I should be wearing it," she said.

"Why?" I asked.

"There are many bad men around here," she said. "A girl needs a pistol."

"So what are you doing, Reyna?" said Angel. "Listening to music and dreaming of a boyfriend?"

"Maestro!"

"Yes or no?"

"Yes," she sighed. "All the other girls my age are married and having babies. I don't even have a boyfriend."

"Ask Ricardo what age girls get married in his country."

"Twenty-seven or twenty-eight is normal," I said. "Although a few get married at seventeen or eighteen."

"Here it is very unusual not to be married by the age of fifteen," she said morosely. "Soon I will be sixteen."

Gunshots rang out in the middle distance. "Drunks?" I inquired.

"Crazies," she said, handing us fresh hot flour tortillas with beans.

"In Ricardo's country and in the United States, the men help with the cooking and the housework," said Angel.

"It's true," I said.

"Que suave!" she said, how cool. "I had to serve my brothers when I was just a little girl. I hated it."

We ate the food in the gathering darkness, thanked her, and said good-bye. I wished her luck in finding a husband but warned her not to marry a drunk. (A few months later, by email, Angel told me that she had ignored my warning, dropped out of school, and married a belligerent young alcoholic.)

Angel had another errand in Burapaco. From Reyna's house we

walked over to a barbed wire fence surrounding a larger property. Angel called from the fence; a man came out and opened the gate. He and Angel stood talking in the front yard. The man's name was Enriquez and news had just come through that his nephew, a good friend of Angel's known as El Güero (The Light-skinned One) and a major figure in the San Bernardo mafia, had been gunned down in Tijuana.

Angel offered his condolences and then we walked back in the dark, talking about his dead friend. "He was a *campesino,* a man of the country, but very intelligent, very thoughtful," said Angel. "I used to give him rides in my truck when all he owned was a pair of sandals. When he got money he wore cowboy clothes but without the gold and the exotic boots. He wasn't wild or ostentatious. He and his brothers were always very good to my family and to the town. I will miss him. There are so many dead. It is so sad."

"And all over a plant that makes people feel happy and relaxed," I said. "It is crazy. Marijuana is less harmful than tobacco or alcohol."

"Smoking *mota* is a bad habit," said Angel. "It is a vice and I have never done it. But the money from it is wonderful. I think of the money often."

"The money is why people get killed over it."

"Yes, but think of the money we could make if we bought twenty kilos. I can get it at a very good price and growing up in San Bernardo I have all the connections to get it to the border. If you can find a way to get it across, we make nearly ten thousand dollars each. So why not fifty kilos? That way we make more than twenty thousand each."

He was about half joking and half serious, as near as I could tell, and I felt the temptation too. It wouldn't be difficult for me to get it across. An old and trusted friend of mine is a well-connected midlevel dealer in Tucson with a smuggling operation on the border. It would take one phone call if I wanted to go into business with him. I knew someone else who knew a corrupt U.S. Customs agent in Nogales who could be paid to wave a vehicle through the border. And I used to live on the border and I knew several obscure smuggling routes in remote places. I felt the beginnings of a new kind of gold fever but mercifully I was too afraid of prison for the fever to take hold.

"I know ways to get it across but it's too risky for me," I said.

"Too risky?" Angel laughed. "Ricardo, listen to yourself! Look at what you're doing. Look where you're going. You love risk. There is no other explanation."

Angel's vice was gambling. He loved casinos. He dreamed of doing drug deals. For him the point of taking risks was to make money. I'm not a gambler. Casinos bore me and I wasn't going to risk prison to make money. But I was prepared to stake my personal safety for a different reward: the heightened awareness, the thrill of the unfamiliar and the melting away of boredom that comes with going to dangerous places where I didn't belong. And I was beginning to wonder if this too was a vice.

11

Bandit Country

IT SEEMED LIKE SUCH a solid and foolproof plan. I would retrieve my truck in Álamos, meet Manuel Flores in San Bernardo, and he would guide me along the bandit road to Chinipas, where I had friends of Joe Brown to look up.

When I got back to San Bernardo with my truck, Manuel had some bad news. A war had broken out between the San Bernardo mafia and the Chinipas mafia. He thought it would be unwise for anyone from San Bernardo to show up in Chinipas at the moment and that I would be safer going alone without him. "You'll be fine," he said. "They are good people in Chinipas. If you treat them with respect, they will treat you with respect. But if you walk past someone on the street and don't say hello to them, they will be insulted and this can lead to trouble. If someone asks you to have a drink with them, have a drink."

I was doubtful. I had after all sworn to fornicate with a goat before going into those mountains alone. And what about the bandits?* The week before they had held up a Coca-Cola delivery truck right outside San Bernardo and killed the driver. But Manuel said not to worry. The bandits operated only occasionally and were strictly amateurs. "They just block the road with their trucks or a big log and

---

* Mexicans no longer use the word *bandido* for bandit. *Bandido* is now reserved for corrupt politicians and officials. For highway robbers or road agents, at least in the Sierra Madre, they use *asaltantes* (assailants) or *gavilleros* (members of a bandit gang).

when you stop they jump out of the bushes with their guns," he said dismissively. "They are just marijuana growers who have lost their crops to the army, not like the bandits we used to have. They were masters of disguise and strategy, true artists of robbery. Jesús Arriaga, the one they called Chucho el Roto—now there was a bandit worthy of the name. He could disguise himself as a priest, a woman, a crippled old man, and they say he never killed anyone. How are the bandits in England?"

"There are none, not for two hundred years or more."

"Really? Well how about the United States? There must be some bandits still out there on the remote highways, right?"

"No, no bandits there either."*

He was genuinely surprised and taken aback by this information and then he burst out laughing. "How barbarous are we Mexicans!" he cackled. "What an unmothered shambles [*que desmadre*] is our country! Oh, how screwed are we!"

As a precaution Manuel advised me to go back to Los Tanques, where the less horrendous of the two roads to Chinipas begins, and pick up a hitchhiker. It was always safer to travel in numbers, he said. Like any predator, the bandits preferred their prey alone and separated from the herd. He also advised me to keep 150 pesos (fifteen U.S. dollars) in my wallet and hide the rest. "If you give them 150 pesos, they will let you go, no problem," he assured me. "These are poor excuses for bandits."

I spent that afternoon and evening in Manuel's house, talking about the situation in the Middle East, African wildlife, Abraham Lincoln, Lady Diana Spencer, Pancho Villa, and other notable bandits such as Heraclio Bernal, "The Thunderbolt of Sinaloa," whose exploits generated more than thirty *corridos*, and La Carambada, a female bandit who disguised herself as a man. After relieving her victims of their cash and valuables she would then insult their

---

* There were in fact bandits operating in the United States but I had forgotten about them. They were the Mexican and Mexican American bandits who robbed, raped, and kidnapped the Mexicans crossing the border illegally.

machismo by baring one of her breasts and crowing, "Look who has robbed you."

When I suggested leaving the house to buy beer, Manuel said, "No, no, no. You are my guest. You relax here. I will go and get us beer."

When I suggested going out for tacos, he said, "Relax, my friend. It will be my pleasure to go and buy some food and cook it for us."

How about a look around San Bernardo? "Ah, but the weather is hotter than fornication, is it not? You will be more comfortable if you stay inside the house."

In the middle of the night I was woken by gunshots a few blocks away, perhaps down by the river. They were shooting semiautomatic pistols and short bursts of machine-gun fire. I lay there on Manuel's fold-out cot in his living room trying to work out if it was a gun battle or people shooting off their guns for fun. In the morning Manuel said he must have slept through it but it was probably just high-spirited drunks. We drank coffee and said our good-byes and I drove back to Los Tanques to find myself a hitchhiker.

Manuel said they would be waiting by the fork in the road in the middle of the village but no one was there when I arrived. I pulled over, parked, and waited. A group of men watched me from across the road, presumably wondering why a strange *gringo* with Arizona plates was sitting in his truck in their village on a Sunday morning. I got out and walked over to explain myself.

"Good morning, gentlemen. It is hot enough, no? Ay, how barbarous is the sun." They nodded and murmured that it was so. "Gentlemen, do you know my friend Roque Rosas? He is a teacher in Guarajay but he grew up here and I think he has family here."

"Oh yes," they said. "We know Roque. His house is right over there but he is in Guarajay. Are you here to see him?"

"No. I am going to Chinipas to see my friends there. Do you know anyone who needs a ride there? I am a little unsure of the directions."

They pointed to the empty patch of ground next to my truck. "That is where you can find people going to Chinipas."

I got back into the truck and thought to hell with it. So what if I had vowed to fornicate with a goat? A man couldn't be expected to keep all his promises. I had names to drop in Chinipas. I was a friend of Joe Brown. Hadn't Manuel said I would be fine? And if I ran into any bandits I would simply hand over the 150 pesos in my wallet and hope they didn't find the four hundred dollars in the money belt around my leg or decide to steal the clothes off my back. Those American bird hunters that Joe Brown had mentioned were left naked by the side of the road not far from San Bernardo.

A kilometer up the road I spied a dirty, scruffy, unshaven *campesino* with a drooping baseball cap and a big black mustache. He was walking toward Los Tanques and when he saw my truck coming he stopped and raised his arm. I was in luck.

My insurance policy sat down beside me and I asked his name. "Onofre Carrillo Fuentes," he said.

"Carrillo Fuentes?" I said, "That is a famous name. Are you related?"

"His family is kin to ours."

The man's name we didn't speak was Amado Carrillo Fuentes, who was born into a mafia clan in the Sierra Madre of Sinaloa and turned himself into the biggest, wealthiest, most powerful drug lord in Mexico. He is estimated to have earned $25 billion from his years in the drug trade and paid out $500 million a year in bribes to various police chiefs, army generals, state governors, and politicians at the highest level of the government. He was nicknamed El Señor de Los Cielos, "The Lord of the Skies," because he had a fleet of full-sized passenger airplanes that he used to fly cocaine from Colombia into Mexico and is thought to have ordered the executions of at least four hundred people. In 1997, at the age of forty-one, Amado Carrillo Fuentes died during a plastic surgery operation in a private hospital in Mexico City, although many Mexicans believe that he staged his own death.

"Is he still alive, do you think?" I asked Onofre.

"*¿Quién sabe?*" He shrugged and looked guardedly out the window. Then I remembered that I wasn't supposed to be asking questions about drugs or looking interested when they were mentioned. Those were the things that an undercover DEA agent might do. Or a journalist. The last thing I wanted was Onofre telling people in Chinipas that I had been asking a lot of questions about his mafioso relatives.

OF ALL THE atrocious roads I drove in the Sierra Madre the steepest, rockiest, and most deeply potholed was that road to Chinipas. Its mother's profession was in no doubt whatsoever and to make things worse it was also covered in at least six inches of fine white powdery dust. It was a hot sweaty day and my air-conditioning was broken so we had the windows open partway and before long the dust had coated our tongues, eyelashes, and throats.

After an hour or so of climbing, with bandits never far from my mind, we rounded a switchback and there was a pickup truck half-slewed across the road. Its hood was up, which might have been a bandit ruse but it wasn't. It was a genuine breakdown and Onofre knew the two men standing by the truck staring at us. They were from the village of Las Chinacas higher in the mountains.

One was pale-skinned with blue eyes and close-cropped frizzy hair, probably in his late twenties. The other man was older and darker with a bristling mustache and the classic hawkeyed Sierra Madre face, wearing a black fake-silk western shirt with an ostrich-skin belt and boots. They were wryly amused to see a *gringo* in these parts and found it improbable that I was actually British. "If you're from *Inglaterra,* how come you have friends in Chinipas?" reasoned the younger man, squinting against the sun.

"I live in Arizona now and they are the friends of my friend there."

The older man turned to the younger one. "He is *güero* [pale-skinned] and he lives in Arizona. He's a *gringo,* no?"

"No *hombre,* he says he is British. They are not *gringos.*"

"What is your passport?" asked the older man.

"British," I said, unbuttoning my shirt pocket and showing it to them.

They looked it over carefully, nodded, and handed it back. "You are a long way from home," said the younger one.

"A very long way," said the older.

"What is wrong with your truck?" I asked.

"It won't start," said the younger man and went into a lot of mechanical terms that I didn't know in Spanish and probably wouldn't have understood in English. I am a woefully bad mechanic. Changing a tire is the absolute summit of my skills. But I did have a tool kit with me and I loaned the men various screwdrivers and shiny unused wrenches as they poked and prodded and thumped on various parts of the engine. They stripped old pieces of wire and tied them together. They unwound pieces of baling wire from the front bumper and tied them into the engine somehow. The younger man picked up a plastic bag from the side of the road and used it as a replacement gasket seal. As so often happens when men congregate around a broken vehicle, a camaraderie developed with our shared sense of purpose and I thought they might invite me afterward for a beer or a meal in Las Chinacas and what a golden entrée that would be into a remote Sierra Madre village.

The taller man slid underneath the truck with a wrench. The front of his shirt rode up and that's when I saw he had a .45 semiautomatic pistol inside the waistband of his jeans. Well now, I thought. This is known to be a dangerous road. Maybe he just carries that pistol for his own protection.

He got out from under the truck and casually tucked his shirt back in. He got into the driver's seat and tried to start the engine again. Nothing. He asked for my knife. I took it off my belt, unfolded the blade, and handed it to him. He ducked inside the cab of his truck, cut off both the seatbelts and, before I realized what he was doing, he had tied them together and was now tying one end of this improvised towrope to the back of my truck.

"Wait a minute," I said. "My little Toyota has a small engine with four cylinders. You have a one-ton truck. Look how steep the road is. My truck can't pull you up that mountain."

He exhaled impatiently and his eyes turned steely. He pulled the gun out of his waistband and made a show of removing the clip and sliding it back in. He pointed it up at the sky, sighted along the barrel, stuck the gun back in his jeans, pointed to my Toyota with his chin, looked me dead in the eyes and said, "Yes it can."

"Okay," I said. *"Andale pues,* let's give it a try."

I felt oddly liberated and removed from myself. Responsibility for my actions was no longer mine. There was nothing I could do except obey the man with the gun.

I was already in first gear in 4WD low, the lowest gear I had. I eased out the clutch, felt the tires grip, and lo and behold I was hauling a one-ton Chevy up the worst and steepest road I had ever seen. A letter of praise to the Toyota motor vehicle company started composing itself in my head and Onofre beside me was saying how *valiente* the little truck was and then the seat belt towrope snapped in two.

No problem. Onofre hopped out, tied the ends together, and up the next switchback we crawled. The seatbelts broke again. Onofre tied another knot into them. A hundred meters farther they broke for the third time. The road got even worse and the seat belts broke again and I noticed a burning smoky smell coming from somewhere.

Onofre tied the seat belts again and got back in. I let out the clutch, felt the tires grip but now there was no going forward. I was held in place by that one-ton weight behind me and the burning smell was getting stronger. I got out and walked back. "I'm sorry," I said. "It won't go forward."

The men got out and I tried a few more times and white smoke started coming out of my engine. The man with the pistol told Onofre to untie the seat belts. He looked frustrated and pissed off but he said I could go. The younger man said the smoke was coming out of my transmission and that was not good.

Onofre stayed behind with them and I continued up the switchbacks, alone now in a wounded vehicle on a bandit highway deep in the Sierra Madre and a very long way from a Toyota mechanic or Toyota parts. It was all Fords and Chevys up here. I had gambled that a Toyota could make it all the way through the Sierra without breaking down.

I made it up the last switchback and found some level ground on the lip of a narrow plunging canyon. I stopped and lifted up the hood, in that absurd gesture that men who know nothing about engines so often feel compelled to make. I knew it was very bad and expensive when your transmission broke but I didn't know where the transmission was or what it looked like. It was down under there somewhere, wasn't it?

Another truck pulled over. The driver was a big, mustachioed cattle rancher type, concerned for a fellow motorist and as friendly as he could be. He looked down into the engine and got underneath it. He said I had probably overheated the transmission a little and it was nothing to worry about. I thanked him for his help and we wished each other a good journey. He got back into his truck but he couldn't get it to start. Nor could he get the hood to open.

His ferrety-looking son worked at the release catch with two screwdrivers and got it open. The rancher picked up a discarded nylon feed sack from the side of the road, put it over the radiator cap, gave it half a turn, and the radiator gushed boiling water all over his hands and arms. He roared and cursed the grand raped mother and all the saints in heaven.

I grabbed a water jug from my truck and doused it over his hands and arms. I let his engine cool down and then I poured water into his radiator, feeling every inch the backcountry mechanic. It still wouldn't start. He picked up a rock and pounded on the battery terminals and that did the trick. We said our good-byes again and away he went.

I got back into my truck and tried to put it in first gear and discovered that I was jammed in neutral. I wrestled with the gearstick in a fierce sweaty panic but I couldn't engage any of my gears or any words in my vocabulary except, "Fuck fuck fuck. Oh bad bad bad."

The nearest human being capable of replacing the clutch and transmission in a Toyota truck was probably in Hermosillo, two days' drive in the other direction. Was it possible to get a tow truck up this road? And even if it was, how could I possibly afford the price of a two-day tow and the parts and labor on a new transmis-

sion? Should I abandon the truck here and hitchhike back down out
of the Sierra and then take the bus to Tucson and do some magazine
stories to make some money to buy another truck and then come
back to the Sierra? Or should I try hitchhiking my way through the
rest of the Sierra? Insurance scam! I would get out of here somehow,
report the truck stolen, and buy another one with the insurance
settlement. I dug my Mexican insurance policy out of the glove box.
I wasn't covered for theft.

I turned off the engine. Now I could force the gearstick into first
gear in 4WD low, although I still had no access to reverse or any of
the other gears. But this was something. I was able to proceed at a
slow crawl. I knew it was foolish to go deeper into the mountains
and farther away from Toyota mechanics but I couldn't face turning
around and going back.

I made it into Las Chinacas with smoke coming out of the transmission again and asked a teenage boy on a donkey if there was a
mechanic in the village. The boy just looked at me and then jabbed
the donkey in the ribs. Three men with hard suspicious eyes came
out of their huts and then something peculiar happened to my
brain. I had overloaded its circuits somehow. Driving as fast as possible, which wasn't very fast at all, I left Las Chinacas in a manic,
giddy, panic-stricken condition that I've never experienced before
or since.

I was desperately trying to think clearly and logically about what
I should do. I knew I had all the relevant data but my mind had seized
up like my transmission and refused to think. Sweat was pouring out
of me and my brain was bouncing around in my skull from the rocks
and potholes, and that fine white dust was streaming in the windows
and sticking to the sweat on my face. I caught a glimpse of myself in
the rearview mirror and it looked like someone else, a madman with
wild, terrified, red-rimmed eyes and white pancake makeup. What
in the name of seven sodomized saints was I going to do? Keep going.
Don't stop. One gear is better than none.

Then I got lost. I was somewhere up on the high divide between
Sonora and Chihuahua in the pine forest. I had passed several forks

in the road with no signs and I had lost my map somewhere but I knew that Chinipas was east and downhill and I was going north and uphill.

I saw a cloud of dust moving down the road toward me and then a red pickup truck took form and we stopped beside each other. My truck was trying to stall. I had to keep revving the engine. The driver was a clean-cut man of about thirty wearing a cowboy hat. Three boys sat beside him on the bench seat. In the bed of the truck were four figures wrapped completely in bedsheets, shrouded like mummies or ghosts.

"Is this the road to Chinipas?" I said. "My truck is screwed and I have very good friends in Chinipas of the family Russo, and the family Almada and the family Alvarez. They are friends of my friend Yo Bron. How are you, sir? Excuse me. I am lost and it makes very hot and this goat-bastard truck have screwed the mother of fornication and . . ."

I heard myself manically jabbering away in ever more broken and obscene Spanish. The man waited for me to stop and said, "The road to Chinipas is back that way. You missed the turning."

Then the four figures in the back started unwinding their sheets and revealed themselves as his wife and three girls. First their faces emerged, then their hair, then their elaborate satin dresses in pink, turquoise, and baby blue. The whole thing looked utterly surreal and Felliniesque and the woman must have seen the expression on my face. "We are going to a wedding," she said. "The dust is very bad."

"Yes," I said. It felt like someone or something was gripping and squeezing my brain. "A wedding."

"The turning to Chinipas is the second on the left," said the man.

"Yes, good, thank you, many thanks."

The man nodded warily, his wife and daughters shrouded themselves again, and they drove on. Using the slope to roll backward, still trapped in first gear, I managed to execute an eight-point turn on that skinny mountain road and on I crawled for Chinipas.

It was downhill hairpins all the way with plunging vertical dropoffs to the side. The dust was in my brake linings and they squealed and shrieked like wounded pigs but there was no sparing them on that road. My mania curdled into a kind of demented bravado, where I no longer cared what happened to me or my truck. It was all in the hands of fate now and I dared fate to do its worst. I shit in the mouths of ten saints! I shit on the twenty-four testicles of the apostles of Christ! Whatever happened would happen and I didn't give a goat-fornicating goddamn.

NINE HOURS AFTER leaving Los Tanques, I drove across the axle-deep Rio Chinipas, passed an encampment of soldiers, and entered the town. I was expecting a rougher, scurvier version of San Bernardo but Chinipas was beautiful, an old colonial town at the bottom of a gigantic canyon, whose west wall I had just descended.

Crawling through the streets in my only gear, I was overtaken by a man clopping over the cobblestones on a big bay horse. I followed him to the plaza, which had a lovely old whitewashed church, elaborate wrought-iron benches, and flowering trees full of birds. There were a few *narco*-looking trucks cruising up and down but compared to San Bernardo it felt calm, sober, and civilized, with women and children ambling around with ice creams and balloons and the clack of pool balls from a corner-front recreation center. I parked next to a faded old hotel called the Centenario, poured water on a bandanna, and tried to wipe the mask of dust off my face. I felt battered, rattled, and apprehensive but back in control of my mind.

Old men, I thought. They will be less prickly and territorial and more likely to remember Joe Brown and his friends. I went into a small store, bought a Coke, and drank it on a bench outside, carefully making eye contact and saying hello or good afternoon to everyone who walked past. I noticed a man in his sixties with a red polyester western shirt who seemed to have a kind, benevolent face. We exchanged nods and he turned into a shady courtyard next to the store. I followed him in there and introduced myself.

His name was Victor Manjarrez Rey and he knew all about Joe Brown, the books he had written, and the film that had been made from one of them. It was well known in Chinipas, he said, that Joe Brown had become a rich and famous man. He also knew the three names that Joe had given me.

Chapo Almada had died. Oscar Russo had abandoned the ranch at El Trigo in the mountains above Chinipas, where Joe had lived and written *The Forests of the Night,* and was now living down on the desert in Ciudad Obregon. Che Che Alvarez, who was born at El Trigo, had also left the ranch and was living in Chinipas. We were sure to see him later on the plaza.

I told him about my journey and said the clutch and transmission on my Toyota were very bad. Victor shook his head, apologized for the behavior of his countrymen, some of whom were "too free with their pistols," and said he would fetch a mechanic to look at my truck. Then he walked me into the Hotel Centenario, introduced me to the charming old woman who ran the place, and asked her to give me the room facing onto the street so I could keep an eye on my truck.

He helped me unload my bags and asked about the big heavy box of books in the back. I said that I was a writer like Joe and interested in the history of the Sierra Madre. "This is a very historic town," he said. "Tomorrow I will show you some of the historic sights and introduce you to a man who knows the history of the area very well."

It took several trips to unload everything and one of the last items was a plastic crate filled with boxes of candies and chocolates, donated by a friend of mine to hand out to children. The old lady saw me bringing them in. "Oh what a lot of candies you have," she said.

"For the children," I said.

"I'm a little girl," she said flirtatiously and rewarded me with a beaming smile when I gave her a box of chocolates. She showed me to a huge room with high ceilings, a creaky old ceiling fan, and five beds all covered with bedspreads featuring African wildlife scenes. All the other rooms in the hotel were unoccupied.

There was no hot water or air-conditioning but I was thoroughly charmed by the Centenario, with its long tiled interior courtyard full of potted plants and trees, its air of decaying colonial elegance. It felt like such an achievement to finally get to Chinipas, a place I had wondered and worried about for years. I first heard about it when I was living in Álamos. An American friend of mine had flown into Chinipas in a Cessna piloted by his girlfriend. They walked from the airstrip into the plaza and sat down opposite the Hotel Centenario. A unit of soldiers appeared. My friend got up and asked the officer how the hotels were in Chinipas. "There are no hotels here," said the officer, standing in front of the open doors of the Hotel Centenario. Then the entire unit of soldiers walked them back to their plane. A week or two later another private plane tried to land at Chinipas and was shot out of the sky.

Joe Brown talked about Chinipas as being somewhere deep in the dark heart of the Sierra. "If you ever make it to Chinipas . . ." he would say. He had fond memories of the place but said it had been taken over by *narcos*. I had already disobeyed his direst warning by arriving in Chinipas alone, and now felt completely unprepared for the calm, friendly, attractive town I found that Sunday afternoon.

An hour later Victor came back with a mechanic, a solemn thoughtful young man who questioned me closely and then sat in the driver's seat. With a horrible grinding noise he wrenched the gearstick out of four-wheel drive and into two-wheel drive, where he was able to run through all the gears easily. It seemed like a miracle. I flashed back to Ruben rising unsteadily to his feet after the runaway mule wreck.

"Where are you going after Chinipas?" asked the mechanic.

"Up to Témoris," I said.

"You can make that road in two-wheel drive," he said. "I don't want to put it back in four-wheel in case it gets stuck again. I think what happened is the transmission overheated and now it has cooled down."

He added some transmission fluid and I asked him how much. "No, no," he said. "There is no charge."

I suggested to Victor that we go for a beer. "It is Sunday," he said. "They don't sell beer in Chinipas on a Sunday. But there is a restaurant where you can eat and maybe they will have a beer for you."

He took me over there and the women smiled and welcomed me and served me a plate of pork stewed with red chilies and an ice-cold

Tecate from a refrigerator in the back. "For the dust in your throat," they said smiling. What a delightful town this was.

"Joe said there had been some *delincuencia* in Chinipas with the *narcos*," I said. "How are things now?"

Victor stiffened uncomfortably. His guard came up. "There were a few problems in the past but no, no, everything is *tranquilo* now."

Che Che Alvarez, in tire-tread sandals and a well-worn cowboy hat, with a magnificent lugubrious ruin of a face, met us on the plaza later that night. His eyes had a soulful haunted quality and it was no surprise to learn that a river of alcohol had run through him, now slowed to a manageable stream, or that he lived with chronic pain. He had smashed up his back in a vehicle accident and could no longer do any work that involved bending and lifting, which described most of the work that he knew how to do.

"Joe Brown is my godfather," he said, which I hadn't realized. "When I was fourteen he took me to get baptized and confirmed in Navojoa." In a soft, gentle, quietly amused voice, he told a few stories—Joe getting stabbed in the pool hall, Joe winning a fistfight in a cantina, Joe's love of *charreada* or Mexican rodeo, Joe throwing a case of beer out of his plane for the cowboys at Guasaremos, Joe and his whores. "Was there ever a man for the whores like Joe Brown?" He laughed.

Che Che had things to attend to and I was completely exhausted so we agreed to meet the following afternoon and have some drinks in his godfather's honor.

PEOPLE IN CHINIPAS were extremely proud of their town and its history and on the whole they were delighted to find a curious outsider. It had been founded by Jesuit missionaries in 1676, and most of the current residents were at least partially descended from the Europeans who came here in the late nineteenth century to work the Palmarejo gold and silver mine, which came under British ownership in 1886. The Santinis were from Italy. The Schultzes were Germans. The Russos were Sicilians who stopped in New York for a generation before coming to Chinipas and turning into Sierra Madre Mexicans.

The O'Leary family now spelled their name Alire and remembered nothing of Ireland. The Bridge family from England became Breach and the Willis family was now Villis. All this and a great deal more was explained to me by a tall, well-groomed, aristocratic-looking man called Félix Almada, who was the secretary of the *municipio* and a relative of Joe's late friend Chapo Almada and the noted Chihuahua historian Don Pancho Almada.

The mining machinery was all built in English factories, shipped to Guaymas on the Sonora coast, transported by mule and donkey to San Bernardo and then up and over the mountains on people's backs. Victor took me to see the old machinery, the ruined hacienda where the British mining bosses had lived, and the twenty-two-kilometer passenger railway they had built between the hacienda and the mine. As for the gold and silver, that was transported by mule trains over the mountains to San Bernardo and heavily guarded against bandits.

We got back to the plaza in mid-afternoon and everything felt different. The women and children were off the streets. Soldiers and state police were standing on the corners with loosely held machine guns. Big pickup trucks were gunning their engines, blasting *narco-corridos* and jockeying for position outside the two agencies that sold beer. You could feel it in the air, that volatile combination of alcohol, cocaine, and machismo.

"Hey *gringo*!" yelled a young man driving a jacked-up Chevy, with three others beside him on the bench seat. "You are Che Che's friend. Come and have a beer with us."

"First I have to meet Che Che but it will be my pleasure to drink with you later."

"Hey *gringo*! How can one donkey have nine names?"

"I don't know."

"Bastard, whore, son of a bitch, cuckold, son of a whore, faggot, cocksucker, son of the grand fornicated bitch, son of a fornication between a whore and a black dog. It's a good one, no?"

"It's fantastic."

"Come and drink with us. Have some *perico*."

"I would like to but first I must meet Che Che."

"No, come now."

SOME TOWNS AND counties in the mountains of Chihuahua have banned alcohol sales altogether but this has only stimulated the bootlegging trade and done nothing to reduce public drunkenness. At least in Chinipas there was a respite on Sundays. But every other day of the week, I discovered, men started drinking in their trucks at about two in the afternoon and by six in the evening, when the beer agencies locked down their shutters, they were raging drunk. With as much beer and liquor as they had the foresight and money to buy in advance, they would then go down to the riverbank and continue drinking. The soldiers and state police were in Chinipas to prevent drug trafficking and murder and they left the riverbank alone as a free zone.

Che Che and I fell into a routine. We would buy a six-pack in the late afternoon and drive up the river a mile or two to get away from the mayhem. In town or on the riverbank, there was always someone demanding that you drink with them and it was always risky to refuse. And if you started drinking with them, it was almost impossible to leave if there was still alcohol to drink, and you were still standing. So Che Che and I would steal away up the canyon and listen to a CD of old *corridos* about Pancho Villa and the revolution, sipping our beers slowly as the canyon walls changed their colors with the sunset. Tentatively at first, then more easily as we got to know and trust each other, we would get into the subject of drugs and violence.

The mafia had gunned down Che Che's nephew recently, shooting him in the back with an AK-47. Che Che didn't elaborate on the reasons why but said that he was so tired of the killing and the grieving.

"How many friends of yours have been murdered?" I asked.

Che Che counted out their names on his fingers and stopped at fifteen.

"What about relatives?"

He threw up his hands. "All the Enriquez are kin to me. And the Parras."

"There must be so many widows with children. What do the widows do?"

"Many many widows. They go and live with their own families."

We talked about the old days in the Sierra, before the drugs and pickups and machine guns. Che Che felt nostalgic for those simpler times but allowed there was a lot of killing back then too. At El Trigo, for example, a man killed his wife and decapitated his children with a machete because he found out that his wife had been with another man. "There were many killings for jealousy and many feuds. Also we had *lunáticos* who wandered around the mountains killing people. But life was better then. People were happier and more content. Before the drugs came in, the only thing people needed money for was to buy soap and clothes. Everything else you grew or made."

With a wry smile, he told the story of his own adventures in the drug trade. He had been growing marijuana up at El Trigo for years, operating as an independent. After the harvest he would pack his bales on a string of mules, drive them down into Chinipas at night, and then buy a truck with the proceeds.

"I never grew enough to buy a good truck," he said. "Only old screwed-up trucks. And the road back to El Trigo is so bad that by the time I got back up there, most of those trucks were destroyed. I had a whole collection of broken trucks up there."

Then one day a soldier followed him and found his plants. Che Che asked how much and had to give him all the money he could muster. The soldier came back with more soldiers and they cut down all his plants and took them away to sell to the mafia, or so he assumed. "They took my money and fucked me. You can't make it as an independent anymore. You have to be with the big mafiosos. They're the only ones who can fix the soldiers and the state police now."

He had left El Trigo four years ago because it got too dangerous. The mafia was killing independent growers. *Narcos* were feuding. Marauding gangs were cruising the mountain backroads at night, killing anyone who got in their way. And every one of these killings and rapes, by the code of the mountains, needed to be avenged by the victim's male family members. There used to be a lot of killing in Chinipas too, he said, but now the army were there and the state police and it was safer.

"There is less money in Chinipas because the law makes it harder to grow and sell but people don't get shot in Chinipas anymore. The killing happens out on the ranches and in the *monte* where there is no law."

My anarchist sympathies were dealt another blow. The Sierra Madre, of course, was a particular anarchy with its own violent history and vengeful culture—the type of anarchy, as Joe Brown said, that gives anarchy a bad name. Now the law had come to Chinipas and although it was corrupt, thieving, heavy-handed, and in league with the mafia, Che Che and Victor and everyone else I talked to in Chinipas preferred it to what had gone before.

LEAVING CHINIPAS, I gave Che Che four hundred aspirins for his back pain and a bottle of Scotch and he gave me a sealed letter for Joe Brown. I thanked Victor for all his help and tried to give him 350 pesos, equivalent to thirty-five dollars. He refused and looked embarrassed that I had offered it. Eventually I persuaded him to take a hundred pesos for his family.

The next town down the road was Témoris. They assured me that it was safe, that I would be fine there without an introduction. The only problem was the road to Témoris. "Unfortunately there are bandits on that road," said Victor. "But it is good that you are leaving early in the morning. The bandits sleep late and do most of their robbing in the afternoons."

12

The Secret Sex Lives of
Narcotraficantes

I STARTED THE LONG climb out of that gigantic canyon in fresh, confident spirits, buoyed by Chinipas and my fine new friendships with Victor and Che Che. The road was steep but freshly graded and my gears were functioning smoothly, at least in two-wheel drive. I was on my way to the safe haven of Témoris and all the bandits on the road were supposed to be asleep.

In the small village of Agua Salada, Salty Water, I picked up a hitchhiker for protection. Where else in the world, I wondered, did you increase your safety by inviting a complete stranger into your vehicle? He was a polite, intense young man wearing gray flannel trousers, a white button-down shirt with no tie, black socks, and black dress shoes worn down at the heels. I guessed he was a missionary but he turned out to be a traveling salesman of patent medicines.

"All natural, all from plants," he said, resting his hands on the all-important backpack on his lap. "Very good for nervousness, insomnia, constipation *y todo,* and everything."

He picked up his medicines from a distributor in Chihuahua City and sold them all over the Sierra Madre, traveling by bus if there were buses, otherwise hitchhiking and riding in logging trucks.

In the towns he stayed in hotels, and in the villages he slept in the houses and huts of the people who bought his medicines, prevailing on their hospitality. He would travel alone through the Sierra for a month or more, until he had sold all his medicines, then go back to Chihuahua City to resupply.

I told him I was traveling through the Sierra Madre and writing a book about my experiences. "There is a lot of *delincuencia* in the Sierra, is there not?" I added.

"Have you been robbed?" he asked.

"No. Have you?"

"Yes."

"How many times?"

"*Frecuentamente,*" he said. Frequently.

"It is good that we are traveling in the morning," I said. "The bandits are still in bed with their hangovers, no?"

"That is not true," he said. "I have been robbed many times in the mornings. I think it is safer to travel in the afternoons."

"Why is that?"

"The bandits rob people all morning, then go home, have a big lunch, and take a long siesta. They are very tired from working so hard," he said, and then burst out into awkward, hysterical laughter that ended with guillotine abruptness. This stretch of road, from Chinipas to Témoris, was fairly safe, he said. He had only been robbed here once. But the next stretch, from Témoris to Bahuichivo, was *muy malo* and he had been robbed there four or five times in the last year. "Usually they block the road with a big log and point their guns at you. They search you and take your money. Then they pull aside the log and let you go."

"Are they poor? Are they *campesino* growers who have lost their crops to the army?"

"Some of them," he said. "But many of them are well-dressed with fine boots and hats and the best guns—goat-horned AK-47s, AR-15s, Colt pistols, *todo*. It's a good business and that's why people go into it."

"Do they take trucks too?"

"No."

"Why not?"

"Because they have too many Chevys already!" He gave another short burst of hysterical, high-pitched laughter. In addition to the roadblock bandits, he said, there were also bad men who drove around in their trucks looking for people to rob and lone travelers were their favorite targets. It was very bad if they came across a woman.

"Have you been robbed by them too?"

"A few times. Also by a man on a mule with an AK-47. And sometimes by the people in the villages."

I suggested that it must be hard for him to make a living when he was getting robbed so *frecuentamente*. "Fortunately the people like my medicines a little more than the bandits like my money," he smiled. "They are excellent medicines, all natural and very effective. If you would like to buy some, I will be honored to give you a special price, since you are kind enough to give me a ride."

I thanked him for his generous offer and assured him that I was in perfect health with no insomnia, nervousness, constipation, or anything. We continued up the switchbacks. By the side of the road, set back in the rocks, was a shrine with burning candles and a dusty wreath of plastic flowers. A few cattle and goats grazed the steep rocky slopes. Farther up the switchbacks the Virgin of Guadalupe was painted on a cliff. We reached the rim of the canyon, with an immense view behind us, and started out across a high forested plateau. The pine trees by the side of the road were a pale chalky color from the dust, which lay a foot deep on the road.

In the approximate middle of nowhere we came to a tiny roadside shack with a sign painted on a piece of raw lumber: "Store—Cigarettes & Soda for Sale." A woman was standing outside it holding a broom. Behind the store was a small cornfield cleared from the pines and a house. The traveling salesman, whose name escapes me and my notebook—it was one of those long convoluted Mexican names like Hermenegildo or Abrahamoswaldo—pointed to the two brand-new trucks parked outside the house.

"It must be a very good business, that little store."

"Or they must grow very special corn," I said.

"Or rob many many travelers!" Again he laughed hysterically until the guillotine blade came down.

In the highland cattle village of Los Llanos there was a stone-faced Tarahumara waiting by the side of the road, dressed in jeans and a polyester western shirt like most male Tarahumaras these days. Only in Batopilas Canyon have I seen Tarahumara men who still wear the traditional loincloth, pleated girdle, and blouson shirt as everyday clothing, although Tarahumara women nearly all dress like their grandmothers and great-grandmothers, in hand-sewn skirts of colorfully printed cotton, often worn three or four at once, with matching long-sleeved blouses and head scarves.

I pulled over and the Tarahumara climbed into the bed of my truck without saying a word. On the outskirts of Témoris he thumped twice on the side of the truck, indicating this was where he was getting off, and I saw the dust had turned his face whiter than mine and collected in his eyelashes.

Témoris was a grubby, placid, little town with chickens scratching in the front yards, coffee-can flower gardens, and dogs sleeping under rusty old pickup trucks, saving their energy for all the barking they would have to do at night. I parked alongside the plaza, which was a small elongated rectangle. A man rode by on horseback. *Norteño* music blasted out of a cruising truck. No one gave me a second look. I said good-bye to the patent medicine salesman and he grasped my shoulder with a fervent look in his eyes and said I was a good and humble man and a true friend to the ordinary Mexican people. Then he went off to ply his wares door to door and that was the last I saw of him.

I DIDN'T KNOW anyone in Témoris. I had no introductions and no names to drop and for once there was no need. Drawn by the spectacular *barranca* scenery and the exotic Tarahumaras farther down the line, foreign tourists came through here all the time on the Chihuahua al Pacifico railroad, also known as the Copper Canyon train, although very few of them disembarked in Témoris. Nor did most of the tourists have the vaguest idea that they were passing through one of the biggest marijuana- and opium-producing regions in the world, with roving bandits and a murder rate far higher than the worst American ghetto.

Bandit gangs used to rob the train on a regular basis, sometimes masked, sometimes wearing military uniforms with telltale sandals. They would go through the carriages demanding money and jewelry at gunpoint and sometimes making their escape on horseback. This was in the 1990s. Now there are guards with machine guns on the train and it appears that the robberies have stopped but the train company, the Mexican authorities, and the guards themselves have done so much lying and covering up about the robberies over the years that it's hard to believe anything they say.

I started riding the train in the mid-1990s when bandit attacks were at their height. The guards, who only carried pistols then and were clearly under orders not to alarm the tourists, told me that there had been some trouble a few years ago but now the train was perfectly safe. The Mexican passengers and the newspapers said otherwise. In January 1999 I noticed fresh bullet holes in one of the carriages and asked the guard if they were from the recent bandit attack that had resulted in the murder of a Swiss tourist. He assured me that the story of the Swiss tourist was a false rumor and those were very old bullet holes.

Here was the formula again: first an event occurs. Then it never happened. According to the newspaper reports at the time, on both sides of the border, masked bandits with automatic weapons stormed the train in November 1998, jumping aboard as it slowed down in a tunnel and spraying bullets around to announce their presence. For some reason none of the train guards showed up for work that day. Ernst Schmidt, sixty-eight, from Arbon, Switzerland, traveling with his wife, Sonia, started videotaping the heist. The bandits told him in Spanish to stop. Schmidt spoke no Spanish and continued videotaping. Some of the other passengers thought he had mistaken the robbery for a staged entertainment. The bandits shot him three times, killing him, and wounded three other tourists from Austria (the *New York Times* says Australia), Italy, and Germany. One of them was pistol-whipped. The other two were accidentally injured by ricochets and flying shrapnel.

Carl Franz, author of *The People's Guide to Mexico* and the Web site of the same name, confirms that the Mexican authorities were routinely suppressing information about the train bandits to avoid frightening tourists but he has no reports of any robberies since 2000, when there were four at Easter. He says the authorities clamped down after the murder of the Swiss tourist, but the story I kept hearing was that the bandits stopped robbing the train because the mafia had started executing them for it. The train robberies, and especially the murdered tourist, had brought unwelcome attention from the authorities and the media at a time when many mafiosos were investing and laundering their money through hotel building and other projects in the booming new tourist economy in the Copper Canyon country.

No one familiar with the Sierra Madre finds this an unlikely story but as always the facts are elusive. What's more important is that the story of the mafia-executed train bandits is widely told and its message was clearly understood: don't mess with the tourists. If you mess with the tourists, you mess with the mafia.

A corridor of safe passage had opened up, broadening out from the train tracks to include the deep *barranca* towns of Batopilas and Urique and some of the more accessible Tarahumara settlements. There was still plenty of marijuana and opium grown in the corridor, and the murder rate was still astronomical, but drug production had found a way to coexist peacefully with a tourism boom. It was a curious arrangement and relied on the naïveté of the tourists, who were carefully steered away from the drug fields and *narco* hangouts by their tour guides, and the fear of mafia reprisals among those who might be tempted to prey on the tourists.

I wasn't quite there yet. Témoris was an island of safety, separated from the main tourist corridor by that *muy malo* bandit highway to Bahuichivo, but already I was feeling waves of relief wash through me. It felt like the purest luxury to be taken for a tourist and get out from under the weight of all that suspicion and hostility—who is this *gringo* with the notebook and what is he really doing here?

I CHECKED INTO a small, clean hotel called the Marshella, unloaded my truck, took my first hot shower in nearly three weeks, and ate a fine bowl of *albóndigas,* meatball soup, in the hotel restaurant. It was prepared and served by the Marshella's owner, a friendly, efficient, welcoming woman in her thirties called Esmeralda Pérez. I asked her how things were in Témoris these days. She said the army was here now. The soldiers were smoking and selling a lot of the marijuana they were cutting down, and in league with the mafiosos, but the town was a lot safer now and that was the most important thing.

I stepped outside for a walk and there in the plaza was a man arranging small plastic jars into pyramids on a blanket. On closer inspection I saw that the jars contained rattlesnake oil, rattlesnake oil with bee venom, powdered rattlesnake, shark cartilage, coyote fat, and "bull extract." The man also had bars of soap that claimed to be made from a hunchback's hump, with a drawing of a dancing hunchback on the label.

I knew that hunchbacks were considered lucky in Mexico. I knew that people paid money to rub their humps for luck and that every hunchback in Mexico was assured of making a living in this way if he or she wanted to. But hunchback soap? Were these live or dead hunchbacks getting drained of their hump fat by the soapmaker? It was far too weird to contemplate and I assured myself that it was normal everyday soap with a fraudulent label.

Then the man went to his truck and came back with a glass jar full of clear liquid and a dead rattlesnake curled up in the bottom of it. I knew what that was. I had learned the hard way. When Tom Vaught and I were coming back from our treasure hunt we saw a similar jar in a curio shop in Casas Grandes, Chihuahua. At first we thought it was snake oil but the woman told us the rattlesnake was soaking in *lechuguilla.* It was very good for muscular pains and stiffness in the joints, she said, and only ten pesos for a shot. It had a rank, foul, oily taste and we kept burping up the most horrendous fumes for the next four or five hours.

Appalled as I was by the hunchback soap, I couldn't help buying a bar for a souvenir, along with a jar of snake oil and bee venom, which the man assured me would cure arthritis, muscular pains, and skin trouble. "What about the coyote fat?" I asked. "What does that do?"

"That works very well for aches, joint pains, and gout."

"And the bull extract?"

He grinned and raised up his right arm at the angle of an erection and tried to slap it down with his left hand.

Before you start scoffing at Mexican folk remedies, let me remind you that you should also be scoffing at the five best-selling herbal or alternative medicines in the United States—saw palmetto (for prostate health), Saint-John's-wort (an antidepressive), echinacea (defense against the common cold), ginkgo biloba (memory function), and glucosamine chondroitin (joint health). In the first large-scale double-blind trials that they have been subjected to, at the National Center for Complementary and Alternative Medicine, all five of them were found to be completely ineffective. Yet I know many people who swear up and down that these medicines have helped them. My feeling is that we can persuade ourselves of absolutely anything, from the efficacy of snake oil to the existence of God, and that the world is a more interesting place because of it.

THAT NIGHT, AFTER sitting on the plaza at sundown and taking the temperature of the town—a few surly youths in marijuana leaf caps (one with the slogan *Soy La Ley,* I Am The Law, printed under the leaf), three or four cruising trucks full of drunks, no one particularly interested in my presence—I decided to risk going to a *cantina* and then discovered that both *cantinas* in Témoris had been closed down because of violence and drunken mayhem in the past. Instead I went to bed with a dry scholarly volume entitled *Defiance and Deference in Mexico's Colonial North: Indians under Spanish Rule in Nueva Viz-caya,* by Susan Deeds. Eighty pages in I came upon a bandit story that read like a fever dream in a Gabriel García Marquéz novel.

In 1685 Antonia de Soto was a mulatta slave in the city of Durango. She was a restless teenage girl with a boyfriend called Matías de Rentería, a Tepehuan Indian from the Sierra who worked as a laborer for the same master. The young lovers ran away together, heading north over the eastern flanks of the Sierra Madre and pursued by an overseer sent by their master. In the silver mining town of Parral, in present-day southern Chihuahua, Antonia found a sorceress who gave her some herbs and magical wild hyacinth flowers called *ca-comites.* Worn under the clothing, over her breasts, the flowers made Antonia unrecognizable to the overseer and they were able to get away from him.

They went deeper into the mountains, through country that had been inhabited by Tarahumaras and Tepehuanes for many centuries but was now the raw frontier of the Spanish empire, with missions, mines, and cattle ranches springing up, all hungry for Indian labor, and a floating migratory population of displaced Indians, runaway mulatto slaves, Spanish chancers, mixed-blood Mexicans, traders, thieves, bandits, and bad men of every color and stripe.

Along the way Matías introduced her to peyote. We think of pey-ote as a hallucinogenic drug but for the Tepehuanes and the other Sierra Madre tribes peyote was a god with powerful magic and they still think of it that way today. In her first vision Antonia saw Matías subdue a charging bull and they learned to dance together under the tutorship of a woman with a guitar. It became their custom to take peyote every Sunday and Antonia's visions started to follow a similar pattern. First she would see serpents. Then the Devil would appear as a devastatingly handsome white man. He invited Antonia to make a pact with him and promised her freedom in return. She agreed to the pact and when the peyote wore off she discovered that she had turned into a man.

She was able to fight bulls and perform daring feats on horseback. On one occasion Matías tried to attack her, for reasons that are unclear, and she fought him off easily and nearly beat him to death with a cattle prod. She started dressing like a man and over the next two years she worked as a cowboy on various ranches in northern Durango, riding with Matías and other Indian and mixed-race cowboys. As a mule skinner she helped pack and transport a shipment of silver all the way from the mines in Durango to the Caribbean port of Veracruz and back, a round trip of nine hundred miles or more.

> Throughout these travels, she continued to rub flowers and rosettes over her body and to use particular arrangements of magical stones and incantations to call forth the devil. He usually appeared in the form of a white man, but sometimes she could only hear him speaking to her and once he materialized as a growling bear. Most often he came on horseback carrying a machete. In these encounters he spoke to her and empowered her to gamble, to break horses, and to fight bulls and even men. On one occasion in the mining camp of Urique in western Chihuahua, Antonia and three companions overpowered a mule train, killed three men, and made off with part of the silver shipment. When one of her accomplices stole her silver-laden saddlebags, she pursued and killed him. Later, in the midst of a heated argument, she killed a co-worker in Sinaloa. She had become more than just a man; now she was a violent bandit.

How do we know all this? What are Susan Deeds's sources? While she was still in her early twenties, Antonia de Soto decided to break her pact with the Devil and give up the swashbuckling life. She turned herself in to a priest in Parral and later made a full confession to the Inquisition, begging forgiveness. She was returned to her master, who promptly sold her to a military officer, and in 1693, after a long series of hearings, the Inquisition absolved her of her sins against God and transferred her case to a civil court.

For Susan Deeds, the significance of Antonia de Soto's story has to do with race (the Devil is white, not black, as the Jesuits were teaching), gender (only males had power and freedom in that time and place), class (sorcery was most commonly practiced by women of lower social status), and what it reveals about freedom of movement, lawlessness, and the culture of male violence in northern Mexico at that time. I didn't disagree with any of that but what struck me were the similarities with the present-day culture of the Sierra Madre and in particular the persistence of banditry, lawlessness, and magical belief systems.

It occurred to me that my biggest impediment to understanding the Sierra Madre, both past and present, was my obstinate and thorough-going atheism, my utter lack of confidence in any belief system that required a leap of faith into the unprovable and improbable. On the whole, despite the menace of fundamentalism, I was glad such belief systems existed and absolutely certain they would never go away. I was prepared to accept that religions often contained deeper truths and insights into the human condition than science, technology, or the modern secular faith in progress, but I couldn't imagine what it was like to really live in a magical universe, controlled by God and the Devil, full of signs and portents, angels and demons, amenable to prayers, spells, magic stones, and flowers.

Angel Flores, who is a believing Catholic, was the first one to point out my shortcomings in this area. "You ask all these questions about how the Guarijios live and what they do but you don't ask questions about their spirituality. You don't understand that everything that happens in their world is caused by spiritual forces—if your sick baby lives or dies, if the army comes to cut down your crops, everything."

He was right. What I believed in was reason and logic and old-fashioned British common sense and these were limited and inadequate tools for understanding the reality of where I was. That was one reason why things kept appearing surreal to me. If I truly believed that an effigy of Jesus in a church was connected to the living consciousness of Jesus in his afterlife, and that this Jesus entity needed respite from all the human suffering he had seen, then it was only a short step to covering the eyes of the effigy. You start looking around for two coverings each about the size of an eyepatch, perhaps with an adhesive backing so they don't slip off. In the little store that sells exercise books, toys, pencils, and balloons you find some blue stickers of the right size with the image of a small bearded figure on them and no one in your village knows or cares that these little figures are called Smurfs.

THE NEXT MORNING I got chatting to Esmeralda and said I was looking for a knowledgeable, trustworthy guide to the area and I could pay two hundred pesos a day. Normally it would take a day or two to set up an arrangement like this but an hour later a man in his early thirties called Baldimir arrived at the hotel. He had close-cropped hair, a goatee, baggy jeans, and a red cap-sleeved T-shirt. On the front of the T-shirt was a cartoon of Albert Einstein holding a beer and the slogan "Let's Get Relative" in English. Baldimir, whose nickname was Jo Jo (pronounced Yo Yo), was stocky with well-defined muscles and an open, friendly, intelligent face. There was nothing effeminate about him but I was fairly sure he was gay and I certainly hoped he was, for reasons of curiosity. I had no idea what it was like to be a gay man in this violent and fanatically macho culture.

First he took me down to lower Témoris. It is in effect a split-level town with two different microclimates. I was staying in upper Témoris, where pines and apple trees grow. Lower Témoris, four hundred meters down into the canyon of the Septentrión River, was semitropical with lush vegetation and banana trees. "In upper Témoris, the people are colder, more reserved, more indifferent," said Baldimir. "Down here, the people are hotter. They fuck and fight more. They dance and laugh more. It is the tropics."

Between upper and lower Témoris, set back in the canyon wall and accessible by a steep and slippery little trail, was an old Indian burial cave littered with human bones. In more remote caves in the area, said Baldimir, you could find human bones that had been cooked and visibly chewed on by human teeth. The Indians in the area had practiced *"canibalismo,"* which was true over most of the central and western Sierra Madre. Warfare was endemic among the tribes and the first Spaniards observed the ritual eating of enemies in drunken peyote-fueled victory celebrations and the ritual marriage of virgins to skulls and skeletons. If there was ever a time of peace and harmony in the Sierra Madre, it doesn't appear in any of our records.

Then we drove to the shrine of a bandit folk saint called Salais, a mound of rocks decorated with candles, flowers, and crosses under the oak tree where they hung him. Like Jesús Malverde, he is supposed to have robbed from the rich and given to the poor. Now they say he works miracles for his followers. "Do the *narcos* also believe in Salais?" I asked.

"No, Salais is more for sickness and love. The *narcos* around here like Malverde and also San Judas Tadeo (Saint Jude of Thaddeus, who is usually described as the patron saint of lost causes). They have built a shrine to him and they say he does many useful things. He makes the soldiers not see the crop. He brings rain and stops rain when the plants need sun. He helps you steal someone else's crop and stops others from stealing your crop."

Baldimir was a font of information on the folk beliefs of the area. There was a huge three-headed snake that people said could eat three cows at once and lay waste to a herd in a single night. In the Septentrión River lived a giant serpent that paralyzed its prey with its terrible breath and then crushed them to death with its coils. It fed on cows, oxen, and the occasional man or young woman. Never take the bones from a burial cave into your house because they will call out for water in the night—"*Agua! AGUA!*"—and scare the piss out of you.

He said there were literally hundreds of stories in the area about lost gold mines and buried treasure. Mysterious colored lights in the night showed where gases were escaping from a hidden mine and there were innumerable earthenware jars full of gold coins buried in the earth or secreted in caves. "There weren't any banks so people did hide their money inside walls, fireplaces, holes in big trees, places like this," he said. "On the other hand these people were nearly all poor. Very very occasionally it does actually happen that people find gold coins but it is always by accident."

Witchcraft and sorcery were rampant among the older *campesinos* and the Tarahumaras. The main work of sorcerers was to counteract each other's spells, provide information on buried treasure, and put hexes on the soldiers to prevent them from finding marijuana fields. Baldimir was gently skeptical but charmed by all these beliefs and he thought they served a useful purpose. "People need these fantasies," he said. "They escape into a magical world because this one is too hard, too brutal in its logic. It does not allow enough hope. But things are changing now with television and satellite Internet in the schools. The younger people don't believe a lot of things their parents and grandparents believe."

In his twenties Baldimir traveled all over Mexico. He got to know its cities well and enjoyed them but decided to come back to Témoris because he loved the Sierra so much. "To live in a beautiful landscape is very important to me and I find the culture here so fascinating, so marvelous."

"What about the violence?" I asked. "Isn't that an integral part of the culture?"

"It's true. Vengeance is very important. And now you have all these men with automatic guns, doing too much cocaine, drinking too much, and they are going around robbing and raping and killing people for no reason. But of course every one of these rapes and killings needs to be avenged. And if they can't get the blood of the man who did it, the blood of one of his family members will do. Most of the killings here are because of these vengeance feuds, but there are also many killings over drugs and mafia business too."

He laughed and shook his head. "This is crazy, no?" he said. "Well, the Sierra is also a crazy place and to live here you have to accept this."

I dropped him off mid-afternoon because he had some work to do. He was making a living painting houses and planning weddings and *quinceañeras* (the coming-out parties of fifteen-year-old girls) with occasional stints in tourist hotels farther down the train tracks in Divisadero. Toward sunset he knocked on my door and suggested we go out for a beer. Since there were no bars or *cantinas,* this meant buying beer from the store and driving up to the top of a high mesa overlooking the town. It was like the riverbank in Chinipas, a free zone away from the town where people got utterly crazed on alcohol and cocaine and drove their trucks up and down. A group of Tarahumaras roared around in an indescribably battered truck and pulled up next to us, offering us cans of beer and bellowing, "Long live the sons of fornication! Come and drink with us, you goat-fornicators!"

"Go for it, my friends!" yelled back Baldimir with maximum heartiness. "We are all sons of fornication! We will drink with you later."

He directed me to a secluded place on the rim of the mesa and we watched the sun set over the canyons, which he said looked like "a thousand Matisses." He said he was writing a book too and I asked him what it was about.

"I am homosexual," he said, just making sure I had figured it out. "So my book is about the experience of growing up and being gay in the Sierra Madre."

"An excellent subject," I said. "Do you know the book or the film *Brokeback Mountain*?"

"Here in Mexico it was called *Secrets of the Mountain* and I have many secrets to tell from these mountains," he said, laughing.

The homophobic violence in *Brokeback Mountain* wouldn't happen in the Sierra Madre or anywhere in Mexico, he said. Homosexuality can make people uncomfortable. Gay men are often treated with scorn and derision and during droughts in Témoris there is a saying that it won't rain because there are too many *jotos* (faggots) around. But violence and hatred against gays is almost completely unknown in Mexico.

Coming out was the most difficult thing, accepting that he was gay and telling his family. His brothers were all good macho cowboy types and it took them a long time to get used to it. For one thing, they didn't understand that it was possible to be gay without being effeminate. "Now it is great," he said. "I have a very supportive network of friends and family members who accept me and love me. But in a small town like this I do have to restrain myself."

"Sexually, you mean?"

"No, in my emotional attachments, in my hopes of finding love. Sexually you would be surprised. There is no shortage of sex here but it's only sex. Afterward they don't know you and the next day it never happened."

Then he dropped a bomb into my brain. "Many *narcos* are bisexual and they are my specialty, you might say. At a certain point in the night, with all the drinking and cocaine, another side of them comes out. And they're risk-takers by nature. They don't expect to live long and they will try anything. You know there is an active and a passive position in homosexual intercourse? Well the *narcos* are always passives. Always, always."

"How interesting. Why do you think that is?"

"I think it's the eroticism of reversal for them. Normally they are the *chingón*, the one screwing-over other people, the *hombre muy macho*, and it excites them to turn the whole thing around."

"Are there any *narcos* who are exclusively gay?"

"In Parral there's a famous gay *narco* who dresses all in pink—pink hat, pink jeans, pink boots, pink cowboy shirt. He goes to nightclubs with all his cute young boyfriends and he is greatly feared. But he is the only purely gay *narco* I know about. And I will bet that he is *activo* in bed. The others that I'm talking about have sex mostly with women, but they have this other side to them and I know about it very well."

He grinned and cracked another beer. "I will tell you a story," he said. "This happened in Chinipas last year. I was walking along the street and this big truck pulls over next to me. The guy is pure *narco* and he says in this deep gruff voice, 'What are you doing? Do you want to go to the riverbank?'

"I know his family are heavyweight mafiosos in Chinipas and they have killed many people. I get in the truck and see he has a pistol in his belt. Baldimir, I tell myself, what are you doing? But I want the thrill. He offers me cocaine. I say no. He offers me *lechuguilla*. I say no, only a beer or two for me. So he drives over to the agency and buys twenty-four beers. The *narcos* always have to do everything big, dramatic, excessive."

At this point the story became incredibly graphic with a lot of below-the-belt detail. It turned out that the *narco* was a bisexual underwear fetishist who liked to be insulted in the filthiest terms imaginable. So Baldimir found himself minus his underwear, in fear for his life, saying things to an armed tumescent *narco* like, "You filthy whore. You faggot scum. You double pig-fucking swine." Afterward the *narco* threw him out of the truck and dismissed him coldly, saying, "You failed to insult me. Now go away."

THIS WAS AN unforseen facet of Mexican machismo but in general I was growing very tired of it. At first it seemed amusing and outlandish, the way they growled and swaggered and cursed and talked about their testicles and each other's mothers all the time. Nowhere in the world had I encountered men more fixated on either subject. The bus driver between Creel and Batopilas, I remember, had a separate wife and family at both ends of his route and a withered bull's scrotum hanging from his rearview mirror, which he would stroke for luck before swinging the bus around the next hairpin curve.

Then it got wearying, the constant crude sexual bantering and self-aggrandizement of the macho, his contempt for women, his bristling pride and enjoyment of violence, his needless cruelty to dogs and horses and livestock. What I didn't know, mainly because machos were so touchy about other men being around their women, was the female perspective on all this but I made some headway the next morning.

Esmeralda and her waitress sat down for a well-deserved cup of coffee after preparing, serving, and clearing away some two dozen breakfasts. I was still working on a post-breakfast cup of coffee at the next table. One other man, a truck driver passing through town, was finishing his breakfast at another table. Esmeralda had already told me, in one of those conversational leaps that women make to let a man know they're not available, that she had recently married a Canadian engineer working in a mine near Témoris. Foreign mining corporations, mainly Canadian and North American, were buying up old mines all over the Sierra Madre and working them with new and often highly toxic technologies like cyanide heap-leaching, notorious for poisoning rivers and aquifers.

"Esmeralda, I'm curious about something," I said, making a conversational leap of my own. "Do you find Canadian men very different from Mexican men?" The two women looked at each other with widened, slightly scandalized eyes at my boldness. Then Esmeralda laughed. "What an interesting question!" she said, getting up and pouring more coffee all around. "It is true that my husband has some very different customs and they are very strange to me."

"What customs?"

"Well, he wants me to eat at the table with him. He asks my opinion about things. I'm not used to this. At first it was very difficult."

I don't think the two women had discussed this between themselves, because the other woman looked absolutely fascinated and amazed by what she was hearing.

"The father of my child is a typical Mexican man," continued Esmeralda. "We never married but we lived together. He was always going out drinking with his friends and seeing his other girlfriends, but my husband doesn't do this. When he goes out with friends, he brings me with him and his friends bring their wives and girlfriends. And my husband doesn't have a mistress. Only me."

"Are you sure? How do you know?" said the waitress.

"I'm sure of it," said Esmeralda.

"But he's still a man, isn't he?" said the waitress. "Why wouldn't he have a mistress?"

"It is their custom. Sometimes I see him looking at other women but that is all. It is the same with the other Canadians at the mine. They only have one girlfriend."

So it continued. Esmeralda described what I considered normal relations between the sexes and her waitress found it almost impossible to believe. "The father of my child would spend all his money getting drunk with his friends," said Esmeralda. "But my new husband shares his money with me. He says it is our money. We pay the bills and then he gives me half of what is left over. This is not the custom in Mexico. It has all taken a lot of getting used to. At first I was afraid."

"What were you afraid of?" I asked.

"Many things. Among them, it is the custom for a man to kiss another man's woman on the cheek, just to say hello. My husband kisses my sister on the cheek and his friends kiss me on the cheek."

"Really?" said the waitress. "And nothing happens?"

"Nothing! The first time this happened to me I was terrified. People get killed for that here. Mexican men are very jealous. And they imagine things that don't exist."

The man with the newspaper, finishing his breakfast, was eavesdropping now and he joined in. "That's not true."

"Yes it is true," chorused the women defiantly.

"So," I said, feeling like a moderator on a panel. "It is the custom for Mexican men to have mistresses but they get very jealous if they suspect their wives or girlfriends of seeing another man. What if the wife or girlfriend really does take a lover and the man finds out?"

There were sharp intakes of breath. The women looked alarmed by the very thought of it. "Maybe he would just beat you," said Esmeralda. The other woman looked at her doubtfully. "It would depend on the man," said Esmeralda. "He would beat the woman badly and throw her out but he might not kill her."

"What would a Canadian man do?" asked the waitress.

"I don't know," said Esmeralda. "But my husband never gets jealous and I will never give him reason to be jealous."

"Are there other women here who have married the foreign men in the mine? It sounds like a better life for a woman."

"There are some others, yes," said Esmeralda. "I can't speak about the other foreigners but my husband is a good man and I'm very very happy with him."

13

The Liver Does Not Exist

STANDING OUTSIDE THE HOTEL on my last night in Témoris, getting ready to say good-bye and good luck, Baldimir and I got into an argument about money. "What is it with you Mexicans!" I remonstrated. "We had an agreement."

"No, no. Listen to me."

"Two hundred pesos a day. Esmeralda is my witness."

"No, no, no." He held up his hands and turned his head away.

"Come on," I said. "Take the money."

"No, we are friends now and I am glad to help you."

"Buy something for your mother, for your nieces."

"Thank you but I don't need it. You wouldn't believe how much money people spend on weddings and *quinceañeras* around here, especially the *narcos,* and they are happy to have someone who can plan the whole thing. Sometimes they like it better that a *joto* is doing it, because they know we are good at these things."

"You mean, making everything *fabuloso*?"

"Exactly!" He laughed.

"How extravagant do the weddings get?" I fetched out my notebook again.

"Oh, a big *narco* wedding can go on four or five days. They hire these fifteen-piece brass bands from Sinaloa who play around the clock and know a hundred different *corridos.* The music is so loud it hurts your whole head. And the drinking is ridiculous. Three hundred cases of beer, twenty cases each of tequila and whiskey—Scotch whiskey, not American. That is the status drink for them. And if they run out, someone flies off in a Cessna and comes back with another twenty cases. The *narcos* love to make the big gestures. That is really why they get into the business. It's not the money but the gestures they can make with the money."

Again I told Baldimir that he should be writing all this down and finishing his book. If it was any good at all, I promised, I would help him get it published. I was a little vague on what gay men were reading these days but surely there was a market for the sexually explicit memoir of a wedding planner in the Sierra Madre who specialized in seducing drunken mafiosos.

Baldimir said he still had a long way to go on the book but in the meantime he wanted to design and market a novelty doll called Marimar, based on the cross-dressing cowboy killer I had told him about. "He has stubble on his face, a cowboy hat, and a pink flowery dress. You pull a string out of his back and he says, 'Go to hell, you sons of fornication!'"

"You will be a rich man." I laughed. "And of course you will give me some of the profits for giving you the idea."

"Oh, of course. We can have him saying different things when you pull the string, like, 'It won't rain because there are too many *jotos*,' and, 'Your ass is mine, whore boy.'"

"We will be millionaires!"

But first I had to drive this bandit road to Bahuichivo and then somehow get through the remaining five hundred miles of the Sierra Madre, including its deepest *barrancas* and the Golden Triangle, the supposed epicenter for drug production and violence, where the states of Chihuahua, Durango, and Sinaloa converge. Baldimir, like everyone else, said the mountains of Sinaloa would be my biggest problem. That was where the mafia was strongest, suspicion of outsiders was most extreme, and life was at its cheapest. Homicide was the leading cause of death for adult males in Sinaloa and nowhere were they more trigger-happy than in the mountainous eastern part of the state.

As the sound of the word Lolita lit a fire in Humbert's loins, so the snaky sound of Si-na-loa put a cold quivery feeling right in the bottom of my guts. Virtually all the top Mexican drug lords had come out of the mountain mafia clans in Sinaloa, and they were revered and protected by the people there as heroes and benefactors of village churches, schools, and medical clinics. Chapo Guzman, the self-described "humble bean farmer" who was officially the most wanted drug lord in Mexico after his prison breakout in a laundry basket, was still able to spend time at his ranch in La Tuna north of Badiraguato, Sinaloa, because the local people would tip him off about impending raids and strangers in the area and local officials would allow his security detail to set up checkpoints on the road. Questioned about this by a *Los Angeles Times* reporter, the second-ranking municipal official in Badiraguato issued a thoroughly Mexican denial: "We do not know in the slightest whether or not this famous Chapo even exists."

I didn't know what I was going to do about Sinaloa. I had no contacts there. Even on the map it looked sinister and forbidding and far too close for comfort. Just across the state line from Chihuahua was a village called Mátalo, which means Kill Him.

Durango wasn't going to be any picnic either—"a very hard country, full of killers," in Joe Brown's words, and home base for the Herreras, one of Mexico's oldest and most powerful heroin-smuggling clans. Then at the southern end of the mountains were the peyote-worshipping Huichol Indians. They were said to be rude, obstructive, and hostile toward outsiders and even more so now that more and more Huichols were growing the crop that pays. A few years ago two Huichols had murdered an American journalist, Philip True, and sodomized him with a stick, according to the first coroner's report in the bizarre, tangled legal aftermath of that killing.

I tried not to think about what lay ahead. It was far too daunting and unnerving. First things first: these bandits on the road to Bahuichivo.

Contradicting the patent medicine salesman, Baldimir said I should be fine so long as I set off early in the morning. Like Victor and Che Che, he was of the opinion that the bandits stayed up late at night drinking and blasting parakeet and were in no shape to rob anyone until noon.

It made sense to me so I got up at first light and was on the road soon after dawn. Thinking back through Baldimir, Esmeralda, Victor, Che Che, Angel and Manuel Flores, Gustavo in Álamos, Nelda and Efren Villa, I couldn't get over how kind, generous, helpful, and hospitable they had all been to me. Nothing in moderation: that was the basic rule of things in the Sierra. The climate swung from killing droughts to catastrophic floods and back again. The landscape wasn't content to be steep; it wanted to be vertical. Everything was pushed to extremes and the people were no exception. I remembered Joe Brown had a theory about this: "Some of the worst people in the world live in the Sierra Madre and a few of the very best. It's like the good people have to be extra good to make up for all the evil, murdering sons of bitches."

The drive to Bahuichivo passed without incident. Again a series of dire warnings. Again nothing happened. My confidence at traveling alone in the Sierra increased further. Even if there were bandits all you had to do was hand over your money, so what was the big deal?

Bahuichivo was a raw highland logging town bisected by the train tracks. Tarahumara women sat on low rock walls nursing their babies, their one- and two-year-olds, and occasionally their three- and four-year-olds. Waiting for the train, slumped against their instrument cases on the platform, were five hungover-looking *norteño* musicians in matching green cowboy suits. There were also a few peasant farmers and ranchers on the platform and two German backpackers, the first outsiders or foreigners that I had seen since Álamos.

I went into a small grocery store and my attention was caught by the calendar on the wall. Issued by a veterinarian in Casas Grandes, Chihuahua, it was illustrated with a line drawing of a man with slightly bent knees and both his arms up to the elbow in the vagina of a cow. There was nothing cartoonish about the drawing. It was an earnest rendition of a vet at work, presumably manipulating a

197 The Liver Does Not Exist

breeched calf, and intended to inspire confidence in his skills and experience.

I bought some bananas, an avocado, some cheese and crackers, and a newspaper. Then I found my way to a low, squat adobe building with a small barred window and the word CERVEZA on the wall. I hunched down and peered through the bars. Inside was a tough-looking woman in her forties, two infants, a wizened crone asleep in the corner, and cases of Tecate stacked to the roof.

"One cold beer, please," I said, desperate to rinse the acrid road dust out of my throat.

"Ten pesos," said the woman.

"Ten pesos?" I was used to paying thirty-five pesos for a six-pack. Was this a special *gringo* pricing arrangement? An old man in a tattered straw hat took his place behind me. I turned around and asked him how much a beer usually cost in Bahuichivo. "Ten pesos." he said. "Fifty pesos for a six-pack."

"Why is it so expensive?" I asked, wondering if it was the transportation costs to such a remote place.

He flung up his right hand in a gesture of dismissal. "The economy is screwed. It's the politicians."

"They are corrupt?" I asked. "Or they make bad policies?"

"They are sons of whores. I wouldn't piss on them if they were on fire. A man can't afford to get drunk anymore."

"Here," I said. "Take this fifty pesos and buy yourself a six-pack." Finally I was able to persuade a Mexican to take my money.

In the newspaper was a story from Guachochi, a town to the south in the Golden Triangle. A unit of the AFI, Mexico's newly minted equivalent to the FBI, formed because the existing federal police agency was so thoroughly corrupt, had been sent into Guachochi to do something about the lawlessness, violence, and drug trafficking.

Yesterday its commander, one Arnulfo Ortiz Guzmán, "in the most extreme grade of drunkenness," had smashed his green Chevrolet truck into a telephone pole, swiped two parked cars, and severely injured a fifty-eight-year-old woman. I read on, knowing by now that there was bound to be some further quirk to the story, that little detail that affirms you're in Mexico. And here it was: the incident had occurred at eleven in the morning, strongly suggesting that the AFI commander had been up drinking and blasting parakeet all night. And two months ago another high-ranking AFI officer, "visibly inebriated," had hospitalized a woman in a hit and run. On the opposite page was a photograph of what had been a wooden shack and was now a pile of splintered wood. Another drunk driver, although not a federal agent this time, had lost control of his 1984 Dodge van and plowed into it, seriously injuring the two children inside.

I turned the page and read a story about the siren of Guachochi, a mermaid with the body of a goddess, honey-colored hair, and the tail of a fish, who lived in the Lake of Herons and called down rain and snow from the sky. Some local farmers were blaming the drought on the fact that no one had seen her lately.

EASTER WAS APPROACHING, the Holy Week as they call it, when drunk-driving fatalities reach their annual high-water mark and the police stack up the dead bodies on the roadsides for collection by the morgue wagons. In Anglo countries a drunk-driving death is considered a particularly senseless waste of life, an avoidable tragedy that calls for tougher laws and stricter policing. Mexicans are more likely to shrug and say, *"Ya le tocaba."* His number came up, his turn to die arrived. A driver's blood alcohol content, a blind headlight on an onrushing truck in the night, the question of seat belts or guardrails or absent warning signs—all these are minor circumstantial details, specks of chaff blowing in the mighty winds of fate. Death comes for you when your number is up, and everyone knows Death works overtime at Easter.

My plan was to spend Holy Week at the bottom of Urique Canyon, the deepest *barranca* of all, measuring 6,135 feet from the rim to the river, approximately a thousand feet deeper than the Grand Canyon of Arizona although not as wide. Tourists went unquestioned there, despite the fact that marijuana growing was the main economic activity, and it was supposed to be a good place to see the Tarahumara Easter rites. They varied substantially from village to village across the Sierra but traditionally included body painting, all night drumming and dancing, ritual drunkenness, wrestling matches, mock battles, and the burning of a Judas effigy with a huge wooden erection. In some villages, mainly at the goading of priests or missionaries, the Tarahumaras were now charging tourists to film and photograph a brief sanitized performance of their traditional rites, with minimal drinking and a dickless Judas, but down in Urique Canyon, or so I had heard, in the villages of Guapalaina and Guadalupe Coronado, Tarahumaras were still celebrating Easter with full pagan gusto.

The road from Bahuichivo snaked its way down the side of the monster canyon, working from one ledge to the next with sheer vertigo-inducing drop-offs and stupendous views that extended for fifty miles or more across the crags, battlements, side canyons, and cave-riddled cliffs, all of it colored in different shades of pink, brown, orange, yellow, tan, and white. The river was a thin band of green more than a mile below.

The term Barranca del Cobre or Copper Canyon refers to one section of Urique Canyon. It is overlooked by the train at Divisadero and named after the lichen that grows on its walls, which is the same shade of green as tarnished copper. To make things more confusing, Copper Canyon is also the name given to the entire complex of huge canyons in this part of the Sierra Madre—Urique Canyon, Batopilas Canyon, Sinforosa Canyon, and three others. Taken as a whole this canyon system has four times the volume of the mile-deep, mile-wide, 277-mile-long Grand Canyon.

The Mexican government has designated the whole area Copper Canyon Natural Park, an honorific title that means absolutely nothing in terms of protection, conservation, or public facilities. Logging was now regulated, at least in theory, but foreign mining companies operated with a free hand and local ranchers and farmers were busily stripping off the vegetation and killing off the wildlife.

The other name for this country is the Sierra Tarahumara. Fifty thousand Tarahumaras are estimated to live here in the *barrancas* and the highlands that separate them. Many of them are semi-nomadic, moving down to the warmer canyon bottomlands in winter and still occupying seasonal caves. From Lumholtz onward, outside observers have been fascinated by this cave-dwelling aspect of Tarahumara life but the shine and mystery went out of it for me on my first visit to Tarahumara country. Their huts were cramped, squalid, and leaky. Their caves were spacious, well-ventilated, and rainproof.

Being poor, hungry, and fifty thousand strong, living by slash-and-burn agriculture and goat herding, the Tarahumaras were particularly hard on the thin rocky soil and the native plants, and their hunting practices were to kill anything they saw that could furnish a meal. Even so they could barely keep themselves and their children fed, especially in drought years, and were growing increasingly dependent on outside aid and charity organizations and leaving the Sierra in ever greater numbers to find work.

When the first Spaniards arrived in northern Mexico some Tarahumaras were living in the *barrancas* but most of the tribe was farther east in the gentler, more fertile river valleys that ran out of the Sierra Madre onto the Chihuahua plains. The Spaniards introduced deadly new diseases, forced labor in the mines, and Jesuit missionaries, come to rescue heathen souls from darkness. The Tarahumaras did the sensible thing and withdrew deeper and higher into the mountains.

The Jesuits followed them, built more missions, and succeeded in converting some Tarahumaras to Catholicism but by "withdrawal, evasion, deceit, dissimulation, feigned ignorance and slander," as Susan Deeds characterizes it, most Tarahumaras resisted conversion and maintained their independence as a people. They would give Jesuits permission to come and talk to them and then be gone at the appointed time. They would refuse to answer questions or engage in discussion, and then state flatly that they wanted to go to hell, not heaven. They mocked the padres, saying celibacy was just a cover story for their impotence. They would try to goad them into fighting by throwing rocks at them and insulting their manhood. And thanks to the geography of the Sierra, there was always a backcountry hinterland where Tarahumaras could go and live as they pleased.

When the Jesuits were expelled from Mexico by the Spanish crown in 1767, their nineteen mission churches in Tarahumara country were abandoned and it wasn't until 1900 that the Jesuits returned. During that time the Christianity introduced by their predecessors had warped and twisted and bound up in strange ways with traditional Tarahumara beliefs, and encroaching Mexican settlers had pushed the Tarahumaras into the most remote and inaccessible part of the Sierra Madre—the deep *barranca* country.

What the Tarahumaras have always wanted is to be left alone by *chabochis*. That is what they call us—Spaniards, *mestizo* Mexicans, Anglos, non-Indians in general. The word refers to our facial hair (Tarahumara men are beardless) and the fact that we are children of the Devil. We are greedy and quick to violence, and we create disharmony wherever we go. It is best to avoid us and we can't be trusted but there's no point hating us. We can't help it. It's not our fault. We didn't ask to be fathered by the Devil.

Driving down into Urique Canyon you could see how far we had pushed them. Clinging to the few, small parcels of horizontal land in that vertical country there were Tarahumara *ranchos*—a hut, a corn patch, a goat pen. One had sheer thousand-foot cliffs falling away on three sides of it and a few gravity-defying goats on the terrifying slope that led down to it. This family hadn't moved here for the scenery. It was a place of last resort, of final retreat.

BY THE TIME I reached river level and the old adobe town of Urique, founded by a gold prospector from Chinipas in 1690, the sun was behind the canyon wall and the long dusk had begun. I had been to Urique just a couple of years before and I was a little sad to see that progress had found its way down here. The municipal authorities, flush with money from a new Canadian-owned mining project downriver, had just finished tearing up the old cobblestoned streets and replacing them with concrete. Twenty-four-hour electricity had arrived and televisions were glowing and jabbering away at high volume in the front rooms. Horses, mules, donkeys, cows, pigs, goats, and chickens were still wandering about the town as before, foraging on weeds and refuse, but the public health committee had painted a big new slogan on a prominent wall: DO NOT THROW DEAD ANIMALS IN THE RIVER.

On the plaza a short balding man with a mustache and an air of calm efficiency introduced himself as Rafael and led me down the street to his hotel, the Cañon de Urique. He showed me a clean, basic room with hot water and a comfortable bed for ten dollars a night. I washed the dust off my face and hands and went across the street to his restaurant. His wife cooked me a tough old piece of chicken and I drank down a couple of beers and watched a game show on his new television. The contestants were men dressed up as women. They squawked in shrill voices and were constantly adjusting their wigs and fake breasts. A boy of nine or ten was fetched out of the audience by the host, who put his arm around him and asked him some questions. One of the cross-dressing contestants, with exaggerated mincing sneakiness, came up behind the boy and squeezed his buttocks. There was a honking sound effect, the boy jumped up in alarm, and the audience shrieked and howled with laughter. Rafael and his wife joined them with a sedate little chuckle.

I finished my meal and asked him for a *trago,* a swallow of tequila to aid the digestion. Urique was a dry town, he said. You could only buy beer with a meal, or in the *cantina,* and liquor sales were banned entirely. Then he produced a bottle labeled Bailey's Irish Cream and poured me a shot of the local *lechuguilla* from it. "This was made by the Indians," he said. "It is all from totally natural ingredients and very pure."

It tasted like kerosene and went down like poison fire. Two days later my throat still felt scorched and wounded from that single shot.

Behind Rafael's restaurant was a garden with some fruit trees and white plastic tables and chairs and it was there, on the Tuesday of Easter Week, that I met two young men called Pancho and José. They had gel-spiked hair and were wearing cargo pants and Nike sneakers. They beckoned me over to their table, poured me a plastic glass of beer, admired my pen, and then took it as a token of our newfound friendship.

"You want to buy some?" said Pancho without further ado. "One hundred dollars a kilo. We have a new machine in town that packs the kilos very tight."

"Ah, no thank you. I'm not here to buy *mota*. I'm here to see the Tarahumara Easter fiesta."

"How about grenades? I have some very good grenades and a rocket for them."

"The rocket shoots the grenades?"

"Yes. It works very well, very strong." He held up his arm and slapped it.

"It's not my business but why would anyone need rocket-propelled grenades in Urique Canyon?"

Pancho gave me the patient, pitying look. "Helicopters," he said. "Sometimes the army comes in helicopters. We used to string cables across the canyons to bring them down but these work much better."

"I don't need to shoot down any helicopters."

"*Hombre,* you can use them for anything you want. Maybe there are bandits on the road ahead. You stop and BOOM!"

"How about some parakeet?" chimed in José. "We can get some right now from Pancho's aunt."

"No thank you. I gave it up because of the hangovers. But tell me, how are the police here? Do they make trouble?"

"There is no problem," said José. They both grinned. "My brother is a police officer and we are training to be police officers ourselves."

IN JOE BROWN'S day, the largest town in each *municipio* would have a single resident *comisario,* or constable, and he was responsible for law and order over hundreds of square miles of rugged, roadless mountains. His only real work, according to Joe, was to confiscate bootlegged *lechuguilla* and then sell it back to the townsfolk out of his office. That was the extent of the law unless there was a killing and the killer was considered too dangerous or troublesome for the victim's family members to kill. In that case, the local people would send for the *judiciales,* the state police, and they would ride up into the Sierra on mules.

"They were really good at what they did," said Joe. "Good trackers, good outdoorsmen, good at packing mules and good at sneaking up on a man's camp. They nearly always got their man and they never brought him out alive. There's no capital punishment in Mexico so they would give him *ley de fuga,* law of flight. They'd throw a rope around a boulder and hang him off the nearest cliff and then report back that he was killed trying to escape."

Now there was a station full of municipal police officers in places like Urique and Chinipas. Pancho and José would soon be joining their ranks. Once they had their badges, guns, and the power of arrest, their potential earnings would increase but they were already well on their way, selling kilos and rocket-propelled grenades. Units of the state police and AFI were stationed in the Sierra Madre now too but this didn't mean that law and order had arrived. What it usually meant was more armed ruthless men looking for a piece of the drug action and a rise in teenage pregnancies and drunk-driving accidents. Trying to distinguish between police officers and drug traffickers can be a futile exercise in Mexico. The traffickers don't just buy protection against arrest. They hire state and federal policemen to transport loads for them and carry out executions. Amado Carrillo Fuentes, The Lord of the Skies, used federal police officers as his personal bodyguards.

The army, which came through the *barrancas* every harvest season, was a slightly different proposition. Judging by the way people complained about them, they were less corrupt than the police but that didn't mean the soldiers couldn't be bought or that they burned all of what they chopped down. According to the DEA, drug corruption was still "rife" in the Mexican military and it was only a few years since General Jesús Gutiérrez Rebollo, appointed as Mexico's drug czar by President Zedillo and described as an "honest man" and a "butt-kicking general" by his U.S. counterpart Barry McCaffrey, was found to be in the pay of Amado Carrillo Fuentes, who was using him to arrest his rivals and seize their shipments.

In Joe Brown's day there was a simpler form of lawlessness in the Sierra. Now things were more complicated, based on shifting arrangements of corruption financed by organized crime, linked to global black markets, and affected by national and international politics. There were enormous amounts of money at stake now and this was what drew the law into the Sierra Madre and also made it imperative to co-opt the law and keep it at bay.

I had an interesting conversation about all this with a tourist guide in Urique. I will have to conceal his name because I didn't tell him I was a writer and what he told me could get him into trouble. He was stopping for lunch in Tita's Restaurant on the plaza with a group of burly middle-aged Texans. I was eating by myself in the courtyard with an ineptly stuffed hawk nailed to the wall over my head. The guide seemed eager to get away from his clients and take a break from speaking English. We started talking about the tourism business and then the conversation ended up where it so often does in the Sierra Madre.

"Everything is running smooth here at the moment," he said. "The army patrols are mostly for show. The big *narco* goes to the military headquarters in Chihuahua City. He says, 'I need this area protected,' and they work out a price. Then the army goes and makes trouble in other areas with the independents and the rivals of the big *narco*. The state police are making more trouble here at the moment but this is usually because a *narco* has done business without paying them. They are putting men in prison for this, putting their wives in prison also, breaking up families and sending the children to orphanages and foster homes. This is a better lesson to the others than just killing the man."

"How is it that tourism and drug trafficking can be together here without trouble?" I asked.

"Because the guides and the *narcos* know each other and we respect each other. I am glad to see the marijuana growing because I don't like to see hungry people with hungry children. The sawmills are closing down and apart from tourism, which employs only a very few people, there is no other way for the people to live. So the guides will often help the *narcos*. If we see an army patrol or the police, we tell the *narcos* and they can take their load another way. Do you know of the Swiss man?"

"The one who was killed on the train?"

"He was a client of mine."

"Really?"

"Yes, he was an angry bad-tempered man who spoke no English or Spanish. His wife spoke a little of both but he wouldn't let her speak. I was glad to get rid of him but that is not my point. Do you know what happened to the bandits who robbed that train and killed him?"

"I heard the mafia killed them."

"All seven of them. One of them they poured gasoline on and burned to death. Another one they shot fifty times and made the sign of the cross on his body with the bullets. Another one they killed his mother and father. This is a very clear message, no? There are still bandits here but everyone knows to leave the tourists alone. We want tourists to come here. They bring money. They don't cause any trouble for the *narcos*. Maybe the *narco* doesn't want his son in such a dangerous business so he builds him a hotel or something like this. Tourism is good for everyone."

"You mentioned bandits. How are they able to operate?"

"There is some law in the towns now but outside the towns the law doesn't exist. It is very dangerous to drive these roads at night because of bandits. That is why I am able to get a permit for my pistol, to defend myself against bandits. It is very very difficult to get a permit for a pistol in Mexico but I can do it because of where I work."

The Texans arose from their table, three or four beers to the wind. The guide snapped back into English: "Okay, guys. We will have a quick look around Urique and take some photographs and then it will be time to go back up."

・ ・ ・

ON THE WEDNESDAY of Holy Week, Urique started filling up with people. Most of them were friends and relatives of the locals but there was also a retired dentist from Minnesota who was traveling around the Sierra Tarahumara doing volunteer dental work in rural health clinics ("extractions mostly"), and two artists from Santa Fe, New Mexico, Craig Johnson and Armando Espinosa Prieto. They had secured permission to film and photograph the Tarahumara Easter rites in Guadalupe Coronado, and would prove extraordinarily helpful at infiltrating me behind the scenes there.

By the late afternoon of Ash Wednesday it was rare to see an adult male in the streets of Urique without a can of Tecate in his hand and I couldn't figure out where they were buying it. An old Ford pickup truck, battered, dented, and heavily laden with half-drunk young men, pulled up alongside me and said hello. I asked them where I could buy beer. They handed me a Tecate and beckoned me to join them. I knew exactly what I was getting into and I was more than ready for it. I had been governed by fear and caution for too long. It was time to climb aboard the wild, drunken roller-coaster of a Mexican fiesta night, when anything might happen and any notion of control must be cast to the winds. Octavio Paz, as usual, describes and dissects its essence better than anyone.

> Friends who have not exchanged more than the prescribed courtesies for months get drunk together, trade confidences, weep over the same troubles, discover that they are brothers, and sometimes, to prove it, kill each other. The night is full of songs and loud cries. The lover wakes up his sweetheart with an orchestra. There are jokes and conversations from balcony to balcony, sidewalk to sidewalk. Nobody talks quietly. Hats fly in the air. Laughter and curses ring like silver pesos. Guitars are brought out. Now and then, it is true, the happiness ends badly, in quarrels, insults, pistol shots, stabbings. But these too are part of the fiesta, for the Mexican does not seek amusement: he seeks to escape from himself, to leap over the wall of solitude that confines him.

• • •

There were four across the bench seat and nine of us in the bed and they were all brothers, nephews, and cousins of the Ramirez family. "How crazy are we bastards!" they kept yelling. "Like wild horses of the Sierra! Ay-ay-AY! Ah-*HUAH!*" Around the town we careened in that old shitheap truck, slewing around corners, scattering dogs and chickens, yelping and howling, singing our own *narcocorridos* because the radio was broken and we needed music. We had cocaine, beer, *lechuguilla,* and marijuana and we puffed and snorted and guzzled in a mad headlong dash to get as wild and wasted as possible. At first I said no to the cocaine but that didn't last long. There was no other way to keep up.

Then we ran out of beer and pulled up outside the house of someone's grandmother. She passed a case of Tecate out of her front room window, followed by a gram of cocaine tied up in a little plastic bag. Then we ran out of *lechuguilla* and stopped at the house of a middle-aged woman who sold us a bottle from her back door and another bag of cocaine. The Ramirez boys explained that there were many widows in Urique and it was their custom to sell beer and *lechuguilla* illegally to support themselves. When cocaine came along, they expanded their repertoire and started selling that too.

Our stalwart driver, a Ramirez in his mid-forties with a deep gravel voice and one of those fierce hawkeyed faces, was drinking, snorting, smoking *mota,* and singing as hard as anyone. With great skill and determination, he wove a passage between the parked cars and staggering pedestrians and the other trucks full of yelping drunks.

It seemed like we had just stopped to buy more beer and now it was all gone again. The call went up for money. I dug into my wallet and handed over some bills. Another case of Tecate was procured from the grandmother and we opened the cans with a round of toasts. "Long live the sons of violation! Fuck the army and double-fuck the stinking *judiciales*!" The first firecrackers of Holy Week exploded overhead, the *lechuguilla* was passed around, and that was the first time I heard the most Mexican of all drinking toasts: *"El hígado no existe!"* The liver does not exist!

Then it was late at night and we stopped outside a small dance hall. Three of them jumped down and beckoned for me to follow them inside. The band wore red cowboy suits and played a perky *cumbia*. The Ramirez boys sat me down next to three teenage girls. "This *gringo* is our friend," they said, and with that they were gone.

I stood up unsteadily, smiled, wished the young ladies a good evening, and headed for the door, the fresh air, my bed in the Hotel Cañon de Urique. The streets were full of white cowboy hats catching the moonlight, rumbling trucks, and girls in short skirts. I was accosted by a drunk Tarahumara who was excited by the prospect of taking off his clothes on Good Friday and painting himself like a devil. He danced the sacred hopping dance of the *pascola* and asked for money.

"*Por que?*" I asked. Why?

"*Por favor,*" he said. Please. It struck me as a good and tidy answer and I pulled out my wallet and found it was empty. How was that possible?

I walked on and saw a crowd of people gathered around a truck. I recognized some of them as Ramirez boys and then I recognized the truck. The driver had finally succumbed and T-boned it into a wall. The front end was crumpled and he was having a hard time getting out of the cab. At first I thought he was injured but then I saw that he was just too drunk to move. His hand kept flopping off the door handle.

A bystander got the door open. The driver got out, reeled around in a circle, fell over, got up on his hands and knees, and vomited copiously. His fellow celebrants clapped him heartily on the back, hauled him to his feet, handed him a fresh beer, and they all lurched off down the street together to plunge deeper into chaos. A few moments later KABOOM! Another truck crashed into a different wall.

14

God Is Drunk

THE VILLAGE OF GUADALUPE Coronado was blessedly quiet and tranquil on Maundy Thursday. I sat down in the shade, leaned back against a wall, and watched the Tarahumaras decorate the old Jesuit church. They gave it a fresh coat of white paint. They climbed up ladders to crown it with palm fronds and creamy white rosettes woven from agave cactus leaves. The inside of the church had already been made gorgeous with arches of flowers, vines, cactus rosettes, and pine boughs brought down from the high mountains. The statue of the Virgin Mary had been covered so she wouldn't have to see the suffering of her son, who was resting in a brush arbor and getting his broken leg repaired by two women. All the wooden fingers had broken off on Christ's hands.

Outside the front entrance of the church was a basketball court, where men had erected two arches and decorated them with more greenery and rosettes. The sound of a scratchy violin came out of one of the buildings. Dogs ambled to and fro. Chickens scratched and clucked. Tarahumaras were coming in from the outlying *ranchos,* where most of them lived.

All around the village were big earthenware jars full of fermented corn beer, *tesguino* as the Tarahumaras call it. It is a sacred drink for them, a gift from God who likes drinking it as much as they do. Before broaching a jar, they sprinkle some *tesguino* on the ground for God, because he gets angry if he isn't served first. The Tarahumara God, also called Onorúame, is not a kind, benevolent deity but bad-tempered and truculent, prone to sending droughts, floods, and plagues at the slightest provocation. It is necessary to sacrifice bulls and goats to him when he is hungry, otherwise mountains will fall down, blood will rain from the skies, the sun will die, and the people waste away in sickness.

Holy Week is a particularly dangerous and uncertain time because this is when God gets into his annual drinking bout with the Devil. Normally the Devil has less power than God and uses it to make people fight when they are drunk. But when God is drunk, the Devil is capable of harming him. It is up to the Tarahumaras to avert this cosmic catastrophe by performing the Easter rituals correctly and also getting drunk so that their souls can leave their bodies and protect God. Not that Tarahumaras need any extra encouragement when it comes to drinking *tesguino*.

Lumholtz was the first in a long line of anthropologists to be astounded by the quantity and frequency of Tarahumara beer drinking, and how absolutely central it is to their society and religion. He spent two years with them during his sojourn through the Sierra and concluded that without alcohol, the shy, reticent Tarahumaras would be incapable of reproducing. He observed also that "absolutely no act of importance" occurs in Tarahumara culture without beer being drunk. Newborn babies are given *tesguino* to drink and shamans sprinkle them with *tesguino* to make them strong. Every social and work gathering is attended by beer drinking. Hunters drink beer for luck. Beer is left out for the dead to stop them pestering the living for it.

John Kennedy, writing nearly a century later, calculated that the average adult Tarahumara, male and female, from age fourteen onward, participated in sixty to ninety drinking binges every year, with each binge lasting between ten hours and thirty-six hours. "I observed that the Tarahumara etiquette of *tesguino* drinking requires that all adults present drink as much beer as possible," he wrote. "The ideal of enjoyment is a state of complete inebriation."

• • •

THE OTHER GREAT Tarahumara pastime, making a complete mockery of all our notions of health and fitness, is running long-distance races. They call themselves the Rarámari, the Running People, and in Lumholtz's day they would routinely run races of 100 miles, 140 miles, sometimes 170 miles, kicking a carved wooden ball the whole way and gambling heavily on the outcome. Now the kickball races are shorter, seldom more than thirty or forty miles, and gradually dying out, but the tribe is still producing runners with extraordinary powers of endurance.

In 1993 an American photographer and outdoor guide called Rick Fisher took a group of Tarahumara runners to the annual hundred-mile ultramarathon at Leadville, Colorado. Running in sandals cut from old tires and stopping for beers at the eighty-seven-mile mark, they finished first, second, and fifth and blew the collective mind of American ultrarunning. The winning Tarahumara, Victoriano Churro, was fifty-five years old and he ran the hundred miles of rough mountain trail, ranging in elevation from 10,000 feet to 12,640 feet, in twenty hours and three minutes.

The next year Fisher took seven runners and I went with them. When we got to Leadville, the Tarahumaras went to the city dump and cut themselves some new running sandals from old tires. Then they sat around for several days smoking cheap, harsh, filterless cigarettes, grumbling that they weren't allowed to drink more Budweiser and refusing to do any training for the race.

At the 1928 Olympics, Mexico entered two Tarahumaras in the marathon and imagined the gold and silver to be a foregone conclusion. But the runners didn't understand that the race was only twenty-six miles. They crossed the finish line a few minutes behind the winner and kept on running until the officials stopped them. "Too short, too short," they said. They also complained that running in circles gave them bad dreams at night.

The Mexican Olympic committee tried again. This time they made sure to explain the race was twenty-six miles and the Tarahumaras sent three women because they couldn't imagine men racing over such a short distance. Tarahumara girls still run twenty- and thirty-mile races carrying a hoop to fling the wooden ball forward. A few modern scientists have conducted physiological studies of Tarahumaras, hoping to unlock the secret of their endurance. The results are not conclusive but suggest that it results from the arduousness of daily life in the Sierra Tarahumara. Children of five and six cover twenty miles a day in rough country herding goats. Adults routinely walk forty miles a day carrying heavy loads on trails that are too steep for horses. Without loads they power-walk at incredible speed up and down the trails, but they don't run unless they're chasing a wild animal or racing with a kickball, which is why they refused to do any training in Leadville.

Nor did they do any stretching or warming up on the morning of the race. They stood there in the predawn darkness, wearing loincloths and loose white tunics, silent and perfectly still, looking like men from another time. They were surrounded by hundreds of professional and amateur ultrarunners in polypropylene clothing and state-of-the-art running shoes, yelling last-minute instructions at their support crews and talking to the TV cameras about total dedication, positive mental attitude, short-twitch muscle fiber, and the importance of a strict nutritional regimen in combination with a scientific training program incorporating track, trail, strength, and speed work. When I told the other runners about the tire-tread sandals and the pile of cigarette butts and beer cans in the Tarahumara quarters, some of them smiled, sighed, and shook their heads. Others turned sour and hostile, saying the Indians were getting "special treatment" and destroying the sense of "community" among American ultrarunners.

None of the sports journalists gave the Tarahumaras a chance of winning, despite their unexpected triumph the previous year. Everyone's money was on Ann Trason, a thirty-three-year-old Nike-sponsored Californian who held six women's ultramarathon world records and had won five races against the best male runners. According to *Sports Illustrated*, the gender gap in ultramarathon running was "the distance between her and the men eating her dust."

After thirty miles Ann Trason was in the lead and well inside course-record pace, grim-faced and sweaty, but running with great poise and grace. Sitting right on her heels were two Tarahumaras, twenty-five-year-old Juan Herrera and forty-two-year-old Martimiano Cervantes, neither of whom had yet broken a sweat. They took turns harrying her, overtaking her and dropping back, trying to upset her rhythm. This was how the Tarahumara hunted deer, running after an animal and harrying it until collapsed from exhaustion, "utterly jaded and its hoofs dropping off," in Lumholtz's phrase, at which point it could be finished off with a knife.

After fifty miles Ann Trason had opened up a four-minute lead over Juan and ten minutes on Martimiano. Kurt Madden, in fourth place, was half an hour off the pace and the other five Tarahumaras were just behind him. Then Trason ran up and over 12,640-foot Hope Pass at record-breaking speed and increased her lead further. The Tarahumaras were convinced she must be a witch. How else could a woman run over mountains faster than a man? After sixty miles Juan's face was contorted in pain and his legs were beginning to hobble. We gave him ibuprofen, chocolate, coffee, and *pinole,* a roasted, ground corn powder that is a staple Tarahumara food. Martimiano threw up, sat down, and wanted to quit but we promised him a beer at the next aid station and he got up and started running again.

At 76.5 miles Ann Trason was still running at record pace but Juan had made a miraculous recovery and cut her lead to sixteen minutes. We gave him more painkillers, sugared coffee, and *pinole* and drove on to the next aid station. It was dark now and the runners were going over Sugarloaf Mountain and a TV helicopter was tracking them and calling through radio reports to the ground crew. She's five minutes ahead. She's two minutes ahead. The lead is fifty seconds. At the aid station we were wild with excitement. The sports journalists were astounded. Ann Trason hadn't slowed her pace but Juan had gone over Sugarloaf like no one before or since.

The lead stayed at fifty seconds. Juan was right behind her, pressing and harrying, and then at the foot of the mountain he swept down past her. He reached the aid station six minutes ahead of her and forty-five minutes inside course-record time. Martimiano was an hour behind in third place and the rest of the field at least two and a half hours off the pace.

The approach to the finish line was an avenue of howling crowds, high-powered lights, and television cameras. As Juan came into view, a disembodied, grotesquely amplified voice started screaming out his name into the night, "Let's give it up for JUAN HERRERA! He's twenty-five years old and running at Leadville for the first time. JUAN HERRERA! He has smashed the course record! Let's have a big Leadville welcome home for JUAN HERRERA!"

He crossed the finish line twenty-five minutes inside the course record. Ann Trason came in thirty-six minutes later, having beaten her own women's course record by more than two hours. Martimiano came in third and looked only lightly fatigued. He had been drinking beers at the last few aid stations and now he drank a couple more and lay down on the floor of the medical tent and went to sleep. All seven Tarahumaras finished in the top eleven and all except Juan drank beers along the way. That was the last time any Tarahumaras were invited to run at Leadville.

TARAHUMARAS ALSO HAVE an extraordinary ability to sit still in silence and do absolutely nothing. In Guadalupe Coronado I spent a great deal of Holy Thursday wondering if they were waiting for the ceremonies to begin, as I was, as Craig and Armando were, or merely existing in some blank meditative state that carried no trace of anticipation or impatience. The workers had finished decorating the church hours ago. The ceremonies were supposed to begin hours ago. Everyone was there who needed to be there. Occasionally someone would get up and amble across to the tiny store for a Coke. Then they would sit down again and no one would talk or move for another half hour.

Finally things started happening. Drummers appeared, men whirled rattles. A group of men holding carved wooden AK-47s assembled on the concrete basketball court. The AK-47s had tin rattles attached to them and the men shook them and thumped them on the ground in rhythm. These were the *soldados,* we surmised, the soldiers. Another group of men came out holding painted spears and beating hoop drums. One of them was wearing a tall pointed hat made of wild turkey feathers. These were the *fariseos,* the Pharisees.

Four centuries ago the Jesuits had tried to bring Christianity alive for the Tarahumaras by staging Easter morality plays. They formed the Indians into companies and showed them how to reenact the persecution of Christ, the Crucifixion, and the Resurrection. In the Jesuit days, the soldiers and the Pharisees were the joint persecutors of Christ. But many drunken Holy Weeks had passed since then and now the Pharisees and the soldiers had ended up on opposite sides, representing good and evil, although their affiliations are switched in some villages. Here it was obvious who was who. You can always tell the evil bastards in the Sierra Madre by their AK-47s.

They each formed a line by the church. A dog walked slowly past them. A drunk man danced by himself to the music of a scratchy violin. Somebody thumped on a drum and another man tried to coax some music out of a broken flute. The two lines crossed behind the church and then emerged running, dragging their spears and rifles, and then reassembled again in the same two lines as before. Again they went behind the church and this time they ran out brandishing their weapons. There was a brief mock battle, startling a dog that was caught in the middle of it. Then they dispersed and went into various houses and open-air ramadas to drink more *tesguino.*

Dancers appeared wearing polyester slacks and seed rattles around their ankles. A man in a basketball shirt started twiddling around with three notes on an out-of-tune guitar. A lunatic came past singing to himself and digging holes, burying a small yellow plastic toy and digging it up again. Another hour went by. The energy faded away.

Then the soldiers reappeared whirling rattles and shaking their AK-47s. They went inside the church while the Pharisees tried to assemble themselves outside. Individuals kept wandering off, arguing with each other, breaking into impromptu dances. The soldiers came out of the church to see what was happening and they started wandering off too. It was clear that some ritual needed to be performed in the church but they had lost momentum. The *capitán*, the man in charge of the ritual, held a staff and wore a black cowboy hat. He yelled at the soldiers and the Pharisees, shook his staff of authority, and pointed to their positions. They ignored him and went back to the *tesguino* jars. A few drunks bumbled around, asking us for money. Some visiting Mexicans in a pickup truck blasted a *narcocorrido* through the village. Another hour went by.

NOW IT WAS dark and the Pharisees and the soldiers were in a condition of lively drunkenness. They pounded on drums, whirled their rattles, cracked jokes and laughed, pretended to sodomize each other, whooped with their palms over their mouths, came up to us asking for money with dried milky smears of corn beer on their faces, making rude jokes and obscene gestures. When sober, Tarahumaras are extremely quiet, modest, polite, shy, and retiring. Now they had swung to the opposite extreme. The *capitán* lost his temper and started raging and cursing at them, shaking his staff and becoming so upset and frustrated that he was on the brink of tears. A group of shawled and head-scarved women filed into the church, knelt in front of the saints, and began a constant chanting prayer.

Soldiers, Pharisees, and villagers went into the church, came out again, wandered about, whooped, and capered. It took all the force of the *capitán*'s personality and a lot more staff shaking but eventually he managed to wrangle them all into the church. Outside the church we waited and waited and waited. Inside confusion reigned. Finally a procession emerged with a phalanx of chanting women at its core, the village governor at its head, Pharisees along the side, white flags, candles, flashlights, images of the Virgin Mary and Jesus, an incense burner trailing pungent *copal* smoke. Drunks joined the procession from the audience and played the fool. Dogs trotted alongside it. The women kept up their chanting and the musicians played a vague, noodling, fractured music. The procession went around and around

the church for an hour or so and this, we presumed, was the reenactment of the Via Dolorosa, the Road of Sorrows that Christ walked to
Calvary carrying his cross. It was a strange and moving spectacle,
a curious blend of devotion, pageantry, drunken high spirits, and
barely controlled chaos.

People drank late into the night and started drinking again on
the morning of Good Friday. Christ was dead, the Virgin Mary was
wearing a black cloak, and God was drinking with the Devil. It was
time for the *diablitos*, the little devils, to paint themselves and wreak
havoc.

Craig and Armando had gone through endless negotiations and
paid a considerable amount of money to be allowed to film and photograph the painting of the *diablitos* and they very kindly invited me
to tag along. We followed two women along a trail out of the village,
struggling to keep up with them. After twenty minutes or so, we
reached a small *rancho* known as Casa Blanca, where a group of men
were stripped down to their underwear and cut-off shorts, swilling
back *tesguino* and daubing themselves and each other in black-and-
white stripes, zigzags, and whorls, using firewood ash for the black
and limestone clay for the white. Musicians were playing—guitar,
violin, and hoop drum—and some of the devils were dancing and
whooping, and shaking their wooden AK-47s. When we arrived
they rushed toward us, threatened us in jest with their AK-47s, and
then grew genuinely angry and belligerent and started demanding
money. Armando and Craig kept explaining that they had already
paid, that the village governor had the money. The women said it was
true, the trouble was resolved, the painting party resumed.

Judas was leaning against the wall of a small adobe building. He
was made of wood and straw, standing about eight feet high with a
two-liter plastic bottle of murky corn beer for a bladder, old leather
boots dangling on pieces of string, and a carved wooden erection about
two feet long. The devils called him Papa and took turns hoisting him
on their shoulders, with the erection jutting out over their heads like
a ship's prow. They danced around until his weight collapsed them
into the dust, whereupon Judas's bladder would fall out, or his penis

would fall off, and the poor *capitán* would have to enforce his authority over the reeling crew of laughing, disobedient devils and get them to put Judas back together again. The *capitán* was unsteady on his feet and knocking back *tesguino* as fast as everyone else.

The women stayed off to the side with the *tesguino* jars, drinking heartily themselves and passing around plastic glasses and tin cups full of *tesguino* to the men. Now they came over to us offering *tesguino*. It is de rigueur to down your *tesguino* in one and that's what we did. It was a grayish-brown color and tasted a little like Guinness but more sour and milky with strands of corn silk and chunks floating in it. The alcohol content was fairly low. I had five glasses in fairly quick succession and felt as if I had drunk three Tecates, at which point I called a halt. It was impossible to take notes because devils kept grabbing my pens and refusing to give them back, so I was determined to burn these extraordinary scenes into my memory.

They painted themselves from head to toe and some wore crazy cardboard hats with visors and cardboard deer horns, painted black and white, decorated with turkey feathers and tied under the chin with blue nylon twine. Across the buttocks of the village teacher were the letters N-O-S-E. *No sé*. I don't know. The women were getting drunker and drunker and one grandmother held a corncob at her groin like a penis and chased around a little boy. I had read about this joking sexual relationship between Tarahumara grandmothers and grandsons but was nonetheless startled to see how raunchy it was. She pinned the boy against the wall and pretended to hump him, producing good-natured laughter all around.

Another devil hoisted Judas on his shoulders. The guitars plunked and the violins sawed, the AK-47s went *chank-chank-chank,* and two bored teenage boys tried to drown out the music with a boombox playing *narcocorridos*. The devil dancing with Judas fell over backward, cracked his head open on a rock, and started bleeding profusely. He got up, staggered about, drank some more *tesguino,* grabbed up his wooden rifle, and started dancing again.

The *capitán* called for the procession to begin. It was time for this crew of lurching drunks to carry the tall, heavy, unwieldy Judas down a steep, treacherous trail to the bottom of the canyon, and then march him along the dirt road into the village. It took them three tries to get Judas over the low rock wall surrounding the *rancho*. Now they had to climb down a notched log serving as a ladder. One of them got Judas on his shoulders, started backward down the ladder, then fell eight feet and landed on his back on a pile of boulders. He got up and dusted himself off. They put Judas back together. Five minutes later the weight of Judas toppled another devil and he split the side of his head open on a rock. You could have put five stitches in the wound but he wasn't bothered and none of the Tarahumaras paid any attention to it.

Finally they reached flat ground and the dirt road. Taking turns carrying Judas and falling over, whooping with their palms over their mouths, and giving a stylized version of the Tarahumara chuckle— "Heh-heh-heh! Hah-hah-hah!"—drinking from plastic bottles of *tesguino,* periodically rushing out from the bushes with their AK-47s and pretending to ambush us like bandits, the devils made their shambolic way toward the church.

As THE LAST rays of the sun faded from the rim of the canyon, thousands of feet above, a painted devil rode past me on a bicycle shaking an AK-47. Fires were burning now and Judas was installed opposite the church. Transgression, madness, and danger were in the air. Devils ran after children with their AK-47 barrels sticking out between their legs like erections. They wiggled their painted asses in the laps of unwary spectators, dry-humped each other, pretended to threaten people, snatched their possessions, and sometimes refused to give them back, all the time whooping and making that stylized laughing sound, "Heh-heh-heh! Hah-hah-hah!"

They approached the front steps of the church, which was as close as they were allowed to get. The Pharisees and the faithful drove them back. The smell of marijuana was in the air for the first time and bottles of *lechuguilla* were circulating along with the *tesguino* jars and cans of Tecate. Some Mexicans had driven up from Urique in their pickup trucks and a vanload of wide-eyed American tourists had come down from their lodge at Cerocahui.

Grandmothers humped their grandsons. People staggered and fell into the fires. The music never stopped and it never formed a coherent rhythm or melody. The first wrestling matches broke out and more Tarahumara heads came crashing down on the hard stony earth. Drunks of every kind—devil, Pharisee, soldier, spectator—became more bold and aggressive in asking us for money, challenging us to wrestling matches, throwing insults and curses, and mumbling incomprehensible gibberish. We shrugged and smiled and edged closer together. We said we didn't understand. A teenage boy from Montana shook his head and said to his parents, "This is the wildest thing I've ever seen in my life."

Their guide was a bullish cowboy type called Doug Rhodes who owned the lodge at Cerocahui, ran horse trips, and had been coming here for *Semana Santa* for many years. "No one here really knows what this means," he said. "It's just what they do and it's different every year because they were all too drunk to remember what they did last year. Have they brought out the dead baby yet? Some years they do. Some years they don't. It gets even wilder in Guapalaina."

"What do you mean?" I asked, unable to imagine how that was possible.

"There's some rougher types downriver, more drug guys," he said. "You get more fistfights and gunfire. Not all the AK-47s there are wooden."

A dust devil swirled across the basketball court and blew a cloud of dust through the open doors of the old adobe church, where I had taken refuge from the melee outside. A human skull rested on a wooden shelf at the back of the church with some other human bones and a sardine can with a candle in it.

"How often do the Catholic priests come to this church?" I asked an old man next to me who was still fairly sober.

"Not for many years now. But we are all good Christians here."

The faithful were lifting up effigies of Christ and Mary onto platforms and getting ready to march them outside in another procession. Then they lifted up a third effigy with a beard and a long green robe.

"Who is that?" I asked.

"That is God," said the old man.

A silver orb dangled from his arm, representing the world. His hand was raised up and turned outward and over the years all his fingers had broken off except the extended middle one. God was flipping the bird. And in some other dimension of the Tarahumara universe, he was getting drunk with the Devil.

The processions continued late into the night. So did the wrestling matches, the dancing, drumming, whooping, and drinking. Around three in the morning, I went down the hill, found a patch of level sandy ground by the river, and slept for a few hours. At dawn the festivities were still going strong. The devils were parading a big jar of *tesguino* up and down the basketball court. A *norteño* band had arrived and were singing *narcocorridos*. I fended off two aggressive drunks wanting money and then two small boys rushed up to me, crying, "Korima! Korima!" which means, "Share!" in Tarahumara, or in this circumstance, "Give us something!"

"You share first," I said in Spanish. One of the boys smiled, grabbed up a handful of dust, and put it my hand. "For you," he said. I did the same, giving him a handful of dust back.

"What's in your backpack?" he said.

"The moon," I said. "Here, I'll give you the moon." I mimed the gesture of handing it over. The boys liked this. They smiled and laughed.

Then they said, *"Korima! Korima!"*

"I've given you the moon and you still want more? What more can I give you?"

"Ten pesos!"

I would have given it to them but the adults had cleaned me out of change long ago.

"I don't have it. The moon was very expensive. But I will give you a pen."

"Ten pesos! Ten pesos!"

I put the pen back in my pocket.

"No, give us the pen."

By late morning the village was strewn with passed-out bodies and people were filling up the floor of the church with water. The devils went into the church and started writhing around on the puddled floor like salamanders, smearing their paint, working it off, becoming human again. The devils kept trying to get up, but the village governor made them lie down in the water and writhe some more. Then he gave the signal. They rushed out of the church and women pulled the coverings off all the images of the Virgin and the saints.

Outside the church, the Pharisees were waiting for them. There was another mock battle and then both groups worked together in tearing Judas apart, pounding on him with sticks, knocking him over, pulling off his boots, setting fire to the straw. The devils grabbed handfuls of straw, ran off and hid them, or rubbed them on people's heads, presumably to ensure that deviltry would not be wiped out completely. They saved the big penis from the flames. Judas and his devils would be back next year, but for now good had triumphed over evil and God was sobering up unharmed.

For the bleary, exhausted Tarahumaras of Guadalupe Coronado, the rest of Easter Saturday and all of Easter Sunday would be devoted to rest and recuperation. For me it was time to leave Urique Canyon and head into the darker, more permanent chaos of the Golden Triangle.

15

Sons of Obscene Perpetrations

A BOLDER TRAVELER WOULD have gone straight south, driving the newly carved dirt roads into the *barranca*-raddled, opium-laced heart of it all, following the mule tracks of Carl Lumholtz, Paul Salopek, and perhaps Johnny Mula, using hitchhikers for introductions and hoping the mafia's injunction against preying on tourists still applied. My route was longer, slower, and more cautious, requiring me to leave the Sierra altogether and reenter it farther south with guides, but it promised something that very few outsiders since Lumholtz had seen: a shaman-led peyote ceremony in a remote Tarahumara community that the Jesuits had never reached.

What if the shaman passed me the gourd? Should I politely refuse or throw caution to the winds and drink it down? That was the big question on my mind as I climbed out of Urique Canyon. I had never taken peyote before but by all accounts it was a serious brain-scrambler, almost guaranteed to make you vomit and then bring on vivid and sometimes terrifying hallucinations with the outside possibility of total psychic meltdown. I had the feeling that taking peyote with the Tarahumaras, way out there in the high wilds of the Golden Triangle, would either be one of the crowning experiences of my life or reduce me to a gibbering wreck.

On the way out of the mountains I stopped for a night in Creel, a highland railroad town that is both the hub of Copper Canyon tourism and the headquarters and chief money laundry for the region's top mafiosos, one of whom is said to keep a tiger in his hotel and feed it live chickens at parties. I drank a couple of beers with the Euro-American backpackers at Margarita's hostel. Then I went up the hill, seeking a more balanced impression of Creel, and rounded out the evening at the Hotel Sierra Bonita disco.

I was the only *gringo* there and soon beckoned to the table of a certain Rogelio. He was in his mid-thirties, cracking jokes and laughing uproariously, buying drinks all around. He had cocaine crumbs in his mustache and pangolin-skin boots* with the toes so pointed that he could have kicked a snake's ass out through its teeth, to borrow an expression I once heard in Texas. He bought me a beer and then another and asked me if I liked marijuana.

"Sometimes yes but tonight no."

"For you I make a very good price."

"For curiosity, how much?"

"Seventy dollars a kilo. Pure sheep's tails."

"That is a good price, but how would I get it through all the army checkpoints?"

"Fuck the army. They are stupid peasants in uniforms. They are drooling idiots. For another thirty dollars a kilo I'll fly it over their heads to Agua Prieta and you can take it across the border from there."

I said I'd think about it and not for the first time I wondered if it would be safer or more dangerous to travel through the Sierra posing as a drug dealer, or perhaps an advance scout for a drug dealer who would bring along the money later. You wouldn't want to get mistaken for an undercover DEA agent, but coming to the Sierra Madre to buy drugs would make more sense to people there than this vague talk of history and researching a book.

From Creel I drove down to Chihuahua City and the ramshackle, handicraft-strewn offices of the Sierra Madre Alliance. Its founder

---

* Pangolin: a tree-climbing anteater from Africa and southern Asia with large horny scales covering its body.

and executive director, an American environmental activist called Randy Gingrich, was the one who had arranged to take me to the peyote ceremony. But a *problema* had arisen, by which I mean a particularly Mexican species of problem. The peyote shaman had run out of peyote. There was more of the holy cactus growing within easy reach but he had delayed the ceremony until he felt the time was right to harvest it. "It could be a few days, it could be months," said Randy. "You never know. It'll probably be a message that he gets in a dream."

There was in fact a clustering fornication of *problemas*. The place we were going was called Choreachi, or Pino Gordo (Fat Pine) in Spanish. It was a Tarahumara *ejido* in one of the last remaining stands of old-growth forest in the Sierra Madre, and much coveted by the neighboring hillbillies for its virgin timber and extreme remoteness, which made it ideal for growing marijuana and opium. Randy was trying to keep the loggers and *narcos* out and a few days earlier his main ally in Pino Gordo, a middle-aged farmer and community organizer called Prudencio Ramos, had been dragged out of his house at dawn by a heavily armed gang of pro-logging goons. They drove him to the nearest police station, eight hours away in Guadalupe y Calvo, and the police obligingly locked him up on false charges.

Now the loggers were bulldozing roads and cutting down trees even though Randy still had an injunction against them waiting to be heard in court. Someone had set fire to one of their bulldozers in retaliation. There were reports of armed thugs cruising around in pickup trucks, looking to avenge their bulldozer, and a notorious Tepehuan killer and gun-for-hire had been spotted in the area. Things were getting very intense up there, said Randy, but we would still go, just as soon as he had worked the phones, filed the protests, and gotten Prudencio released from jail.

Fast-paced, harried, and overworked, with wispy red hair, glasses, a trimmed red beard, and a kind, friendly face that lit up boyishly when he smiled, and flushed when he got angry or frustated, Randy had been struggling for fifteen years to defend old-growth forest and indigenous rights in the far southwestern tail of Chihuahua, where the Golden Triangle begins. The bad guys were local *narco*-timber bosses who were logging off the virgin pines, seizing Tarahumara lands, forcing Tarahumaras to grow marijuana and opium, growing it themselves, and killing people who objected. The good guys who needed help were the Tarahumaras, who were trying to defend their sacred forests and maintain their native traditions and spirituality.

That, at least, was how Randy had to explain it to his board members, his donors, the media, and most of the time to himself. He knew the larger story but it was horribly twisted and complicated, shot through with apparent contradictions and paradoxes, intractable *problemas,* devil's bargains, snakes in the grass, fantastic levels of corruption, disorganization, dissimulation, and sheer drunken madness. If you were a well-meaning, politically correct American liberal environmentalist like Randy and his cohorts, it was liable to make your head hurt. You had to put all that to one side and keep focusing on your core beliefs. It was the only way to stay positive and optimistic and keep going in the face of so many disappointments, setbacks, and unexpected disasters.

AFTER A WEEK of wrangling and delays, we set off in Randy's big four-wheel-drive Chevy Suburban. All charges had been dropped against Prudencio and he was sitting in the backseat, alongside another anti-logging Pino Gordo farmer called Pedro Peña and a Tarahumara activist called Isidro Baldenegro López, who had recently won the $125,000 Goldman Environmental Prize from a foundation in San Francisco.

Prudencio and Pedro were dressed in cheap slacks and sandals and remained silent and impassive in the usual Tarahumara fashion. Isidro was a different kind of Tarahumara altogether. He had grown up in a remote community in the Golden Triangle called Coloradas de la Virgen, but he lived in Chihuahua City now and had spent fifteen months in the state prison. He was a burly, powerful-looking man in his late thirties with a big head and a broad handsome face. He was fastidious about his appearance. At the Goldman prize ceremony, encouraged by Randy, he had worn traditional Tarahumara garb, but now he was wearing a Guess watch, a silver bracelet, and spotless new jeans, boots, Houston Oilers T-shirt, and a baseball cap over buzz-cut hair. He had an assertive, charismatic, slightly domineering presence and a tendency to deliver long monologues on the subject of scores that he had settled or that needed settling. He spent most of that first day's drive fiddling with his new cell phone, checking for reception, calling his estranged wife and telling her he would be there in a few days, calling his pregnant twenty-year-old girlfriend and telling her she worried too much, calling various friends and colleagues and his other two girlfriends.

"I love the women," he grinned. "Three girlfriends is not enough for me. But soon I will have five."

Isidro won the Goldman Prize for the courageous, inspiring although ultimately unsuccessful resistance he led against loggers and *narcos* in Coloradas de la Virgen. After his early victories, when a series of protests and blockades brought illegal logging to a halt, he was arrested by the police on trumped-up guns and drugs charges and sent to prison. Randy orchestrated an international campaign for his release and then nominated him for the Goldman Environmental Prize.

What neither Randy nor the Goldman committee understood at the time was that Isidro was all in favor of logging the old-growth forest in Coloradas de la Virgen. He just didn't want outsiders doing it and taking the profits, especially after they murdered his father for trying to stop them. Isidro felt a sense of ownership toward the trees but he didn't feel the kind of reverential spiritual guardianship that Randy and the white liberal brigade expected him to feel as a Native American from a traditional community. Neither did Isidro's father. At the time of his murder, he owned the local sawmill.

Isidro's attitude toward drugs and *narcos* was also more complicated than it first appeared. He had grown and dealt marijuana and opium all the way through his teens and twenties. He rose to prominence in his community when he allied with a young *mestizo narco* and sometime bandit known as El Towi, The Boy. They formed a mini-cartel to defend the interests of Tarahumara drug growers against the murderous local *narco*-timber baron, Artemio Fontes, who was El Towi's uncle. Isidro, his eyewitnesses, and Amnesty International all say that the police planted an AK-47, a pistol, and 230 grams of marijuana in his house when they arrested him, but at other times in his life these were the tools of his trade.

The Goldman money was all gone now. Isidro had given half of it to the Sierra Madre Alliance and spent the rest, mostly on pickup trucks that he had crashed and destroyed. He was working for Randy now as a grassroots organizer in threatened Tarahumara communities, but the two men had very different visions of what needed to be done.

"For me, ultimately, it all comes down to money," said Randy, as we all feasted together on roast kid goat in a Parral restaurant that night. "If we can get the funding, then we can do all the studies we need and get these areas internationally recognized as the most important biocultural treasures in North America. We can do sustainable agriculture workshops in native communities. We can build lodges for ecotourists and set up native-run sustainable forest management programs. We can get classes on shamanism into community schools—90 percent of children in Choreachi don't even have access to a school at the moment! We can set up women's craft cooperatives and start marketing organic native Tarahumara beans and selling them in whole-food stores in the States. We can save the forest and empower indigenous communities to keep native traditions and native spirituality alive, but in this world it takes millions of dollars."

Randy's vision was formed by the university classes he had taken and reinforced by the publications he read, the talk he heard at conferences and board meetings, the reigning orthodoxies and shibboleths of his field. Isidro's vision, which he explained to me a few days later, came out of his upbringing in the lawless *narco* zone of the Golden Triangle, and was reinforced by the lessons of the prison yard: "Randy has already spent crazy amounts of money on studies and workshops and programs and it has achieved nothing. We don't need more outsiders coming in and deciding what is best for us. I

already know what we need to do. We need to show these local bosses that we won't be taken advantage of. We must stand up to them
and force them to back down. Then they will leave us alone and we
can live as we want."

LEAVING PARRAL, WE passed Randy's favorite local landmark:
a children's amusement park built around a *narco* plane that had
crashed outside town. Randy and I had our differences of opinion.
He thought Mexico was slowly, painfully, awkwardly evolving into
a modern liberal democracy. I thought the whole nation was turning
more feral, violent, and chaotic, that the Sierra Madre held glimpses
of Mexico's future as well as its past. Randy thought I was overly
pessimistic and cynical, and I thought his bio-cultural development
plan had about as much chance of working in the Golden Triangle as
the American plan to install democracy in Iraq. But we enjoyed each
other's company and had become friends, partly because we shared a
similar appreciation for things like a children's amusement park built
around a wrecked drug plane.

"Apparently there's a gay mafioso in Parral who wears all-pink
norteño outfits and is said to be *muy cruel*," I offered.

"Wow, I don't know him. There was a *narco* around here called
El Guante, The Glove, which might be the best nickname I've ever
heard."

"It's right up there with El Cochi Loco, The Crazy Pig," I said,
referring to a particularly vicious Sinaloan drug lord who was dead
now.

"What are you going to do about Sinaloa?" asked Randy. "Do you
have any contacts there?"

"Not yet. Hopefully someone will lead to someone else who can
take me in there, because there's no way I'd go into those mountains
alone."

I had Randy's map open on my lap. In the Chihuahua part of the
Golden Triangle was a village called El Muerto, The Dead One, and
another called Mala Noche, Bad Night. But there were no names

on the Chihuahua map to rival Sinaloa's Mátalo, Kill Him, and this seemed significant. It fit in with everything I'd read and heard about the fiery temperament, touchy pride, and quickness on the trigger of the mountain Sinaloans.

As we climbed the eastern flanks of the Sierra, logging trucks came down past us in convoys, heavily laden with thick pines. "Pretty good-sized trees but that's all second growth, not much good to birds or wildlife," said Randy. "Wait till you see the old growth. There are some real giants up there like Lumholtz describes. He came right through Choreachi and was blown away by the trees."

The road was paved until the sawmill town of Yerbitas, where we stopped for lunch and filled up the back of the Suburban with sacks of beans, corn flour, cooking oil, and other supplies. Then we put it in four-wheel drive and turned north. First built by illegal loggers in 1991, the road to Pino Gordo was fifty-two miles long and usually took six or seven hours to drive, which was about standard traveling speed in the Sierra Madre.

We went for two hours without seeing another vehicle. Then two new pickups passed us in quick succession. Then we had the road to ourselves for another two hours, the big Suburban jouncing and jolting all the way. Through the roadside pines we caught glimpses of Cerro Mohinora, the highest peak in Chihuahua at 10,663 feet and second-highest in the Sierra Madre Occidental. To the southwest was Cerro Milpillas. This was a sacred peak to the Tepehuan Indians and nine of them were murdered there in the 1980s, for trying to keep loggers out. To the north was a huge expanse of mesas and *barrancas* with a few isolated forest fires burning, a common sight in the dry season.

We came to a sign painted in shaky red letters for the *narco* village of Barbechitos and soon afterward we entered the infamous *narco ejido* of Coloradas de las Chavez. One of Randy's colleagues, research-ing the municipal records, found thirty-three outstanding arrest warrants for murder against the *ejido* members of Coloradas de las Chavez. A newspaper article in *El Diario de Chihuahua* counted more than three hundred widows and orphans in a total population of a thousand. These were the murderous *narco*-hillbillies now scheming after the land and timber in Pino Gordo and we were the outside agitators crossing their territory. Fortunately the road stayed on the ridges and most of the people were living down in the swales and valleys. We met no other vehicles and saw only one man. He was a *mestizo* rancher with a mustache and a cowboy hat. He was standing in a plowed field and he gave us a ferocious Lee Van Cleef dagger-stare as we drove past.

On the far side of the *ejido* were the first views of Sinforosa Canyon. The sun was setting, plumes of smoke were rising from the far mesas, and I had never seen the Sierra look so dramatic and forbiddingly beautiful. "Once you've seen Sinforosa, the Grand Canyon never looks big again," said Randy. Measured north to south, or east to west, by the ruggedness of the landscape, the quantity of drug production, or the distance to the nearest police station, we couldn't have been any closer to the heart of the Sierra Madre.

Pino Gordo occupied a broad promontory of land that extended out into Sinforosa Canyon from its southern rim. It was dark when we got there with a high country chill in the pine-scented air. We drove over narrowing dirt tracks, took obscure unmarked turns and eventually came to an isolated log cabin with two aging but serviceable pickup trucks parked next to it. "Two trucks!" exclaimed Randy. "Wow, these guys must really be moving a lot of pot."

Two Tarahumara men came out of the cabin, followed by various women and children who took one look and went back inside. We exchanged soft courtesies and pleasantries, caught up on the news—there would be a big meeting tomorrow about the logging—then one of the men led us across a cornfield to another cabin where we could stay.

"We'll be safe here," said Randy. "No one messes with these guys. They're like the brokers for the Tarahumara growers in the area. They're good at dealing with the *mestizo narcos* who come here trying to swindle the Indians out of their crops."

Isidro knew all about that from Coloradas de la Virgen. "Once we had fifteen kilos of *mota* and the *narco* said if we packed it on mules across the *barranca* to Guachochi, he would give us a truck and five machine guns for it," he said. "It's a two-day journey because you have to be very careful and travel very early in the morning, then a little in the afternoon at siesta time, then a little more at night, then five hours across the mesa to Guachochi. We get there and the *narco* has an old, old car with oil leaking out all over the place and no machine guns. This is how it is in the Sierra. It's easier for them to kill you and take what you have than pay you what it's worth. This is why you must establish your reputation as a man that people do not take advantage of."

Isidro went into the cabin with Pedro and Prudencio. Randy and I started pitching our tents outside. "How many people are growing here?" I asked him.

"I think nearly everyone except for Prudencio and the elders. I'm not sure about Pedro."

"And of their own free will?"

"Oh yeah. In other parts of the Sierra you had guys from Sinaloa coming in and forcing Tarahumaras to grow or else. In Coloradas de la Virgen, Artemio Fontes was killing Tarahumaras who didn't want to grow, or wanted more money than he was paying them. But not here. The problem they have here is the army. The *mestizos* in Coloradas de las Chavez get left alone and the soldiers come over here and cut down all the Tarahumara opium and marijuana they can find."

"So why don't you raise the money and make the connections so these people can pay off the army and live as free and independent dope farmers? Isn't that what they want?"

"Hah! That's actually not a bad idea but I can't see my donors and board members going for it."

The cabin had a low doorway, loose dirt floors, and two rooms divided by a wooden door. We stacked up the food in the front room, as a gift to our hosts, then opened the door to see our three Tarahumara companions sitting on a brand-new couch with the plastic covering left on. Their faces were blank and their eyes were glued to a small black-and-white television hooked up to a car battery. It was the first couch or television that Randy had ever seen in Pino Gordo.

The picture was a pale fuzz with darker moving shapes. At first the sound was white noise, but listening more closely we realized it was an American football game broadcast in English and the dark shapes were the players. An hour and a half later the Tarahumaras were still glued to it. Let no one doubt the power of television.

THE NEXT MORNING we were walking through the forest on the way to the meeting when a pickup truck rumbled into view and stopped about fifty yards away. Two *mestizos* with white cowboy hats got out simultaneously and started walking down the trail toward us. "Who are those goat-bastards?" I hissed in a panic. "What do they want with us?"

"No, no," said our host, smiling. "They are good people. They are friends of a man from here who is in prison. They are looking after his opium field. In this way the man can still feed his family."

The opium gardeners went by with a wary nod.

"Is the man in prison for growing?"

"No, he killed a man at a *tesguinada*. It wasn't his fault."

"Why not?"

"He was drunk."

This I had read about. The Tarahumara believe that the body and mind are controlled by a group of souls of various sizes and capabilities. When a person drinks *tesguino,* the biggest soul, the one responsible for the proper functioning of the brain and large physical movements, leaves the body because it doesn't like the sour milky smell. This is why drunks say stupid things and have poor balance and also why a man who kills someone when drunk is not considered responsible for his actions. His main soul had left his body.

"Usually they don't report killings that happen at *tesguinadas,*" said Randy. "If the killer goes to prison, that leaves two families that need supporting. So what they do instead is make the killer support the victim's family so he has to work twice as hard."

"How often do these killings happen?"

"It's pretty commonplace, unfortunately. The guy who did it usually feels terrible about it the next day."

We walked on through the forest. Stupidly, I had been expecting it to look like the protected old-growth forests I had seen north of the border, where almost no one lived, all human activity was strictly regulated, and something close to wilderness had been preserved. This forest was keeping nearly a thousand poor, hungry people alive. There were indeed some impressively fat pines, although the Tarahumaras had cut down a lot of the biggest ones because they made the best roofing shakes for their cabins. There was a healthy bird population, including some rare ones like thick-billed parrots and trogons that depended on old trees, but the Tarahumaras had hunted out or scared away most of the mammal life—in three days I didn't see a single squirrel—and the land was brutally overgrazed by their goat herds and scarred with erosion.

Randy had set up and financed many workshops and programs intended to make Tarahumara farming practices less destructive to the land, and they had all foundered on the question of corn and goats. Tarahumaras will sacrifice a goat when they determine that God is angry or hungry. They will eat goats on special occasions but they don't keep the animals for their meat or milk. Instead, they use them to fertilize their cornfields, penning up the goats overnight on one patch of the field, harvesting the manure, letting them out to graze the next morning, usually with a small child to herd them, and then penning them on an adjacent patch the next night.

"It's really not an efficient system and if they would only rotate their crops instead of just planting corn, corn, corn, year after year, they wouldn't even need all the fucking goatshit," said Randy, laughing and flushing red with frustration at the same time. In another Tarahumara community called Caborachi, his volunteers had set up a test project on a struggling farmer's land, rotating beans and corn and intercropping winter vetch to fertilize the soil. The man tripled his yields, the whole community saw it, and the next year, despite the offer of free seeds and volunteer labor, they all continued with corn and goats, including the farmer whose yields had tripled.

"Randy, you can't discount culture. They're very conservative, stubborn people and suspicious of outsiders. That's how they've managed to stay Tarahumara."

"I know, but they're also a practical people. I mean, they didn't have any trouble adjusting to pot and opium. They were new crops brought in by outsiders. If we can just show them that a few small changes will really benefit their lives . . ."

So we proceeded, two white men yammering away in English about who the Tarahumara really were and what was best for them. We emerged from the forest and came down into the center of Choreachi. Once it had been a mountain meadow. Now it was a goat-ravaged dustbowl containing a handful of small buildings and a crowd of people gathered in the shade of their crumbling walls. A few old men were still wearing loincloths. Many younger men were wearing marijuana-leaf caps or belt buckles. The women and girls were all dressed traditionally with the frequent addition of fuzzy yellow or pink acrylic socks.

The long wait began. A young man with a pistol in his jeans and a rooster-patterned shirt ambled over and asked if I wanted to buy *mota*. A small boy chased a runaway piglet to general amusement. Pedro walked up to me and shook my hand. I felt something wriggle and opened my hand and there was a horny toad blinking at me. Pedro grinned his winning grin, and then I played the same trick on a boy of eight or nine and had to stop him from killing it.

Randy and I went for a walk and found the peyote shaman plowing a cornfield behind two oxen. He was an old man in a loincloth and a blue suit jacket, walking with a pronounced limp. He took a wrong turn in the dark one night last year, fell into a ravine, and broke two bones in his leg. Randy found him half-crippled two months later, got him to the hospital, and paid the doctors to fix his leg. That was why the shaman had invited Randy and a guest to the peyote ceremony. As to when that ceremony might be, the shaman shrugged and stared out across the land.

The meeting got under way in mid-afternoon in the usual Tarahumara fashion. People stood up and gathered in a circle. The men took off their hats. The governor made a speech in Tarahumara and Isidro translated it for us into Spanish: "We are sad because we are the owners of those trees, not those people over there, and they are cutting down so many trees. We want this logging stopped. We want those men to leave. The women are afraid because those men have guns."

After the governor's speech, people voiced their comments and opinions, shouting them out with a stylized formality. They marked their thumbprints in a school exercise book to record their objections to a family that had moved onto *ejido* land without permission. The governor called for four witnesses to go to the authorities in Guadalupe Y Calvo and say they had seen Prudencio's armed kidnapping. He didn't seem overly particular about whether the witnesses had actually seen it or not.

Randy gave a speech in Spanish: "With your permission, I will go to New York, Washington, D.C., and London and invite biologists, researchers, and organizations to come here and bring money to help you."

Isidro said it was very important to be organized and united and fight the enemy on all fronts. The governor asked me to say what I was doing there and I said I would be writing about their struggle and hoped that the whole world would learn of the injustices done against them, and put pressure on the Mexican government to set them straight. I felt like a fraudulent windbag, but I couldn't say what I really thought, that it was too late and their struggle was doomed no matter what I wrote, or how much money Randy raised, or what they did or didn't do. Their enemies were simply stronger and more cunning, with more powerful allies in the courts and the government, and the forces of capital and history on their side.

What I didn't understand until later that day was that they considered their most effective enemy to be the commissioner of their own *ejido,* a Tarahumara born in Pino Gordo called Raul Aguirre. They maintained that through an incredibly byzantine series of maneuvers, Raul had succeeded in legally moving the boundary lines of Pino Gordo so that 95 percent of its timber reserves were ceded to the *ejido* of Coloradas de las Chavez, where his associates held the logging concession. It wasn't *mestizos* from Coloradas de las Chavez who had kidnapped Prudencio at gunpoint, as I had assumed, but Raul Aguirre's Tarahumara supporters in Pino Gordo. It was a bitterly divided community and only the anti-Raul faction were at the meeting.

The governor closed the meeting with a few remarks on other topics. He knew the people had very little corn to make *tesguino* but God was not in agreement with *teporoche* (a rough liquor made from sugar and baker's yeast) because it made people fight. He called for a big fiesta to bring the rains. They would sacrifice a bull and put its heart on a cross and the rain would come and soon they would have corn again to make *tesguino*. This would please God and he would bring more rain.

Then the meeting was adjourned. The gambling and the kickball races began. People were soon cracking jokes and laughing, chatting, grinning, and yelling encouragement and good-natured abuse at the runners, their troubles temporarily forgotten or moved aside, their habitual reserve and silence suspended.

"*Heh-heh-heh!* Look at that old donkey trying to run."

"*Ho-ho-ho!* He'd better run faster or his grandmother will catch him."

"*Hah-hah-hah!* Run, donkey! Your grandmother is after you!"

RANDY AND I wanted to see the logging damage. Prudencio lived nearby so we gave him a lift and loaded in a few sacks of food to keep him going through the dry season. When the logging trucks came into view, Randy parked the Suburban, got out, and started taking photographs with his big, long-lensed camera. The drivers of the logging trucks didn't look happy about this and neither did I, but Randy wanted to show that he wasn't intimidated and they were under outside scrutiny. We drove on and photographed some stumps and freshly bulldozed logging roads. I was expecting a clear-cut horror show but this was fairly selective logging, done with an eye to future timber harvests if not endangered bird species.

On the way back we found the road blocked off by two pickup trucks. Each truck had seven or eight young Tarahumara men standing in the bed and looking hostile. At the wheel of the lead truck was the logging contractor from Coloradas de las Chavez, a tall pale-skinned *mestizo* with glittering hazel eyes. Sitting beside him was the notorious Tepehuan *pistolero*, who looked as if he could hardly wait to carve out our livers and start chewing on them.

"Where are you going?" said the *mestizo,* with no preliminary courtesies. "What are you doing here?"

"We're giving our friend a ride to his house," said Randy, gesturing to Prudencio.

"Then what?"

"We will look at the *barranca.*"

"This land belongs to Coloradas de las Chavez. You are here without permission. What are you doing here?"

"I have just told you that. Now we will be going."

Randy drove off the road and swung around them. He's been coming here for fifteen years and he hasn't gotten himself killed yet, I thought. He must know what he's doing. But mostly I thought fuck-fuckfuck. As I knew they would, the two trucks turned around and followed us.

We reached the gate of Prudencio's *rancho,* high on the rim of Sinforosa Canyon. We got out and started unloading the sacks of food. They pulled up in front of us, got out of their trucks, and there was another exchange.

"I don't mean to bother you but there has been a lot of trouble here with men with guns," said the *mestizo* with a sneering mock politeness. We all knew the men with guns were on his side of the conflict and none of us had any doubt there were guns in those two trucks.

"Also a bulldozer was burned, and a man kidnapped and taken to jail, so we wanted to ask what you were doing here."

"We are delivering food to our friend's house," said Randy. "We are invited guests and we have every right to be here and I'm sure you understand that if anything happens to us here, it will make a lot of trouble for you."

Isidro stepped forward and announced his full name and they exchanged glances and nodded among themselves. We stood there for a few moments in a real, honest-to-god Mexican standoff and then the *mestizo* smiled a cynical smile and said, "Well, I wish you a pleasant visit and I'm sure you understand why we have to be careful. Apparently there are some bad men in the area."

The Tepehuan killer glowered at us. The fifteen Tarahumaras glowered at us. The *mestizo* shook our hands and wished us well and walked back to his truck and they all drove off. Randy watched their dust and said, "Man, it's a good thing they weren't drunk or coked-up. Did you see that fucking Tepehuan? Jesus, what an evil-looking motherfucker. Prudencio, do you know the Tepehuan?"

"He is a very bad man," said Prudencio. "They say he has killed many people."

I said, "Fuck." My vocabulary had yet to rebound in either language.

We carried the sacks of food down to the cabin. A ninety-year-old man came out to greet us, wearing a loincloth, a blue suit jacket, and a tall-crowned cowboy hat. This was Prudencio's father. There was a feather hanging from the roof of his cabin, dogs and chickens wandering around, a pen of goats on a plowed cornfield, and an eighty-mile view across Sinforosa Canyon and the mesas behind it. Prudencio's father went back inside and came out with a plastic bucket of *tesguino* and a gourd. Women and children emerged. A young man came walking down a trail and joined us.

We took our hats off while he threw a gourdful of *tesguino* to the east, west, north, and south. He poured another one on the ground for God and uttered a benediction of some kind in a hoarse croak. Then we were each handed a gourd in turn and expected to drink it down in one swallow. This was not easily done. It was a particularly thick batch of *tesguino,* clogged with chunks of cornhusk that you had to strain out with your teeth and then spit on the ground. An eight-year-old boy drank his *tesguino* along with us. A young mother gave a few sips to her baby.

We drank four or five gourds each and got nicely buzzed there on the rim of Sinforosa Canyon and it occurred to me that this was more or less the moment I had been looking for when I set out on this journey. Here I was in the heart of the Sierra Madre, about as far from consumer capitalism and the comfortably familiar as I could get, drinking *tesguino* with a wizened old Tarahumara and feeling that edgy, excited pleasure in being alive that follows a bad scare. It was an uncomfortable realization. To put it another way, here I was getting my kicks and curing my ennui in a place full of poverty and suffering, environmental and cultural destruction, widows and or-phans from a slow-motion massacre. I tried to persuade myself that I was going to write something that would make a difference and help these people, but my capacity for self-delusion refused to stretch in that direction.

RANDY HAD TO get back to Chihuahua City. One of these days he was going to come up here for two or three weeks and just hike and camp and meditate but there was no time for that now. His last-ditch plan was to go to the government and try to get negotations under way for an indemnification. It was a hideously complicated process but the basic idea was to buy out Choreachi from Coloradas de las Chavez using donor money, give ownership of the land to the anti-Raul faction, and then turn it into a biocultural preserve and eco-tourism destination.

"Randy . . ." I said.

"Hey, I know it's a long shot but I've got to try. What do you do when you're in a leaky boat in the middle of the ocean? You keep on bailing."

We drove the eight hours to Guadalupe Y Calvo, an old mining town that was the capital of the municipality and considerably calm-er than it used to be in the *narco* heydays of the 1980s and early 1990s, when traffic couldn't move because the streets were so clogged with brand-new trucks, and forty flights a day ferried in alcohol, musicians, fine clothes, cocaine, and cash, and flew out opium and marijuana. One *narco* party in 1994, I had read, took over the town for fifteen days straight, with a sore-lipped brass band from Sinaloa playing from early afternoon until the break of dawn every night.

Randy caught a bus and my tour of the Golden Triangle continued under Isidro's guidance. The plan was to go north to Baborigame, where Isidro's wife lived and where the Sierra Madre Alliance had been trying to do something for all the displaced Tepehuans in the area, then on to Coloradas de la Virgen to see where Isidro grew up and the remains of the old-growth forest that had been logged there. Most of the Tarahumaras had moved out of the area now. It was climate change as much as anything. There had been twelve drought years in the last fifteen and it was becoming impossible for subsistence farmers to keep themselves alive. Of all the problems and challenges the Tarahumara were up against, this was the most intractable.

The first thing that happened with Randy gone was that Isidro started drinking four or five six-packs of beer a day, from breakfast onward. It appeared to be a custom of the country. The restaurants were full of men drinking beer with their eggs in the morning. I never saw Isidro sloppy drunk but he did get domineering at times and deliver many repetitive, self-justifying monologues, lengthy denunciations of his foes and critics, and testaments to his own machismo.

The second thing that happened was the Suburban kept breaking down. You'd be driving along and the engine would splutter to a halt and refuse to start again. If you sat there and waited for half an hour, then it would start and you might get twenty minutes of driving before it died again. The three-hour drive to Baborigame, known locally as Babori-goma, *goma* being opium, took ten hours, including a stop-off at a ranch in the middle of nowhere so that Isidro could flirt with some young, frightened Tepehuan girls. This was all Northern Tepehuan country in Lumholtz's day but *mestizo* loggers, ranchers, and drug growers had taken over most of it.

"All along this road here, in all the valleys, there would be opium poppies as far as you could see," said Isidro, referring wistfully to the golden age in the 1980s and early 1990s, when there was almost no law enforcement, the planes were flying in untold millions of dollars, and the homicide rate was going through the roof. Why did drug cultivation increase the murder rate? "Because drugs give people money to buy guns, alcohol, and cocaine," said Isidro.

He didn't think that statement required any elaboration but I asked him to elaborate anyway. "People get more aggressive and paranoid. They kill more easily and then the dead man's family has to avenge the killings. Near Coloradas, there are whole communities that have wiped themselves out in feuds in this way."

I was reading a fascinating book with a similar thesis. Its title translates as *The Sierra Tarahumara, A Wounded Land, The Culture of Violence in the Drug-Producing Zones*. Its author, a professor in Juárez called Carlos Mario Alvarado Licón, based his ideas on prison interviews conducted with convicted murderers from the Sierra. He found that they were nearly all model prisoners, with no prior criminal record, and no remorse or regret for what they had done. Except in cases where they had killed family members, they told of their crimes "serenely" and were convinced they had done the right thing.

> In the Sierra homicide is no dishonor. Killing is a part of life, a circumstantial action, generally vengeance for another killing. However, on occasion it is a symbol of pride, when vengeance was done and the law taken into one's own hands. . . . Homicide is a form of maintaining the social order where the official authority is absent, unjust or corrupt, and particularly where it fails to punish aggression or offense to the family.

These are not traditional Tarahumara or Tepehuan principles but they had picked them up through exposure to the *mestizo* culture. When Isidro's father was killed, his mother implored him to take vengeance. "It was very hard, but I decided not to because if I avenged my father, I would end up losing my brothers and maybe my uncles. It wouldn't bring back my father and would bring more sorrow into my family. My mother didn't understand. She never really forgave me."

Baborigame was an ominous, grim-looking town in a wide valley with heavily logged mountains around it. When Randy first came here in the early 1990s, there was no law, no electricity, and a killing almost every night. Arriving on a small plane, he encountered a gut-shot man waiting by the airstrip, holding in his intestines with a dinner plate. Then he went to a dance where the men were all dancing with AK-47s and Uzis in their hands. Now electricity had reached Baborigame, along with the army and state and federal police, and men no longer went armed. As usual, the arrival of the law, although it was thoroughly corrupt, had resulted in a decline in the murder rate in town, an increase in the murder rate out in the ranches, and a slump in the standard of living.

The torrent of money that had flowed through Baborigame in the 1980s and 1990s had left almost no traces. The streets were unpaved and deeply potholed. The drains didn't work. Aside from a few *narco* houses with bright paintwork and fancy wrought-iron fences, people lived in squalid shacks and adobes. All the money had been spent on guns, trucks, alcohol, fancy clothes, and cocaine, with almost nothing invested in infrastructure or local businesses.

Most long journeys have their sour, depressive times and mine arrived with a vengeance in Baborigame. I was tired and run down and my body ached all over from being rattled and jolted. The constant breaking down of the Suburban wasn't helping but what I really lost tolerance for, as I chauffeured Isidro on his rounds, met his friends, and dodged his enemies, was Mexican machismo. I came to hate it with as much venom as the most strident lesbian feminist. It was the root of the worst evil in Mexico, I decided, the real reason why men killed each other and raped women in such horrifying numbers. Not that those numbers were available. According to Mary Jordan of the *Washington Post,* fewer than 1 percent of rapes are reported in Mexico, because it is not treated seriously as a crime and because rape victims who do go to the police are usually mocked and blamed for inviting the crime, and are sometimes raped by the police, who get aroused hearing the victim's story.

In the Sierra Madre the practice known as *rapto,* where a man kidnaps a girl and forces her to marry him, is still commonplace. Raping an underage girl is not against the law in many Mexican states if the rapist marries her. This is what happened to Chana, a friend of Isidro from Coloradas de la Virgen who was now living in Baborigame. Raped at fifteen and made pregnant, she had to marry the rapist so he could help her to raise the child. This was the code of the mountains but it didn't make for happy marriages. She had another child with her rapist-husband and then he was murdered, leaving her with two children to raise.

Driving around Baborigame with Isidro was a procession of murder sites—"Here was where El Towi was killed. A drunk Tepehuan walked up to his truck and shot him for no reason"—and long-suffering women. Since Baborigame has the same stupid, counterproductive alcohol laws as Urique, a lot of these women were selling bootlegged beer. You would come into the front room and there was always a TV blaring and it was usually broadcasting a game show with a man dressed as a woman, squawking and shrieking, while the bootlegger's children watched solemnly from a ratty old couch with the smell of tortillas and sewage from the bad drains. A wood-burning stove in the kitchen, vinyl on the kitchen table. Pictures on the walls of the Swiss Alps and the Virgin of Guadalupe. A sad, tired, worn-out woman trudging over to the fridge, trying to make ends meet by selling beer to the same drunk machos who had wrecked her life.

On we jolted through the humped streets. A donkey with its ears cut off or perhaps frozen off in a bad winter was drinking from a filthy stream. Three drunk Tepehuans were passed out underneath a beer advertisement that read, "Always In Moderation." Periodically, Isidro would have to duck down in the passenger seat to avoid being seen by someone who wanted to kill him. Another truck pulled up alongside us with another shit-faced drunk at the wheel. "Isidro!" he yelled. "We are sons of the grand raped mother! We are sons of obscene perpetrations! Come drink with me! You, *gringo,* you drink with me too." And these offers had to be declined with the greatest politeness and delicacy because as Professor Licón puts it, "To refuse a drink of liquor from someone that has cost all their salary or savings to impress their friends is almost a declaration of war, a very serious discourtesy and many times an insult that ends in tragedy . . . wounded masculine dignity is the most important motivation to explain the great number of killings in the Sierra."

"In a world of *chingónes* . . ." wrote Octavio Paz, "ruled by violence and suspicion—a world in which no one opens out or surrenders himself—ideas and accomplishments count for little. The only thing of value is manliness, personal strength, a capacity for imposing oneself on others."

We went to Isidro's wife's house where his sister, also abandoned by a man, was living with four or five children. Isidro sat down like a potentate and started ordering the women around. "Go get my beer from the truck," although he could have so easily brought it in himself. There was a foul reek coming from a pot of stew on the stove and although I said I had just eaten, Isidro's wife set down a bowl of it in front of me, and I had to stifle a retch with the first mouthful. I tried crushing dried chillies into it. I tried chewing the meat, but there was just no way to break it down and it was a constant struggle not to retch too visibly. I don't know where that meat came from, perhaps an old diseased donkey who drowned in a sewer and was dragged out and left to dry in the sun for a month.

We got the Suburban fixed and set out for Coloradas de la Virgen, but the Suburban broke down again on the mountain backroads. That was where we encountered the state policeman in the forty-thousand-dollar Lincoln LT truck who knew of Johnny Mula and said he had settled down on a ranch with a Mexican woman. Isidro knew the *judicial* and I had the distinct impression they used to do business together. We drove ten minutes and broke down for another twenty. It was one in the afternoon and Isidro, already into his third six-pack of the day, with a semi-abandoned wife and three girlfriends, one of them pregnant and twenty years old, went into a long insistent tirade about the perfidy of women. They were all jealous, he said, and they would all cheat on you given half a chance. "If you came home and found your woman with another man, what would you do?" he asked me. "Would you kill her?"

"No. I'd leave the house and leave the woman, probably. In my country, if you killed a woman you would get caught and go to prison for a very long time."

"Here no," he said flatly. "If your woman is with another man, you kill her. It is easy to not get caught. The police don't care because there is no money in it for them and they would do the same if it was their woman."

THEN FINALLY WE were in a minivan at dawn, leaving loathsome Baborigame and the whoremothering Suburban behind, heading down into Sinforosa Canyon. The driver and the passengers were talking about the bandits who had held up the van last week and raped a woman by the side of the road a few months ago. We crossed the river and switchbacked up the other side. A few hours more and we reached the wretched shithole of Guachochi, which was full of *narco* trucks, staggering drunk Tarahumaras, and sons of obscene perpetrations, with dead dogs lying in the gutters and wanted posters on the telephone poles of murderers and kidnappers with fantastically evil faces.

Before catching the bus to Chihuahua City, I insisted that we go to Cumbres de Sinforosa, which Randy had described as *narco-Disneylandia* and said was not to be missed. *Cumbres* means summit or overlook and the local *narco* had built a kind of tourist resort there on the rim of the canyon. First we reached a collection of stables, warehouses, and immaculate gardens with peacocks on the lawns, all sealed off from the public behind wrought-iron fences and security gates. Then we drove down a wide boulevard with electric lights to a paved overlook with cabins, gazebos, and wandering donkeys. It wasn't until we reached the very edge and looked down into that gigantic sun-scorched chasm that we saw the *pièce de résistance:* an artificial ski slope bulldozed down into the canyon and carpeted with white Astroturf.

16

The Centaur of the North

ISIDRO HAD TO GET back to Chihuahua City. He was out of money and clean clothes and his pregnant girlfriend kept calling him. I needed to get back there too. My truck was parked outside the Sierra Madre Alliance offices and it was time to be moving south, although I was a little vague on the details of where and how. I had no contacts in the next three hundred miles of mountains but I felt sure that something would work out if I went in there alone and was careful. We caught a second-class bus from Guachochi and eight hours later, having endured a lot more beery advice from Isidro on how to treat women, I shook his hand good-bye, thanked him for his help, and walked away with a rush of relief.

The next morning I checked my email and the next phase of my journey started to take shape. Ruben Ruiz, last seen hobbling away from a runaway mule wreck at the northern end of the Sierra, had tracked down a cousin in Sinaloa. She was a teacher in the coastal city of Los Mochis and had persuaded an English teacher and one of her former students to take me up to their respective home villages in the Sinaloa mountains. This was exciting, dramatic, unexpected news and it trumped all the justifications that had been building up in my mind for sliding past Sinaloa with a nod and a wave and hot-footing it down to the Huichol country at the southern finish line, where I did have some contacts lined up.

Los Mochis was on the west side of the mountains. Chihuahua City was on the east side. The train was the fast, easy way to get there but I was in no hurry. Ruben's cousin said it would take two or three weeks to complete the arrangements. So I decided to drive down through Durango and then take the Devil's Backbone over to Sinaloa. This was the other paved road that crossed the Sierra Madre: El Espinazo Del Diablo. It was supposed to be a vertigo-sufferer's nightmare, twisting and turning along a narrow ridge between two yawning *barrancas,* but otherwise safe to travel.

I knew no one in the entire state of Durango but I didn't feel unduly concerned about traveling there alone. Surely the fact that I had made it this far was proof that the Sierra Madre wasn't as dangerous as people said, that the threat from bandits and killers was greatly overblown, that warnings were ten a penny and an outsider could easily make it through on his own if he was careful and comported himself like a gentleman.

And for once I had some confidence in my cover story. I would be a writer researching a book about Pancho Villa, Durango's most famous son. According to my guidebook, Villa was still revered and hero-worshipped all over the state and visitors should be careful not to say anything against him. So presumably a writer whose deep admiration for Villa had brought him all the way across the ocean from England, to see the sites where the great man had made history, would be met with general approval and perhaps outpourings of hospitality. To buttress my disguise, and because I was genuinely intrigued by the Shakespearean dimensions and complexities of Villa's character, I was carrying nine books about him in my traveling library.

My first stop was Canutillo and the old stone hacienda where Villa lived from July 1920 to July 20, 1923. That was the day he went to the bank in Parral in his beloved black Dodge and was ambushed by assassins. As he lay there full of bullet holes his last words were, "Don't let it end like this. Tell them I said something."

He was killed for reasons that are still murky and debated but probably traceable to President Obregón. The revolution was over and Villa was in retirement. He was breeding fighting cocks and running his agricultural estate at Canutillo with the same iron-fisted discipline that he had imposed on his troops. He said he wanted to farm in peace but he had more than eight thousand rifles, half a million cartridges, and a large supply of bombs and hand grenades at Canutillo, which seemed a little excessive for home defense, even for a man with as many enemies as Pancho Villa, "hated by thousands and loved by millions," as he liked to put it. Obregón, who had emerged victorious from the vicious round of internecine wars, betrayals, and assassinations among the various revolutionary leaders, may have feared that Villa had another uprising left in him and played it safe by ordering his old rival killed.

I was the only visitor that afternoon. The nearby village was deep in siesta and the only sound was the hot dry wind in the trees. Carved in stone by the entrance was an inscription about Villa: "Warrior of my fatherland, fist of the people, colt of fire, cry of the darkening storm, roaring avalanche, may your memory burn and your name crackle . . . gallop for us in your shining phosphorescence raising your flag."

The hacienda was an imposing fortlike building with a chapel tower and a large interior courtyard, looking out over rolling hills, green irrigated fields, and a winding river lined with trees. Behind the hacienda the hills soon turned into ridges and mountains. Villa must have felt secure here with the Sierra Madre at his back. From his earliest days as an outlaw, it had always been his place of refuge and escape, and I suspect he knew its trails and hiding places, from southern Durango to the U.S. border, as well as anyone who has ever lived.

He was born on a hacienda on the central plains of Durango. His parents were *peones,* feudal serfs, and they named him Doroteo Arango Arambula. He fled to the mountains for the first time at the age of sixteen, after shooting the master of the hacienda in the foot for trying to rape his younger sister, or so the dubious story goes in his memoirs, unsupported by any police reports or arrest warrants in the municipal records. In the Sierra he joined a well-known and successful bandit gang, changed his name to Francisco "Pancho" Villa, and learned the arts of armed robbery, cattle rustling, horse thieving, bribing local officials and corrupt judges, and running, hiding, and shooting it out with the *rurales,* the rural police. They were often former bandits themselves, tough, ruthless, and expert in tracking down men in the mountains and taking them unawares, the predecessors of the mule-mounted *judiciales* who so impressed Joe Brown. Villa didn't know it at the time, but he was also getting an education in the arts of guerrilla warfare.

Many years later, after Villa invaded the United States in a vengeful fury and sacked and burned the town of Columbus, New Mexico, a so-called "punitive expedition" was sent after him with ten thousand U.S. troops under the command of General Pershing. Like Geronimo before him, Villa went up into the Sierra Madre where no one was a match for him. Pershing spent eleven months chasing him before turning around ignominiously and going home. "They came here like eagles," Villa observed. "And they left like wet hens."

Inside the hacienda was a small museum with photographs of Villa slumped over backward and spilling out of his Dodge, Villa dead on a hospital bed with his clothes removed and the bloodstained bullet holes clearly visible. Some of his saddles were on display, along with his Victrola, his hatstand, and a bust of Rodolfo Fierro, aka "El Carnicero" (The Butcher), the cool sadistic Sinaloan who was his chief executioner, although Villa was no slouch in this department. God knows how many men they executed between them. And it wasn't only men. During one of his rages, Villa ordered ninety women killed by firing squad in the town of Camargo, for consorting with enemy Carrancistas.

Villa's domestic life at Canutillo was complicated, to say the least. He had married twenty-six times, although some of those marriages were short-lived. Once they were consummated he often had his men destroy the records. Now that he was settling down, he wanted his children to live with him but they were scattered far and wide. He rounded up three sons and four daughters from the surrounding area, separating them from their mothers because he had a new wife. She was Austreberta Rentería, an attractive, young middle-class woman from Chihuahua who had been kidnapped by The Ear-Cutter, one of Villa's more brutal commanders, and offered to him as the spoils of war. Villa admitted during a newspaper interview that he had raped Austreberta the first time they met, and then wept alongside her afterward and proposed marriage, saying, "You are not like other women."

Austreberta was the "official wife" at Canutillo and bore Villa two more children. Also living here was a melancholy semiofficial wife called Soledad Seañez (Villa had killed her fiancé) and Villa's first wife, Luz Corral, although he kicked her out after a while and refused to support her. Then there was Manuela Casas, a mistress who lived nearby and also bore him a child. In interviews, Villa's wives repeat the same themes. He could be a wonderfully tender romantic lover or a cruel tyrant, depending on his mood, but he was unfailingly kind, loving, and attentive to the children—not just his own children but all children.

The outbuildings were starting to crumble around the old hacienda but I was glad to see that the school that Villa built had been modernized and was still in use. Villa, who learned most of what he knew about reading and writing in prison, had always regretted not getting any schooling himself and education was one of his passions. At the apogee of his power, when he ruled Chihuahua like a warlord, printing money, bullying the press, usurping haciendas and selling off their cattle to the *gringos* to pay his troops, he also built more than one hundred schools.

Shortly after he and Zapata converged on Mexico City in 1914 and Villa, a lifelong teetotaler, choked on his victory swallow of brandy, he met a boy in the street whose father hadn't been sending him to school. Villa summoned the father and threatened to shoot him for this offense. The father said that he needed his son to help him gather corn so the family could eat. Villa was having none of it:

> I know nothing about your corn, Señor. But you can be sure that my men will hunt you out and shoot you if that son of yours and his brothers do not go to school. Don't you know that we are fighting the Revolution so that every Mexican child may go to school?

If the greed of the rich deprived you of schooling, as it did me, and so you are unable to support yourself or your family, then steal, Señor, steal whatever you need to send your son to school. If you steal for that reason, I will not shoot you, I will reward you; but if in not stealing you allow your son to stay away from school and follow the road of misfortune and crime, I will shoot you for that.

—Martín Luis Guzmán, *Memoirs of Pancho Villa*

From Canutillo I drove southwest, deeper into the mountains, to the village of San José del Tizonazo and Villa's favorite shrine. He was not a religious man and thought priests were thieves and leeches on the poor, but he would visit the shrine to ask supernatural favors from a saint called The Lord of the Warriors.

There was hardly any traffic on the roads and the sky was full of towering gorgeous cloud formations with shafts of light coming down between them. Vehicles were outnumbered by cowboys on horseback, wearing low-crowned, wide-brimmed hats with almost no curl at the sides. I had never been to Durango before and it threw me into a state of postmodern confusion. It looked so much like the Old West. Was this because the landscape was so similar to parts of West Texas, New Mexico, and Colorado but without the telephone poles, power lines, and billboards? Or was it because so many Hollywood westerns had been filmed on location in Durango for that reason? Sam Peckinpah made *The Wild Bunch* and *Pat Garrett and Billy the Kid* here. John Wayne was in four movies filmed in Durango and bought a ranch here. Farther south I was planning to visit the fake Old West towns that had been built as movie sets.

The use of cow skulls as gate ornaments is a long-established tradition all over northern Mexico and the American West. But at the El Congo ranch, in a remote mountain valley near San José del Tizonazo, they had hacked the head off a cow and hung that on the gate, leaving the wind and the sun and the flies to make a skull out of it. The eyelids had shriveled away but the eyeballs were still there, giving the thing a ghoulish look of wide-eyed horror.

The village was founded by the Jesuits in 1607 as an outpost among the Tepehuans and was now drought-stricken and dying, populated only by a few old men, mothers and children. The men had all gone north to find work in the United States. The village was kept alive by the money they sent back and the annual pilgrimage to the shrine of El Señor de los Guerreros, The Lord of the Warriors, plus the occasional off-season visitor like me.

I parked outside the 350-year-old church and hungry-looking children swarmed my truck, chanting, "Help me, help me! Sir, please help me!" I gave them some candies and pens and one- and two-peso coins. They looked grudgingly satisfied. An earnest solemn boy with a withered arm said he would watch my truck for ten pesos and make sure no one stole anything while I was inside. He assured me he was a good truck-watcher who could be trusted and not like some. I advanced him five pesos and went inside.

First I came to a wall with locks and braids of hair pinned to it, notes of thanks, babies' shoes, ladies' gloves, an artificial plastic foot, curling photographs of the grateful and the needy, and several signed publicity photographs of various cowboy-suited *norteño* bands, one of them holding AK-47s and scowling fiercely at the camera. Then I walked down the nave to the altar. The Lord of the Warriors was a bleeding, haggard Christ-like figure and he was wearing a white silky garment that hung just above his knees and looked like a woman's slip or petticoat.

But why? Why not wrap some cloth around his hips? In the adjoining gift shop, there was a photograph of El Señor wearing a similar garment with a lacy pink border. There had to be a simple logical explanation. I didn't know what it was, but I refused to believe that Pancho Villa's favorite saint was a cross-dresser.

THE SHADOWS WERE lengthening and one of my basic rules of travel in Mexico is don't drive after dark if you can avoid it. I've had too many close calls on narrow roads with drunk drivers, truck drivers with broken headlights, cavernous potholes that you can't see until it's too late, wandering cows, horses, donkeys, and pedestrians. I needed to find a hotel and Santa María del Oro was the nearest good-sized town.

I arrived at sunset, passing a couple of lurid *narco*-mansions on the edge of town, and found a hotel with secure parking opposite the plaza. It was Mother's Day and an outdoor concert and political rally had been laid on by the PRI, the so-called Institutional Revolutionary Party that ruled Mexico as an authoritarian kleptocracy for seventy-one years, until the election of Vicente Fox in 2000. The streets were closed off and about two hundred mothers were seated on fold-out chairs with babies on their laps and older children running up and down the rows.

After a long and fulsome introduction a beautiful young female mariachi took the stage and sang wildly, hopelessly, agonizingly out of tune for twenty minutes. Then a raffle was held and two clowns provided further entertainment. One of them went around pinching the bottoms of small boys, a sight to which I was now thoroughly inured. The other clown was mustachioed, beer-bellied, and, you guessed it, wearing a wig and a dress. I imagined the local PRI boss masterminding it all at a strategy meeting: "Okay, we've got Mother's Day coming up and we're going to have a rally. Get me a girl mariachi who can't sing, a cross-dressing clown, another clown to grab their sons' little asses, and we'll have their votes in the bag."

After the rally I bought some tacos on the plaza and asked the vendor about the road ahead. I wanted to go to Guanaceví, an old mining town up on the border of the Golden Triangle where Pancho Villa had once run a freighting business. "It was very bad a few years ago but now they say things are calmer," he said. "Sometimes the people drink too much and then you must be very careful."

"Is the army there?"

"Not at the moment. They come at harvest time."

That sounded good enough. I would leave in the morning.

LATER THAT EVENING something happened that I still don't like to think about. I was sitting in a restaurant with a bottle of beer, looking out of the window at the plaza. A cute little puppy ran across the road and a full-sized pickup truck ran over its back legs. The puppy lay there yiping and screaming and no one paid it the slightest attention. It had to scramble out of the road by itself, with its useless, mangled back legs dragging behind it. I rushed outside. The puppy had dragged itself under a parked truck and was screaming and screaming. A few feet away a group of men was standing and talking and I went up to them. "Is no one going to help that puppy?"

The men shrugged and looked insulted. What was this *gringo's* problem? It was just a fucking dog.

"Isn't there a veterinarian? Isn't there someone who can shoot that fucking puppy and stop its suffering? What is wrong with you?"

They stared at me, turning angry. The puppy continued its piercing screams. I turned and rushed up to my hotel room and broke down weeping. I was a dog-loving Englishman but it was more than that. Some sort of floodgate opened inside me and I wept uncontrollably, not just about the puppy, but about all the suffering, violence, tragedy, cruelty, hardness, and brutality in these mountains, the hungry children at Tizonazo, the earnest boy with the withered arm, a pregnant fifteen-year-old girl forced to marry her own rapist, that evil-looking Tepehuan killer, the widows and orphans, how worn out and jangled and depleted I was by it all. Finally I pulled myself together and went downstairs with my knife.

Three women were there, pointing under the truck to the puppy and talking to the man in the driver's seat. Thank God for the kindness of women, I thought. The women will take care of it. But the women got into the truck and the man drove them away and the puppy had to drag itself under another truck and that made it scream again. Children walked past happily, smiling and laughing, holding PRI party balloons, completely unconcerned by the screaming puppy with the mangled bloody legs a few feet away. They gave it a casual glance and nothing more. The natural affinity that we imagine between puppies and children is not natural at all but learned cultural behavior.

I knelt down and looked under the truck. The puppy stopped screaming. He looked back at me, frightened and unsure. He was breathing hard and you could see his heart thumping. It was a Sunday night and if there was a vet's office it would be closed and all a vet could do was amputate those legs. I wasn't going to adopt him and he wasn't going to make it on two legs. He was a street dog and the other dogs would beat him to the scraps and he would starve to death. The best thing I could do for him was cut his throat but I couldn't do that either. I was too chickenshit. I went back to my hotel room and watched television and drank myself into oblivion and in the morning there was no sign of him. There was nothing to do but get over it and move on.

THE ROAD TO Guanaceví had once been paved but was now badly pitted and cratered. It climbed over ridges and descended through valleys. There were oak trees and mesquites but the ground between them was parched and cracked and dead cattle lay strewn about. I was hoping for a hitchhiker but I saw no one and no other vehicles on that road until I reached the outskirts of Guanaceví. Described by a Jesuit as "the refuse dump for all of New Spain" after the silver rush of 1627, it was a small, crowded town with narrow, bustling streets and a magnificent old mission.

Villa freighted goods on a mule train between here and Chihuahua City, during one of his periodic attempts to give up banditry and go straight. He also tried mining, brickmaking, working with fighting cocks, and opening a small butcher's shop in Chihuahua City. Villa had a petit bourgeois streak and he enjoyed selling meat to his customers, but then people whose cattle had been disappearing started asking a lot of questions about where he was getting his beef and Villa was forced to close down the shop. Next he descibed himself as a "wholesale meat-seller," which was a nice way of saying he had gone into cattle-rustling full-time.

After he got swept up by the revolution and discovered his genius as a leader of men and military tactician, General Villa came back to

Guanaceví regularly to impose levies on the American-owned mines for money, arms, horses, and supplies. He also held the president of the mining company for ransom. The man was called Frank Knotts and he became something of a confidant for Villa during the long ride north to the U.S. border. Villa told him a different story about how he became a teenage outlaw. A *rural* had struck him with a whip for trespassing, even though he was just riding innocently across a pasture, and he became so enraged that he shot, killed, and robbed the *rural* and fled for the Sierra. At the border Villa exchanged Knotts for twenty thousand dollars and gave him a deer hide and a ring as a thank-you for the good conversations they had enjoyed.

I parked on the plaza and approached a bench full of old men. "Excuse me, señores, how are you? Perhaps you can help me. I'm a writer from England and I'm researching a book about Pancho Villa. I understand that he was here in Guanaceví."

"Oh yes," said one old cattle rancher in a battered straw hat. "Villa was here many times."

"Is there anyone here who knows the history of the town well? Who can tell me stories of Villa in Guanaceví?"

They shrugged and conferred among themselves and shrugged again. "There was a man but he is dead." A few moments later a recording of "Ave Maria" sung by a woman with a soaring operatic voice was broadcast through the town from big speakers on the outside walls of the mission. It was a moment of transporting beauty at a time when I badly needed one. We all stopped talking and listened. "How beautiful that was," I said. They nodded that it was so.

"Are you traveling alone?" said the rancher.

"Yes."

He waved his forefinger from side to side, erasing that idea as a bad one. "It is not safe. There are many people in these mountains with many things to look after. Do you understand?"

"They grow the crop that pays?"

"They are very suspicious men."

I tried to keep talking to him but he got up and left with the others. I looked around the town and I was on the point of checking into the one fleabag hotel when I got cold feet. Was I being paranoid or were my instincts sound? I didn't know but it felt good to get out of there. There were bigger towns farther south on busier highways where I wouldn't be such an obvious target.

I stopped for a late lunch at a roadside steakhouse called Los Caza-dores, The Hunters, south of Tepehuancs. On the other side of the road was a bright watermelon-pink Moorish-style mansion surrounded by wrought-iron fences and security gates. Halfway through my meal, eight men came into the restaurant wearing black leather jackets, gold chains, sunglasses, and cowboy hats. The rest of us went quiet. The waitress brought their beers. One after another, they ordered the full *parillada,* the biggest gut-busting array of grilled meats and innards on the menu. Then the waitress came to the youngest man among them. "A salad and nothing else," he said.

"Salad?" grunted one of the other men.

"Yes, I am vegetarian. Meat has a lot of cholesterol."

The other men were so dumbfounded they didn't know what to say.

ON THE ADVICE of his foreign doctor, Dr. Raschbaum, Pancho Villa became a vegetarian during the siege of Torreón. It was an effort to control his "outbursts," as he called them, the volcanic rages that consumed him and caused him to do things that he later regretted. Giving up meat made a big difference. Not only was he calmer, when there was every reason to be furious, but he also found that he had less drive and energy. So he went back to eating meat and soon after-ward his blood was boiling again.

In those days I was threatened with a serious illness on account of violent attacks of anger provoked by a woman who was with me. It happened in this way. My forces were masters of the plaza of Torreón, and during a fiesta, I met a girl in Ciudad Lerdo named Otilia Meraz, who was satisfied with the propositions I made her. . . .

One day she told me, I do not know why, that an officer sitting before us was a friend of hers before I took her. This was Darío Silva, one of my best friends and one of the eight men who had followed me since the beginning of the struggle, and I did not see how I could endure the revelation. Instead of blaming the woman who told me of her past when there was no remedy for it, or blaming myself for taking a woman who had belonged to others, I blamed Darío Silva and I obeyed my impulse to punish and humiliate him and make him understand that he should not have had the same woman as I, and show her that the men she had known before knowing me were nothing by comparison.

That day, when we were taking our places at the table, I said to Darío Silva, "You are not to eat with us; from now on you will be my errand boy."

Then Villa started thinking that he had abused his power and authority and his anger turned against Otilia Meraz. "I was overcome with such fury that I could hardly restrain myself from inflicting with my own hand the punishment she deserved. But I recovered and contented myself with throwing her out and calling Darío Silva to assure him of my friendship."

There speaks the true macho. How dare she sleep with another man before she met me? The man must be humiliated and the woman deserves to die for such an affront to my masculinity.

It's tempting to hold up Pancho Villa as the very archetype of Mexican machismo. He was a crack shot and a phenomenal horseman who could cover one hundred miles of mountain trails in a day. His nickname was The Centaur of the North. He was a domineering leader of men and a compulsive womanizer who demanded absolute fidelity in return and was known to rape women who didn't respond to his propositions. He was quick to violence, with a touchy pride and a wide cruel streak, and he was absolutely fearless in the face of death, leading all his cavalry charges himself.

In other ways he didn't fit the archetype at all. Drunkenness and machismo are almost inseparable and Villa was a teetotaler, preferring strawberry soda and ice cream. There was also his tender romantic side, his love of children, the ease with which he wept, his boundless compassion for the poor and downtrodden, his disinterest in personal enrichment. Of all the revolutionary leaders, Villa was the only one who didn't start scheming after more power and wealth.

Machismo came to Mexico from Spain, a Spain that had been under heavy Moorish or Arab influence for seven centuries when Columbus set sail. This is not to say that Native American societies weren't patriarchal or oppressive toward women, but the men weren't macho in the Spanish way. Spaniards, like Arabs, believed that women were inferior wanton creatures whose sexuality needed to be strictly controlled and firmly dominated, and that women from other cultures were fair game for rape. Octavio Paz in his analysis of Mexican machismo points to the old Spanish saying, "A woman's place is in the home, with a broken leg," and identifies the conquistador as the model for the Mexican macho, the original *chingón*, the hard isolate killer who raped and seized Indian women and so brought the *mestizo* Mexican race into being. The act of *chingar* could not be rooted more deeply in the national psyche, as Mexicans recognize on Independence Day when they get drunk and hail each other as *"Hijos de la chingada!"* which can be loosely translated as sons of bitches, sons of violated mothers, sons of fornication, sons of obscene perpetrations, and so on, but carries a specific reference to Cortés and his Indian mistress, La Malinche, who betrayed the Aztec empire and was the first mother of *mestizo* Mexico.

If you looked at it in this light, disapproving of Mexican machismo was like disapproving of weather or plate tectonics. But I couldn't help feeling outraged that the punishment for stealing a cow was more serious than the punishment for rape in most of Mexico. I still recoiled at the idea of a raped teenage girl being forced to marry her rapist, like Chana in Baborigame and thousands of others every year. I still thought it was indefensible that so many unfaithful husbands and boyfriends thought women should be beaten or killed for infidelity. It was pointless to make these judgments. It was none of my business. But I couldn't help making them.

• • •

FOR YEARS I had been hearing about Las Herreras, the hometown of the Herrera drug cartel, a mafia of more than three thousand members, nearly all of whom were related to each other. They refined Sierra Madre opium into heroin and sold it in the United States, along with marijuana, Colombian cocaine, and methamphetamine. If you bought heroin in Chicago or Buffalo at any time over the last twenty years or so, it was almost certainly the Herreras who brought it to you. In Durango, according to a 1980s DEA memo quoted in Charles Bowden's *Down by the River,* the Herreras didn't need to bribe the authorities, because they were the authorities, "chiefs of police at the town and municipal levels, directors of state police, mayors and police agents in every law-enforcement agency. Those who reportedly respond to the Herreras have been [high officials in the state of Durango]. Jaime Herrera himself is said to encourage bright young men to pursue political careers."

Of course that was twenty years ago. But now the Herreras were supposed to be even better organized and more successful in their chosen field. Their hometown in the Sierra was said to be fabulously opulent with palatial mansions, luxury auto dealerships, and a strip of designer boutiques to rival Rodeo Drive. From drug dealers, journalists, and photographers, I had heard stories about this town—Las Herreras—and now it was just a few kilometers away on the main road south from Tepehuanes. With equal parts trepidation and curiosity, I took the turnoff and made a brief circuit through the town.

There were maybe two dozen houses with security gates and new trucks and SUVs parked inside them, some very watchful eyes, and a definite *narco* feel but the rest of it was myth. There was no fabulous opulence. Most of the houses were poor and most of the streets were unpaved. The only stores were corner groceries and hardware shops. I couldn't see any bars or restaurants, just old men wearing shabby hats and sandals drinking bottles of Pacifico outside the beer agency. I pulled over and bought myself a beer and stood next to them.

"Oh, that beer tastes good," I said. "How are you gentlemen?"

They nodded and said they were well.

"I'm just passing through. I'm on the way to see the old movie sets."

"Ah yes." They sipped their beers and looked off down the street.

"How are things here in Las Herreras? Are people making a living?"

"Things are well. Things are good."

"That is good to hear. I was farther north and there were some problems of violence and delinquency."

"No no. Nothing like that here."

I noticed the name Lupillo Rivera painted on a wall across the road with a date written out next to it. Lupillo Rivera was a *narcocorrido* superstar based in Los Angeles, and then I realized that it was today's date. "Lupillo Rivera is playing here tonight!" I said. "Where can I buy a ticket?"

"Not here. He is playing down the road in Santiago Papasquiaro."

"Ah, okay. But before I go, can I buy you gentlemen a beer?"

"Ah no. We must be going." They finished their beers hurriedly and nodded their good-byes.

I CHECKED INTO a cheap motel in Santiago Papasquiaro and bought myself a ticket. It was a large agricultural and market town and as I was tall, long-legged, sharp-featured, and white-skinned, wearing jeans and a straw cowboy hat, no one gave me a second look. There were Mennonite colonies in this valley and the Mennonite farmers looked just like me. Standing outside the nightclub, waiting in line to get frisked for guns and knives, I heard someone nudge a friend and say, "Check the Mennonite."

"He must be a *narco*-Mennonite," quipped the friend.

It was a big, new, modern nightclub on two stories with an expensive sound and lighting system, lots of chrome, expensive drinks, and a plush carpet surrounding a wooden dance floor. Apart from a few hard-looking cases in the VIP section, the crowd looked like wannabe mafiosos. They were into the flashy *narco* style, wearing shiny tailored cowboy suits with long draped jackets, ultra-curled *cinco en troka* hats, and pointed cowboy boots, but they looked slightly awkward and unsure of themselves and they couldn't afford the heavy gold jewelry. On the shirts and hats and belt buckles were lots of images of scorpions. There is only one species of scorpion in Mexico that can kill an adult human with its sting and Durangueños are enormously proud of the fact that it lives only in their state.

I took up a position by the bar, kept my demeanor open and relaxed, and nodded and said hello to people. In Sonora and Chihuahua, there were always friendly extrovert drunks who wanted to drink with you and ask where you were from and if people there liked to drink beer. They might turn hostile if you refused, or at any time, and they wouldn't let you leave until you were drunk, but they were always around if you were in the mood to take the chance.

Not in Durango. People here were more closed and guarded. They wanted nothing to do with me. A few awkward exchanges was all I got in three hours at the bar. I hadn't managed a ten-minute conversation since crossing the state line.

Lupillo Rivera, wearing a silk suit and holding a bazooka-sized cigar, swept into the club and took the stage at 2:00 A.M. He was backed by a twelve-piece Sinaloan brass *banda* with matching suits and synchronized dance routines. I found it hard to catch the lyrics but it sounded like the usual stuff: hard drinking and womanizing, coke-snorting and gunfighting, strutting and preening, bloodthirsty heroics. I left early. I have to be in a particular mood to enjoy the ear-splitting *banda* style and I was dispirited by my failure to strike up a conversation or make a friend. Durango didn't feel that dangerous. But there was a high wall of reserve and suspicion and I was stuck on the wrong side of it. The way through, presumably, was a personal introduction but I didn't know a soul in the entire state.

WHEN JOHN WAYNE came across the village of Chupaderos in the mid-1960s, it was an old, photogenic adobe village at the base of the Sierra Madre with a few peasant families living in it. Film crews added an Old West main street and four small blocks of Old West buildings with English signs. The peasants were shunted out and more Hollywood westerns were filmed here than anywhere else in Durango. Now the film crews had all gone, the village was half in ruins, and the peasants were moving back in.

A man with a horse and cart was taking rubble from the ruins of the Feed Store. He said he was going to fix up the place and live in it. There was already a family living in the Saddlery, he said, and a big extended family behind the lace curtains of the Hotel. Dusty red curtains still hung in the upstairs windows of the collapsing Saloon.

I went over to the Barber's Shop, where a couple with three young children were living and running a small store. I bought a Coke and sipped it on the raised, splintered wooden sidewalk. Men on horses and families in battered pickup trucks went by. I asked several people if it felt strange to live in an old movie set and no one understood the question. They just kept saying that many of the buildings were still good and the others could be fixed up with some work.

Farther down the road was another old movie set called Villa de Oeste, Western Town, which had been built from scratch by film crews. This one was more organized, with a parking lot and an admission fee, a gift shop, restaurant, and horse rides. I walked down Main Street. I was the only tourist. A midget gunfighter was crossing the street on his way to lunch in the restaurant. He was about four foot three and dressed all in black.

"Excuse me, I am curious. I was in Chupaderos earlier. Are there people living here too?"

"Not in the same way," he said. "In the past, between films, people would move here and occupy the buildings, put their animals in the corrals. The filmmakers would have to get the police to throw them out when they wanted to make a film here. But now there is security and all the people living here are working here. If you come back this afternoon, you can see our gunfights. It is a good show."

He drew his pistol and twirled it expertly and then holstered it again. He stood there with his hands on his hips, his chin jutting upward and outward, an air of actorly confidence. By an odd string of coincidences I've come to know quite a few dwarves and midgets—little people, as some of them prefer to be called—trying to make a living in the entertainment industry. I was glad to see that this one had found steady work that he evidently enjoyed.

17

Deliverance in Durango

"NOTHING HAPPENS IN MEXICO until it happens," said the wise old dictator Porfirio Díaz as he sailed away from the revolution to France.

I packed up my truck with supplies in Durango City and drove back up into the Sierra Madre, following the paved road toward the Devil's Backbone. One of my guidebooks suggested a detour to a town in the mountains called San Miguel de Cruces and described it as a good "jumping-off point" for exploring the spectacular jungled *barrancas* and old colonial mining towns in an area known as Las Quebradas, The Breaks, on the border with Sinaloa and not far from the Devil's Backbone. The guidebook also said there was drug growing in the area but I was used to that and told myself I would be careful.

After driving for about two hours I came to the village of Navajas (Knives) and then the turnoff for San Miguel de Cruces. There was a fruit stand at the junction and I stopped there to inquire about the road ahead.

"It is calm during the day but at night there are bad men and bandits," said the fruit-seller, mixing me up a papaya and melon concoction. "You do not want to be on that road at night."

"And how about San Miguel? Is there a hotel?"

"Oh, San Miguel is beautiful. There is a hotel and a new resort for tourists up there. They rent cabins, horseback rides, things like this."

"That sounds perfect. Thank you very much."

The road was bad washboard with rocks and potholes and about eighteen inches of fine powdery dust on the surface. The best way to deal with the dust, I discovered, was to run the windshield wipers. There were occasional houses and tiny settlements along the way and I was struck by the lack of color in them. Farther north even the poorest shacks had a coffee-can flower garden out front and the smallest store would try to brighten itself up with paint and signs. Here everything was brown and gray, knocked together with raw lumber, and people's faces were hard and grim.

I rattled and jolted along that road for two and a half hours and then came into San Miguel de Cruces. It had once been a mining town and then a sawmill town. Now it was bleak, shabby, and doomed-looking, with abandoned houses and boarded-up stores. Why had that fruit-seller described it as beautiful? Compared to what? I couldn't find a hotel so I stopped at a small store and bought a Coke. A girl of eighteen or nineteen was behind the counter watching a small black-and-white television. She looked blank and depressed. I asked her if there was a hotel and she pretended she hadn't heard me. I asked again. She sighed and called into a back room.

An older woman came out. There was no hotel, she said, but there was a new tourist center back the way I had come. There was a blue sign. I must have missed it in the dust clouds.

On the way out of town, I picked up a man hitchhiking with his ten-year-old son. The boy got into the bed of the truck and the man sat beside me. He didn't want to talk. He didn't want to look at me. He didn't want anything to eat or drink. He admitted grudgingly that he was from the *ejido* of Vencedores and that was where I would find the tourist center.

I dropped them off and soon afterward reached the blue sign. *Centro Turístico,* it announced, with diagrams of cabins, horses, and fish. It was getting very late in the afternoon and here at last was my sanctuary. I followed a long winding dirt track through the oaks and pines, stopping several times to open and close stick-and-wire gates. Finally I came over a rise and down toward a cluster of cabins by a trout hatchery. Standing there by a battered old Chevrolet pickup truck, looking at me like a great big pork chop that had just arrived on their plate, were the two drunk men who would spend most of that night hunting me through the woods.

I KNEW IMMEDIATELY they were predators. My instincts were screaming at me to turn around and get out of there but the sun was going down and I worried about the bandits and bad men. The nearest hotel, along with the nearest cop, was three hours back down that road. There was nothing to do but fall back on charm and bullshit.

I got out of the truck and walked up to them, loose and casual, respectful and friendly. "Hello, good afternoon, gentlemen. How are you? I'm looking to rent one of these tourist cabins."

They smiled and looked at each other. "You are alone?" said the taller one.

"Yes, let me explain. I write for tourist magazines. I was at the state tourism office in Durango City and they said I should come up here and write about the new tourist center."

"Who do you know here? What was the name of the man who sent you?"

"I don't remember his name. He's the head of the state tourist board."

"And you want to rent a cabin?"

"That's right."

"He wants to rent a cabin," said the shorter one.

The taller one laughed and shook his head. The shorter one laughed and offered me a beer. This was a good sign. My only hope was to make friends with them and drinking together is the key male bonding ritual in the Sierra. "Ah thank you," I said. "I am Ricardo from London, England. What are your names?"

The tall one with the mocking, suspicious, menacing eyes and the silver scorpion fixed to his cowboy hat was Abel. The shorter, fatter, more easygoing one was Lupe. They were workers from the nearby *ejido*, building another cabin for "the boss," as they described it. I had the distinct impression that the new tourist center was more of a private hunting and fishing lodge for the local *narco*-timber boss and his cronies. The cabins were large and well appointed with four or five bedrooms apiece and fully equipped kitchens. The men showed me one and said it would be two hundred dollars for the night. There didn't seem to be anyone else around.

"I don't have enough money on me," I said, although there were five one hundred bills strapped to my leg. "I had better be going." Maybe I could pull over into a thicket somewhere on the way back.

"No," said Abel. "You can sleep for nothing under the trees. There is no problem. Do you have a gun?"

"No, I . . ."

"You're up here alone and unarmed?" He gave a sinister little chuckle, whistled, and shook his head.

"Aren't you afraid someone will kill you?" said Lupe.

"Why would anyone want to kill me?"

That's when Abel smiled and said, "To please the trigger finger," and the fear really took hold of me. That's when Lupe pointed out that "someone" could kill me and throw my body down a ravine and no one would ever know. That's when Abel thumped his chest and told me they were hundred percent killers here.

Then Lupe, playing good cop to Abel's bad cop, said, "No, no. Don't worry. We are friends. We will get drunk together. Do you have beer?"

"I have something better than that, my friends. I've been saving it for a special occasion." I pulled out a bottle of Johnny Walker Black Label, two-thirds full. It was a calculated risk. Getting drunk with them offered the best and perhaps the only chance of making friends with them, but it was equally likely to make them more dangerous, belligerent, and unpredictable. I passed around the bottle. They each took a big swig, nodded in satisfaction, and fetched three more beers from their truck. They shook out piles of cocaine onto their scarred leathery palms, gulped them back with a beer, and didn't offer me any. This was not a good sign.

It swung back and forth for a while. I was trying everything I knew to be charming, jovial, hearty, funny, respectful, and sometimes I would get them laughing and we would be *amigos* again and I would start to think that maybe it would be okay. Then one of them, usually Abel, would get suspicious again. Or a predatory look would come into his eyes and he would stare at me as if he could scarcely believe his luck. Again and again, he asked me if I was really alone and unarmed, and what I was doing there.

"I am traveling through Mexico writing about places that tourists can visit. At the tourism board in Durango, they said I should come here. Don't you want tourists to come here to your tourism center?"

"You say you are British? Where is your passport?"

I showed him my passport. "Where is your tourist permit? You are a foreigner and you must have permission to enter the country. When I was in Texas, the fucking *gringos* threw me out. Where is your permit?" Now we seemed to be going through a strange, drunken, ritualistic reenactment of a scene he must have gone through at the U.S. border. I showed him my tourist permit.

"Are you a terrorist? How do we know you're not a terrorist?"

"No, no." I smiled gently. "I'm a writer, not a terrorist. Look, I will show you a book I have written."

I opened up my traveling library, dug around, and found a copy of my first book. I pointed to my photograph on the inside jacket.

"What are you doing with all these books?" said Abel. His eyes were fierce and crazy. "Are you a terrorist?"

"These are books about Mexico. I have a lot of books about Pancho Villa. He is a hero of mine."

"Pancho Villa?" exclaimed Lupe. "Pancho Villa was my cousin. Abel is related to Pancho Villa also."

"That's amazing! That's wonderful! I never thought I would meet a cousin of Pancho Villa. Villa is my hero! Look!" I started pulling out Pancho Villa books in wild excitement. I heaped up all nine of them and grinned.

"What do you think of Pancho Villa?" asked Abel.

"He was an extraordinary man, a great man, a brilliant general, a true revolutionary, a true hero of the revolution . . ."

"Pancho Villa was a Mexican!" snarled Abel, thumping his chest again. "You're not Mexican. Pancho Villa has nothing to do with you. You shouldn't have these books. You should have books only about your country and that's all. Pancho Villa is for Mexicans only."

He put out his cigarette on the callused palm of his hand and stood there fuming, looking entirely homicidal. "I'm a scorpion," he said, pointing to his hat. "Hundred percent killer. Watch out."

"Calm yourself, *cabrón*," said good cop Lupe. "We're friends here. Everything is *tranquilo*. We will drink."

"So tell me about the tourist center," I said. "What is there for tourists to do here? The sign said horses, fishing."

"All of that," said Lupe. "We have a beautiful waterfall. We have fishing. We have hunting. There are many lions, *onzas*, a few bears, lots of deer."

Abel thumped his chest. "We are hundred percent hunters here. We kill things. Hundred percent! Do you understand me?"

He went into his truck and came out with a .22 rifle and loaded it. "Lupe, get your pistol," he said.

"There's no bullets left for the pistol, *cabrón*," said Lupe. "The bullets are back at the house."

Abel pointed to my truck. "You drive," he said. I got into the driver's seat. Abel sat next to me with the rifle between his knees. Lupe was on the other side. "Where?" I asked. I had gone numb and passive. It occurred to me that I might be driving to my execution but I concentrated on following directions and not high-centering the truck. They directed me up and down various dirt tracks and then told me to park and get out. The air smelled of skunk and I said so. "Here," said Abel, handing me the rifle. "Shoot it. Kill it."

Now I had the loaded gun. This felt better. But I still had no idea what was going on. They pointed down a trail and told me to walk ahead. I walked down the trail and emerged at the foot of a gorgeous waterfall.

"You see?" said Abel. "It's beautiful. Write that. We've got the best fucking waterfall."

"Are there other places for tourists to visit in the area?"

"Fuck them!" snarled Abel. "They're not worth a dick. This is the only place. This is the fucking BEST for tourists! You write that."

He finished his beer and hurled the can into the pool at the bottom of the waterfall. Lupe did the same. My beer was still half full. I was trying to drink as slowly as possible without their noticing I was drinking slowly.

"Now," said Abel. "Up the trail. You first."

I went up the trail and stood by the truck. "Stay here," said Abel. He walked over to a tree about twenty yards away and wedged a cigarette into a crack in its bark. He came back. "Shoot," he said. "Shoot the fucking cigarette."

I aimed the rifle and shot. We went forward and looked for the mark. I was four inches high. Abel grabbed the rifle away from me, sighted it, and shot. He missed the cigarette by a sixteenth of an inch. "I win," he said. "Now we shoot and the loser buys a twenty-four."

"A twenty-four?"

"Twenty-four beers. A fucking case."

I drove back to the cabins. I wedged an empty cigarette packet into the bark of a tree and we walked back about thirty paces. A caretaker of some kind came out of one of the buildings. He introduced himself as Jesús and when Lupe and Abel's backs were turned he pulled down on his bottom eyelid, making the Mexican sign for "Watch out."

"He is sleeping under the trees tonight," they told him.

I shot first. The dusk was well advanced now but despite the gloom and a slight tremble in my hands I was only two inches high and dead center. But was it better to win or lose? Again I had no idea. Then Abel shot. We went forward and found his mark right next to the side of the cigarette packet. "I win. You lose," he said. He ground out another lit cigarette on his palm and bored his eyes into mine.

The caretaker said that I must give the money for the twenty-four to Abel. I shook Abel's hand, congratulated him on his shooting, and handed over the money. The caretaker went inside to get the case of beer. By the time he came out with it, Abel had lost the money in his pockets somewhere and was fumbling around drunkenly for it. Then he snarled at me, "Give me my fucking money, *gringo*."

"That is not correct," said the caretaker. "We all saw him give you the money. You have it somewhere. But that's okay. Keep the beer and you can pay me tomorrow."

"Get your pistol, Lupe," said Abel. "Let's make the fucking *gringo* the target this time. He's got no right to be here."

"Calm yourself," said Lupe.

"Where's my fucking bullets?" said Abel, fumbling around in his pockets again.

"It's no big deal," said Lupe. "We have beer. We have *perico*. We will have a good time."

They gulped down another pile of cocaine. The caretaker pulled down his eyelid again and said it was time for him to be going. "Me too, goodnight, my friends," I said, jumping quickly into my truck, driving across the creek and around under the trees about two hundred yards away. There were fire rings and concrete picnic tables and benches. I parked next to one of the tables and then walked away from my truck, deeper into the woods, and stood behind a tree watching and waiting. I didn't know if they wanted to rob me, kill me, or just frighten me some more, but I was sure they would come for me.

I must have waited there forty minutes. It was fully dark and I couldn't see what they were doing but they kept opening and slamming the door of their truck. Finally I heard the engine, that sound I would come to know so well, and sure enough, instead of driving up the hill toward the village they came across the creek to where my truck was parked. When they saw I wasn't there, they put on their high beams and started roaring through the trees looking for me. That was the first time I ran and hid. They drove around for twenty minutes or so. I ran and hid, ran and hid. Once they came terrifyingly close to the tree I was pressed against. Finally they gave up, turned around, and drove up the road that led out of the tourist center toward the village.

Jesus Fucking Christ, I thought. I'll never go into the Sierra alone again. Never never never.

I went over to my truck and got out a sleeping bag and a thick corduroy shirt that I rolled up for a pillow. I got into the sleeping bag and lay on top of one of the concrete tables, just in case of scorpions. Half an hour later, just drifting into sleep, I heard that engine again and saw the headlights coming down the hill.

In a moment of high-speed panic, I scrambled out of the sleeping bag, stuffed it and the shirt under the picnic table, and bolted for the deep woods. This time there were four of them and they had flashlights. They fanned out on foot and I kept running and hiding ahead of them. Then two of them got back into the truck and two of them continued on foot. They must have spent nearly two hours combing the woods for me but for most of it I was across the creek and halfway up the slope on the other side, hiding in my thicket, peering over the boulder and growling to keep the wild animals away.

Finally they gave up. They went back to where my truck was parked and lit a fire. At first I thought they were setting fire to my truck but since there was no explosion, I decided it must be a campfire or a temporary drinking fire, which they would sit around for a while and then go home.

I waited and waited. The fire kept flickering. I couldn't stop thinking about that warm, fleece-lined corduroy shirt. My arms were withdrawn from my T-shirt sleeves and wrapped around my body. I lay down and hunched up in the fetal position and shivered uncontrollably. This was not going to work. I was going to get hypothermia. I had two choices. I could either walk around all night and keep myself warm that way or I could sneak in there and get my shirt and sleeping bag. The men had to be drunk out of their minds by now. Sooner or later they were bound to pass out.

I made my way down the slope and across the creek and very slowly and quietly through the woods toward the firelight. A magazine once sent me on a wilderness survival course and one of the things they taught us was how to walk silently in the woods. There wasn't much to it. You just had to be incredibly slow and patient, landing each small footstep on the outside of the foot, slowly rolling the weight inward to the ball of your foot and then slowly easing down the heel, so that any little twigs or dry leaves would be very gradually compressed and make no sound. Then you began the slow process of lifting up the rear foot.

The moon was up now and from four hundred yards away I could more or less make out the situation. They had parked their truck to block the exit road that went across the creek and up the hill. Between their truck and my truck was the fire. I waited there shivering until I was fairly sure by the flickering light that they were all lying down. Then I started creeping on all fours, moving as smoothly and silently as I could from one tree to the next, making my way toward the picnic table and bench where I had left my shirt and sleeping bag, pausing frequently to listen. It must have taken me twenty-five minutes to cross those four hundred yards.

Finally I reached the picnic table. The shirt and sleeping bag were still there. I eased out the shirt and put it on. Then I started easing out the sleeping bag but the nylon made a loud rustling sound and I froze and waited. My plan had been to go back into the deep woods with the sleeping bag but the damn thing was too noisy. I lay there beside the picnic table and slowly, slowly pulled the sleeping bag over myself and started to warm up. They were asleep now in their blankets about fifty yards away. Occasionally one of them would put more wood on the fire and then lie back down.

I waited there until the first signs of light. They had parked in the middle of the dirt track that led out, but I saw there was enough room to get around their truck and make it over the creek and out. Down on all fours again, heart hammering but moving very precisely, feeling again this new, highly focused, clearheaded type of fear, I crept over to my truck, got my keys out of my pocket, unlocked the door, opened it, eased into the driver's seat, and then turned the key. There was a sickening hiccup before the ignition caught and then I was swinging past them and the men were rising out of their blankets looking bleary and confused and I was across the creek and gunning it up the hill with my heart racing, expecting to see that big dented

Chevy in my rearview window and knowing I would have to stop to open the first stick-and-wire gate and that's where they could catch me. But I never saw them again.

Their names were José Guadalupe Villa and Abel Carrazco Villa. If anyone feels like going up to Vencedores and asking them about that night, I'm sure they will say nothing happened. A *gringo* of some kind turned up, said he was a writer. We showed him around and then he disappeared off into the woods and left early the next morning without saying good-bye.

I drove out of the mountains and then north across the plains and deserts and I didn't stop driving for fifteen hours until I was in striking distance of the U.S. border. I was ready to write about celebrity bathroom fixtures for a living, designer footwear, what your window treatments say about you. Some other fool could go into Sinaloa. I never wanted to set foot in the Sierra Madre again. The mean drunken hillbillies who lived up there could all feud themselves into extinction and burn in hell. I was out of courage, out of patience, out of compassion. They were sons of their whoring mothers, who had been fornicating with dogs.

Selected Bibliography

Betzinez, Jason. *I Fought with Geronimo.* New York: Bonanza, 1959.

Boudreau, Eugene. *Ways of the Sierra Madre.* Sebastopol, CA: Pleasant Hill Press, 1974.

———. *Trails of the Sierra Madre.* Santa Barbara/San Francisco: Capra Press/Scrimshaw Press, 1973.

Bourke, J. G. *An Apache Campaign in the Sierra Madre.* New York: Charles Scribner's Sons, 1958.

Bowden, Charles. *The Secret Forest.* Albuquerque, NM: University of New Mexico Press, 1993.

———. *Down by the River: Drugs, Money, Murder and Family.* New York: Simon & Schuster, 2002.

Brown, J. P. S. *Jim Kane.* New York: Dial Press, 1970.

———. *The Forests of the Night.* New York: Dial Press, 1974.

———. *The Cinnamon Colt and Other Stories.* New York: Doubleday, 1991.

Buitimea Romero, C., and T. Valdivia Dounce. *Como una Huella Pintada.* Hermosillo, Mexico: El Colegio de Sonora, 1994.

Carmony, N. B. *Onza! The Hunt for a Legendary Cat.* Silver City, NM: High Lonesome Books, 1995.

Deeds, S. M. *Defiance and Deference in Mexico's Colonial North: Indians under Spanish Rule in Nueva Vizcaya.* Austin, TX: University of Texas Press, 2003.

Dobie, J. F. *Tongues of the Monte.* Austin, TX: University of Texas Press, 1980.

———. *Apache Gold and Yaqui Silver.* Austin, TX: University of Texas Press, 1985.

Goodwin, Neil. *The Apache Diaries: A Father-Son Journey*. Lincoln and London, NE: University of Nebraska Press, 2000.

Guzmán, M. L. *The Eagle and the Serpent*. New York: Doubleday, 1965.

———. *Memoirs of Pancho Villa*. Austin, TX: University of Texas Press, 1975.

Hatch, E. L. *Médico: My Life as a Country Doctor in Mexico*. Mesa, AZ: Jeanne J. Hatch, 2003.

Hilton, J. W. *Sonora Sketch Book*. New York: Macmillan, 1947.

Ingstad, Helge. *The Apache Indians: In Search of the Missing Tribe*. Lincoln and London, NE: University of Nebraska Press, 2004.

Katz, Friedrich. *The Life and Times of Pancho Villa*. Stanford, CA: Stanford University Press, 1998.

Kennedy, J. G. *Tarahumara of the Sierra Madre: Beer, Ecology and Social Organization*. Arlington Heights, IL: AHM Publishing, 1978.

Lumholtz, Carl. *Unknown Mexico: Explorations in the Sierra Madre and Other Regions, 1890–1898*. New York: Dover Publications, 1987.

Meed, D. V. *They Never Surrendered: Bronco Apaches of the Sierra Madre, 1890–1935*. Tucson, AZ: Westernlore Press, 1993.

Merrill, W. L. *Rarámuri Souls*. Washington, D.C.: Smithsonian Institution Press, 1988.

Nabokov, Peter. *Indian Running: Native American History & Tradition*. Santa Fe, NM: Ancient City Press, 1981.

Parker, M. B. *Mules, Mines & Me in Mexico 1895–1932*. Tucson, AZ: University of Arizona Press, 1979.

Paz, Octavio. *The Labyrinth of Solitude*. New York: Grove Press, 1985.

Pennington, C. W. *The Tepehuan of Chihuahua: Their Material Culture*. Salt Lake City, UT: University of Utah Press, 1969.

Reed, John. *Insurgent Mexico*. New York: Penguin Books, 1984.

Rivard, Robert. *Trail of Feathers: Searching for Philip True*. New York: Public Affairs, 2005.

Shannon, Elaine. *Desperados: Latin Drug Lords, U.S. Lawmen, and the War America Can't Win*. New York: Viking, 1988.

Spicer, E. H. *Cycles of Conquest*. Tucson, AZ: University of Arizona Press, 1962.

Traven, B. *The Treasure of the Sierra Madre*. London: Prion Books, 1999.

Wald, Elijah. *Narcocorrido: A Journey into the Music of Drugs, Guns and Guerillas*. New York: Rayo, 2001.

Yetman, David. *The Guarijios of the Sierra Madre: Hidden People of Northwestern Mexico*. Albuquerque, NM: University of New Mexico Press, 2002.

Index

About the Author

Richard Grant is an award-winning writer who has published his work in *Men's Journal, Esquire,* and *Details,* among others. He is also the author of *American Nomads: Travels with Lost Conquistadors, Mountain Men, Cowboys, Indians, Hoboes, Truckers, and Bullriders.* Grant currently lives in Tucson, Arizona.